LYNDON JOHNSON AND EUROPE

LYNDON JOHNSON AND EUROPE

IN THE SHADOW OF VIETNAM

THOMAS ALAN SCHWARTZ

HARVARD UNIVERSITY PRESS
Cambridge, Massachusetts
London, England
2003

Publication of this book has been supported through the generous provisions
of the Maurice and Lula Bradley Smith Memorial Fund.

Library of Congress Cataloging-in-Publication Data

Schwartz, Thomas Alan, 1954–
Lyndon Johnson and Europe : in the shadow of Vietnam / Thomas Alan Schwartz.
    p. cm.
    Includes bibliographical references (p.) and index.
    ISBN 0-674-01074-4
    1. United States—Foreign relations—1963–1969.
2. Johnson, Lyndon B. (Lyndon Baines), 1908–1973—Views on foreign relations.
3. United States—Foreign relations—Europe.
4. Europe—Foreign relations—United States.
5. Vietnamese Conflct, 1961–1975—Diplomatic history.   I. Title.
E846 .S38 2003
327.73'009'046—dc21   2002038814

Designed by Gwen Nefsky Frankfeldt

CONTENTS

Abbreviations Used in Text

ABM	antiballistic missile
ACDA	Arms Control and Disarmament Agency
ANF	Atlantic Nuclear Force
ASP	American selling price
BAOR	British Army on the Rhine
CAP	Common Agricultural Policy
CDU	Christian Democratic Union
CRU	composite reserve unit
EEC	European Economic Community
FDP	Free Democratic Party of Germany
FRG	Federal Republic of Germany
GDR	German Democratic Republic
IAEA	International Atomic Energy Agency
ICBM	intercontinental ballistic missile
IIASA	International Institute for Applied Systems Analysis
IMF	International Monetary Fund
MIRV	multiple independently targeted reentry vehicle
MLF	Multilateral Force
NATO	North Atlantic Treaty Organization
NPD	National Democratic Party of Germany
NPG	Nuclear Planning Group
NPT	Nuclear Nonproliferation Treaty
NSAM	National Security Action Memorandum
NSC	National Security Council
SALT	Strategic Arms Limitations Talks
SDR	special drawing rights
SPD	Social Democratic Party of Germany
STR	special trade representative
TEA	Trade Expansion Act

LYNDON JOHNSON AND EUROPE

Lyndon Johnson as the Ugly American

In the summer of 1958, the book *The Ugly American* became a national sensation. Written by William J. Lederer, a retired naval officer, and Eugene Burdick, a university professor, it was an instant bestseller, capturing "the faith and fears of a generation whose lives had been deeply marked by the upheaval of World War II and the onset of the Cold War."[1] In the post-Sputnik atmosphere of crisis, the authors depicted an America losing the Cold War, and they placed the blame not on diabolical Russian or Chinese communists but on stumbling and ineffectual American representatives abroad. These Americans—notably the character of ambassador Louis Sears, or "Lucky Lou," a Southern senator recently defeated for a fourth term and sent off to the fictional Asian country of Sarkhan—lacked any cultural sensitivity, command of the local language, and sense of identification with the struggles of the people of their host countries.[2] From a historical perspective, the book provides insight into the mentality that spawned the U.S. crusade in Vietnam and also captures another phenomenon of the time: the emergence of an inexperienced and provincial America, thrust into a role of world leadership for which it was unprepared. Indeed, the term "ugly American" quickly entered into American discourse to describe the thousands of ill-behaved and boorish Americans, especially tourists but not exclusively so, traveling and working throughout Europe and Asia.

To many historians of and commentators on the 1960s, Lyndon Johnson is the classic "ugly American." Whether in the telling of Johnson anecdotes—returning from a trip to Asia, LBJ told reporters on his plane, "Boys, I don't understand foreigners. They're different from us"—or in stories about his excess and vulgarity—is there a Johnson book that does not include the story of his dictating to a presidential aide while sitting on the toilet?—writers have depicted Johnson as "the quintessential provincial," a man ill equipped by nature or temperament to deal with foreign policy, and who wanted, as Professor Alonzo Hamby concluded, to be remembered as a "conciliator" but who "is likely to be remembered as a warmonger who propelled his nation into its worst military disaster."[3] Henry Kissinger, no stranger to charges of warmongering, commented more sympathetically, if somewhat patronizingly, that "President Johnson did not take naturally to international relations. One never had the impression that he would think about the topic spontaneously—while shaving, for example." More damning was Kissinger's assessment that "the very qualities of compromise and consultation on which [Johnson's] domestic political successes were based proved disastrous in foreign policy."[4]

Vietnam is the obvious reason Lyndon Johnson's foreign policy is considered an abysmal failure, and many historians connect Johnson's personal failings to the flawed decisionmaking of the war. Bruce Kuklick of the University of Pennsylvania has argued that Johnson felt "culturally deprived" among the Kennedys and the East Coast elites and was unprepared to assume the responsibilities of the chief executive. Johnson was so uncomfortable that he became "utterly reliant" on the "best and the brightest" whom he inherited from Kennedy. Whereas Kennedy could be skeptical of his Ivy League advisers, Johnson followed their advice to its logical conclusion: the Americanization of the war in Vietnam.[5] H. R. McMaster paints a devastating portrait of Johnson "as a profoundly insecure man who craved and demanded affirmation," and indicts him for his mistrust of military advisers and his "real propensity for lying" to benefit his political career.[6] Both David Kaiser and Fredrik Logevall in their books on Vietnam emphasize Johnson's personal inadequacies in foreign policy as a major factor behind the decisions that escalated the war. Logevall stresses that Johnson was "deeply insecure about his abilities as a statesman." In describing Johnson's interaction over Vietnam with such allied leaders as British prime minister Harold Wilson, Logevall characterizes LBJ as "a man tone-deaf to the subtleties of diplomacy," without "the slightest sympathy for [Wilson's] predicament."[7] Kaiser cites the U.S. ambassador to Portugal, George Anderson, who described the difference between Johnson and John Kennedy, emphasizing the time Kennedy took to speak with the ambassador and his ability to talk of the issue "very intelligently." By contrast, he said that "President Johnson probably didn't know anything about [Portuguese-American relations and] wasn't interested. He had other things on his mind."[8]

This perception of Johnson and his foreign policy is part of a larger contempt for the thirty-sixth president, a man who epitomized so many of the embarrassing qualities of the ugly American that Burdick and Lederer pictured.[9] Compared with both his predecessor, the cosmopolitan and urbane John Kennedy, and his successor, the sinister but geopolitically astute Richard Nixon, Johnson comes off—especially in the foreign policy realm—as "the last of the really big hicks."[10] Nicknamed Ol' Cornpone in the Georgetown salons, Johnson faced a general prejudice against both white southerners and southern accents that was particularly intense during the racially divisive 1960s.[11] (For example, despite Johnson's success with the Civil Rights Act, *Washington Post* political cartoonist Herblock portrayed him as a white slave master using a whip to beat the White House staff.)[12] Stories painting Johnson as a hick flourished among diplomatic professionals and were told with great relish. During LBJ's trip to Germany for Konrad Adenauer's funeral, the president wanted to bring back to his Texas friends some "real German art." Embassy staffers went out to galleries in Bonn, but Johnson didn't like their selections. "We finally figured out that he was referring to paintings of old farmers with their pipes in their mouths, people in lederhosen, women in peasant costumes, etc. Real junk!" recalled Thomas Stern, who was the administrative counsel at the embassy. After the embassy staff procured the types of paintings LBJ wanted, Johnson insisted that they put a short biography of each artist on the back of each one so his friends would know their great value. Stern and the ambassador's assistant, Fred Fischer, spent a night dreaming up names and fictitious biographies for the artists. "I am sure that somewhere in Texas there are a number of paintings, if they haven't been thrown away by now, by artists from the 'Stern School of Hamburg' or the 'Fischer School of Bremen,'" said Stern. Johnson took the paintings, "as happy as he could be." It was, as Stern recalled, the "greatest scam I ever participated in." Other stories, particularly of LBJ's travels abroad, paint a similar picture of Johnson's provincialism, ignorance, and "ugly American" behavior.[13] The historian Waldo Heinrichs describes LBJ as "lacking a detached critical perspective" and consequently "culture-bound and vulnerable to clichés and stereotypes about world affairs."[14] Indeed, one of his early biographers, Doris Kearns Goodwin, went so far as to argue that Johnson's "inability to conceive of societies with basically different values was the source of his greatest weakness as President."[15]

This book presents a different picture of Lyndon Johnson and his foreign policy, a foreign policy that still remains largely lost in the shadow of the Vietnam War. His friend John Connally, a fellow Texan often painted with the same "wheeler-dealer" brush as LBJ, described in his memoirs "the many different pictures of Lyndon Johnson. You try to put them together. It is like trying to lift an untied bale of hay. No handles. It comes apart in your hands."[16] I argue not that other portraits or accounts of Johnson are wrong—only incomplete.[17] The focus of this study will be Johnson's approach to that region that was arguably the most significant area of the world for American interests during the Cold War: Europe. Because of the overwhelming influence of Vietnam on contemporaries as well as an entire generation of historians and policymakers, there are no English-language studies of Johnson and Europe.[18] Shorter treatments have been critical, deriding Johnson for his "dogged lack of imagination" and for his imprisonment in "Cold War discourse."[19] Johnson is also depicted as not caring about "rich Europeans" as compared with Asians or Latin Americans, to whom Johnson believed he offered something akin to a "global New Deal."[20] However, LBJ's personal preference mattered relatively little. The very structure of the American national security state—its security institutions, military commitments, transnational linkages, and economic interests—inexorably drew the United States into all manner of European questions. As Dean Rusk, Johnson's secretary of state, sometimes put it, "Europeans were not innocent bystanders in the Cold War. They were the issue. The United States was not going to fight the Soviet Union about polar bears in the Arctic; it would go to war over Europe."[21] Although the major issues in Johnson's years were not as profound or apocalyptic as the Marshall Plan or Berlin, the management of the complex Atlantic alliance, in its political, economic, and military dimensions, was one of the most significant tasks for American presidents during the Cold War. And in retrospect, it was the effective maintenance and nourishment of the alliance that allowed the United States to prevail peacefully in the Cold War, a successful chapter in American diplomacy that places the American experience in Vietnam in a different, and less dominating, perspective.

This book also departs from most treatments of Johnsonian foreign policy by following a chronological approach, in part to allow for what Robert Dallek, Johnson's foremost biographer, calls the "need for a more dynamic picture" of how LBJ's attention to foreign policy and external events had "its peaks and valleys."[22] Many impressions of LBJ were created during the first year of his presidency, when it is clear that his attention was largely centered on vital domestic matters, both the tax cut and the civil rights law. One of the most powerful impressions was that Johnson simply didn't care about foreign policy and was not interested in it.[23] The Chad Mitchell Trio, a popular folk group, sang a satirical song early in the Johnson years that suggested that Johnson's teenage daughter Luci must be the "brains behind our foreign policy / Who else but Luci could it be?"[24] On a more serious note, one presidential aide told Eric Goldman, Johnson's in-house historian, that "Lyndon Johnson wishes the rest of the world would go away and we could get ahead with the real needs of Americans." Indeed, Goldman's book, *The Tragedy of Lyndon Johnson,* has been the most influential in shaping this view of Johnson's priorities and knowledge of foreign policy, even though Goldman left the White House in early 1966.[25] David Fromkin of Boston University, in a review essay of more recent books about LBJ's foreign policy, picks up on Goldman's characterization, pronouncing that Johnson did not have a foreign policy but rather "only a set of unoriginal opinions that he articulated with great force and conviction and was unwilling to question even in the face of failure . . . In a changing world, he might have made a poor foreign policy president even without the Vietnam War."[26]

This book will dispute Fromkin's conclusions and show that Johnson not only had a foreign policy but became more adept at conducting it over time. This study also demonstrates that the president did not draw a strict line between foreign and domestic policies but that these issues were always intertwined in the Johnson approach.[27] A careful and dispassionate reading of the archival record—supplemented by the Johnson tapes, European sources, and materials from the former communist countries—reveals Johnson's greater attention to European problems after the passage of his domestic program in 1965. Vietnam obviously consumed much of his time and influenced his other policies, but there was more to the Johnson years than the war in Southeast Asia. When one follows the development of his policy toward Europe from the first days after the tragedy in Dallas until the final days of his administration, Johnson's approach and priorities become far more clear. Ugly American though he may have been, Lyndon Johnson emerges from these various documents as an astute and able practitioner of alliance politics, a leader who recognized how to assemble crossnational coalitions and work toward his overriding goals and objectives.

The historical record also demonstrates the degree to which Lyndon Johnson, for better or worse, shaped and controlled his foreign policy on the world stage. From a very early point in the historical literature, writers have characterized Johnson as either the victim or the beneficiary of his "best and the brightest" advisers. Johnson himself, in one of his self-pitying moments, told *Time* magazine correspondent Hugh Sidey, "I don't believe that I'll ever get credit for anything in foreign affairs, no matter how successful it is, because I didn't go to Harvard."[28] LBJ's own penchant for secrecy and for keeping his intentions concealed until he was ready to act has made it difficult for historians to recognize the personal control he exercised over many of his non-Vietnam policies. As William Manchester, not a great admirer of Johnson, once wrote, "With Lyndon Johnson, the shortest distance between two points was a tunnel."[29] In truth, Johnson ran his administration with impressive attention to detail and the specifics of policy. Noting that, while Johnson was "not averse to delegating authority when he had to," he would "plunge deeply into complicated issues such as the European Common Market, the balance of payments, the monetary crisis," George Christian, Johnson's press secretary, summed up his boss with the words, "In brief, he ruled."[30]

Now, more than three decades after Johnson left the White House, it is time to take a more dispassionate approach toward Johnson and his era, and to recognize both the strengths and the weaknesses in his approach to the international politics of the United States. Dallek convincingly argues that it is "time to free ourselves from conventional judgments about LBJ's personal limitations as a foreign policy leader and start discussing the specific options he did and didn't have. And where he made choices, we need to consider whether they were wise or shortsighted, beneficial or destructive to our national and the world's international well-being."[31] With that challenge in mind, this book explores Lyndon Johnson's approach to Europe, his achievements and failures, and the significance of his legacy in understanding this era in American history.

Retreat from the Grand Design

John Kennedy's presidency was intimately tied to European affairs, both in the drama of its crises, such as the Berlin Wall, and in its rhetoric, as in Kennedy's "Declaration of Interdependence" speech of July 4, 1962. In his outline of a "Grand Design" for the United States and Europe, Kennedy affirmed his desire for "a true partnership" between the United States and Europe as "two pillars of democracy of equal weight with leaders of equal voice."[1] Kennedy's European trip of June 1963 was an extraordinary success, with its dramatic Berlin speech and the huge and enthusiastic crowds that came out to see him. The U.S. mission in Berlin described it as "a great day" for which the problem was the "proper choice of superlatives."[2] *Newsweek* called it the "most genuinely spontaneous, exuberant, and heartfelt reception ever accorded a U.S. Chief of State on European soil."[3] Kennedy was received as if he were "the new prince of peace and freedom,"[4] and even skeptical French diplomats in Berlin grudgingly acknowledged the "extraordinary warmth" of the reception the president received and Kennedy's success in "restoring the direct line" between Bonn and Washington.[5]

Kennedy's assassination on November 22, 1963, stunned and shocked not only a generation of Americans but all the major Euro-

pean allies and adversaries of the United States as well. American diplomats reported the outpouring of feeling by ordinary Europeans, including Russians, who came in large numbers to American embassies
to express their sympathy. Kennedy's popularity in Europe had been
at its highest point shortly before his assassination, with some 83 percent in Germany approving of his leadership, and similar figures
reported elsewhere. The American ambassador to London, David
Bruce, noted that "the recognition of [Kennedy's] position as leader
of the free world was, at last, ungrudgingly accorded him,"[6] and historian Arthur Schlesinger later wrote, "In the summer of 1963, John
F. Kennedy could have carried every country in Europe."[7]

President Kennedy's actual foreign policy achievements were more
modest than many at the time believed. However, in terms of prestige
and popularity Kennedy raised the position of the United States in
Europe to its highest point in postwar history. Henry Brandon, the
influential Washington correspondent of the London *Times,* wrote
that "no other president spoke for Europe, with such understanding,
as he did, and I dare say, none ever will." Kennedy created the impression "of being a living fusion of the American and European cul-
tures."[8] His death was deeply unsettling to Europeans, both because
of their affection for the leader and the man, and because it was a sign
of potential instability and uncertainty in the country on whose protection they relied so heavily. Ironically, however, Kennedy's popularity, and his martyrdom, obscured the fact that his Grand Design for
American and European interdependence and cooperation was at the
time of his death being stalled and deflected by serious obstacles that
his successor would have to confront.[9]

Europe in November 1963

When Lyndon Baines Johnson stepped into the presidency, the European continent was in the midst of a political and economic transi-

tion. Western Europe had recovered economically from the war, and its prosperity brought with it conflicting demands: the Europeans wanted greater influence over American decisions, while the Americans wanted more "burden sharing" from the Europeans. The resolution to the Cuban missile crisis, which indirectly brought an end to the Berlin crisis, had created a situation of "tense stability" between the two blocs in Europe, and now allowed internal processes for change to develop in both alliances. NATO and the European Economic Community were now established facts, but efforts to bring about greater cooperation and integration were limited by France's resistance.[10] There were also stirrings within Eastern Europe for greater independence from Soviet domination, with Romania now following Yugoslavia's path, and the increasingly public Sino-Soviet split allowing more room for maneuvering within the communist orbit. The dividing line drawn across Europe, now more stable because of the Berlin Wall, created opportunities for "coexistence," but these were opportunities fraught with potential danger. For its part, the United States worried about the prospect of alliance disintegration and instability, as the threat that had brought America and Europe together began to recede. With each of America's three major Western European allies—Great Britain, France, and West Germany—President Johnson faced unique problems along with the common challenge of preserving alliance unity in the midst of a possible detente with the Soviet Union and Eastern Europe.

Great Britain remained the closest ally of the United States, the only ally still performing a global role in cooperation with the United States.[11] Kennedy had taken comfort from Prime Minister Harold Macmillan's advice during the crises in Berlin and Cuba, and demonstrated his gratitude in December 1962 with his decision to supply the British with Polaris missiles. (This decision precipitated a crisis with France, which Kennedy at the time of his death was still trying to resolve.)[12] The British ambassador in Washington, David Ormsby

Gore, enjoyed privileged access to the president, the product of a wartime friendship with the Kennedy brothers. Many among Kennedy's diplomatic team, including National Security Adviser McGeorge Bundy and Secretary of State Dean Rusk, once a Rhodes scholar at Oxford, were sympathetic to British perspectives and concerns. But Harold Macmillan resigned in October 1963 in the wake of the Profumo spy scandal, and was succeeded by Sir Alec Douglas-Home, the former foreign secretary. Douglas-Home lacked the experience of wartime Anglo-American cooperation that Macmillan possessed, and displayed a marked clumsiness in public statements. He told an interviewer before he became prime minister: "When I read economic documents, I have to have a box of matches to simplify and illustrate points to myself." As the Conservative Party's compromise choice to replace the legendary Macmillan, Douglas-Home was the last "blue blood" to lead the Conservative Party, a public relations problem in the egalitarian atmosphere of the 1960s.[13] The conservative Tories, who had been in office since 1951, were low in the polls and facing an election in the very near future.

The central problem for the British was their clear overextension as a global power—an overextension in political, military, and economic commitments. British leaders were coming to recognize that their people no longer had the stomach for the economic sacrifices required to administer and defend what remained of the empire on which the sun never set. Since the late 1950s, Britain had been running chronic balance-of-payments deficits, which continually threatened the value of its currency, the pound sterling, one of the two reserve currencies under the Bretton Woods system. The British government faced a contradiction between encouraging domestic prosperity and defending the value of its currency, which was fixed in its relationship to the dollar and gold. Domestic controversy over British commitments abroad, especially the British position east of the Suez Canal and the defense of Malaysia and Singapore, threatened Anglo-

American relations, as the United States feared that British with-drawal would create a dangerous power vacuum in Southeast Asia and the Middle East. Gone were the days of American suspicion of British imperial motives, the suspicion that had precipitated the Suez crisis of 1956. Now U.S. leaders feared that economic weakness would lead the British to abandon their responsibilities and leave the United States as the only "global policeman," a position unpopular with the majority of Americans even before Vietnam.[14]

In dealing with France, sometimes called America's oldest ally, Johnson would soon face a dilemma that the Kennedy administration had only begun to appreciate: the strongest and most senior political leader within the West was the one most adamantly opposed to American policies, not only within the Western alliance but through-out the world, including the Bretton Woods economic order that America sustained.[15] The president of France, General Charles de Gaulle, the leader of the Free French movement during World War II and one of the last surviving statesmen from that era, possessed his own unique vision of France's place within Europe and the world. He was determined to restore French power and self-confidence after the traumas of two world wars and especially France's shattering defeat in the second. His policies had troubled American leaders since he be-came president of the Fifth Republic in 1958 and demanded that the Western alliance be converted into a "codirectorate" or what came to be called a "tridominium," in which the United States, Britain, and France would consult and direct the strategy of the alliance as equal partners.[16]

Despite de Gaulle's vocal criticisms of America's dominance of NATO, the French leader enjoyed considerable sympathy within the United States because of his heroic wartime role, the political and economic stability he brought to France, and his decision to with-draw the country from its futile war in Algeria.[17] De Gaulle's general expressions of support during the Berlin and Cuba crises also earned him credit from Americans prepared to overlook his efforts to increase his distance from the United States on other issues. However, beginning in January 1963, de Gaulle stepped up his assault on America's role within Western Europe. His condemnation of the U.S.-British nuclear agreement at Nassau, coupled with his veto of British entry into the Common Market and his signing of the Franco-German Friendship and Cooperation Treaty, posed direct challenges to Washington's leadership. Kennedy reacted with alarm, fearing the prospect of an independent Franco-German bloc, a "Third Force" that could maneuver between the United States and the Soviet Union. France's June 1963 decision to withdraw its Channel and Atlantic fleets from NATO, its insistence on building its own independent nuclear deterrent, the *force de frappe*, and its attacks on the U.S.-negotiated Limited Test Ban Treaty and U.S. policy in Vietnam all put high-level relations between the two countries in a deep freeze before Kennedy's death. "Never before have the misunderstandings between France and the U.S. been as profound," the French ambassador, Hervé Alphand, wrote shortly before Kennedy's death.[18] Polls in 1963 showed that in contrast to Germany, where 75 percent had "confidence in the ability of the United States to lead the West intelligently through today's global problems," the figure for France was only 33 percent, with 49 percent expressing strong doubts about American leadership.[19] Indeed, Kennedy's European tour in the summer of 1963 was designed to counter de Gaulle's rejection of American "hegemony." And it was clear that the young American president enjoyed a personal popularity within France that belied the official estrangement and made it more difficult for de Gaulle to demonize the United States. Kennedy's successor would not have that advantage.

In the same month that Harold Macmillan resigned from office, the other towering figure of postwar history, Konrad Adenauer, finally stepped down as chancellor of the Federal Republic of Germany. During his fourteen years in office, Adenauer had led Germany to a renewed position of prominence in Europe. Combining a rigid anticommunism with a policy of integration with the West and a refusal to recognize the division of Germany, Adenauer had emphasized political stability and economic growth.[20] American officials had long recognized the central importance of good relations with Germany for maintaining the U.S. position in Europe. However, by 1963 West Germany had earned the characterization later proffered by Chancellor Helmut Schmidt: "economic colossus, political pygmy." Germany's economic miracle had given it increasing clout on global trade and monetary issues, but its divided status and the legacy of the Nazi past limited its ability to exercise open leadership within Europe. Although Kennedy enjoyed enormous popularity with ordinary Germans, his relations with Adenauer were extremely strained. Adenauer and Kennedy repeatedly clashed over issues like Berlin, the Franco-German Treaty, and the Limited Test Ban Treaty, as the young president sought "new ways of overcoming the stagnation and deadlock of the Cold War," while Adenauer worried that the "Federal Republic's hard-won stability, respectability, and security" would be placed at risk by the "restless" Americans.[21]

Adenauer's successor, the genial, cigar-chomping former economics minister Ludwig Erhard, was determined to step back from Adenauer's flirtation with France and pursue better relations with the United States, and he made that the lodestar of his foreign policy. However, Erhard was not a commanding figure, and he lacked the ability to control his heterogeneous party. When Erhard was later criticized for having "no government," Adenauer remarked: "That is quite wrong. There are at least three governments, and he's not in charge of any of them."[22] Within Erhard's own political party, the Christian Democratic Union (CDU), his rivals for leadership, as well as the embittered ex-chancellor Adenauer—who remained chairman of the CDU—wanted to increase Germany's independence by tilting it increasingly toward de Gaulle's France. The division between the so-called Atlanticists, led by Erhard and Foreign Minister Gerhard Schröder, and the Gaullists, led by Adenauer and the Bavarian leader Franz Josef Strauss, was already complicating Erhard's policies. Triggered in part by the West's acceptance of the Berlin Wall, Germans increasingly realized that reunification was no longer a central priority of the West. American interest in improving relations with the Soviet Union, although not strictly opposed by the Germans, was feared by many, since it was believed it would come at the expense of German interests. "We are the victims of America's policy of detente," wrote Heinrich Krone, one of Adenauer's closest political associates, in August 1963, and this refrain became part of the Gaullist critique of Erhard's pro-American policies.[23] German concern about the constancy of the American commitment to Europe rose after the signing of the Limited Test Ban Treaty and the subsequent "redeployment" of some U.S. forces. In October 1963 Kennedy reassured Bonn that he would maintain "six divisions as long as they are required" in the Federal Republic.[24] (Germany also agreed to continue to offset the costs of the American commitment through purchases of weapons from the United States.)[25] Erhard was seeking to confirm this arrangement when he scheduled what would have been his first meeting with Kennedy, in late November.

Johnson Takes Charge

Almost all contemporary observers were impressed with the speed and determination with which Lyndon Johnson assumed the American presidency. Standing well over six feet tall, with a large head and an elongated and weathered face that was the delight of political cartoonists, Lyndon Johnson was an impressive figure and looked older than his fifty-five years. Elected a congressman before John Kennedy had graduated from college, Johnson's age and his southwestern style made him an awkward presence in the youthful, northeastern, and sophisticated world of Kennedy's Camelot.[26] But he had been a faithful and loyal vice president, and had played a more significant role in such events as the Cuban missile crisis than many at the time realized.[27] His travels as vice president had been extensive, and although they had been largely ceremonial, some trips, particularly those trips to Vietnam and Berlin, had had important policy implications.[28] He could also draw on considerable political experience, including his own role as Senate majority leader in the bipartisan support for Eisenhower's foreign policy and the defeat of neo-isolationist efforts by the Republican right to restrict presidential power.[29] Even as harsh a critic as his disillusioned former press secretary, George Reedy, later argued that "despite the mythology to the contrary, [LBJ's] knowledge of world affairs equaled that of any other president and his instincts were frequently superior to those of the 'foreign policy establishment' which grew out of academic participation in World War II."[30]

Having pledged to maintain continuity with the policies of his martyred predecessor, Johnson, in his own approach to American foreign policy, would draw as well from his political hero, Franklin Roosevelt, especially Roosevelt's determination to improve relations with the Soviet Union and lessen the threat of nuclear war. As he told the Soviet deputy premier Anastas Mikoyan the day after Kennedy's funeral, "I can assure you that not a day will go by that we will not try in some way to reduce the tensions in the world."[31] In part because of the Vietnam War, and in part because of Johnson's more dramatic success in domestic affairs, historians have not fully recognized the degree to which he was determined to reduce the threat of nuclear war with the Soviet Union, and how this overriding objective influenced his foreign policy decisions.[32] Johnson had a number of goals as president. He wanted to keep faith with existing treaty commitments, "from South Vietnam to West Berlin." He sought to ensure full civil rights for African Americans. He was determined to promote economic growth and commit the nation to a "war on poverty." However, Johnson took very seriously his central and overriding presidential responsibility: to reduce the danger of a nuclear apocalypse.[33]

This was a concern from the very moment of Kennedy's death. Indeed, in a conversation with Senator Richard Russell, his mentor and close friend, Johnson expressed his fear that, because Lee Harvey Oswald was a communist, Americans might blame the Kennedy assassination on Cuba or the Soviet Union. This would have the result, in Johnson's words, of "kicking us into a war that can kill forty million Americans in an hour."[34] (The figure of 40 million was a reference to the briefing on nuclear war that Johnson received shortly after becoming president, about which LBJ later said, "I wished I hadn't known it.")[35] At the first National Security Council meeting after Kennedy's assassination, Johnson read and reread a statement prepared by McGeorge Bundy: "The greatest single requirement is that we find a way to ensure the survival of civilization in the nuclear age. A nuclear war would be the death of all our hopes and it is our task to see that it does not happen."[36] Speaking before the United Nations in December he proclaimed that "the United States of America wants to see the Cold War end," and one of Johnson's first successes in Congress came with the Christmas Eve passage of a bill allowing the sale of wheat to the Soviets.[37] In a telephone conversation with Bundy the day after New Year's in 1964, Johnson complained about the lack of flexibility in the U.S. position toward the Soviets, comparing the U.S. position with the rigidity of former German chancellor Adenauer.[38] He followed up the conversation with an announcement in his State of the Union address that the United States would cut back production of enriched uranium by 25 percent. In April the Soviets agreed to production cutbacks as well, and Johnson announced these along with additional American reductions.[39] Less successfully, the Johnson administration also put forward proposals for the mutual destruction of obsolescent bomber aircraft, parallel reductions in military budgets, and even a freeze on the numbers and characteristics of strategic delivery vehicles.[40] In May, in a speech given only a day after his "Great Society" speech at the University of Michigan, Johnson affirmed his interest in reducing tensions in Europe and spoke of the need to "build bridges across the gulf which has divided us from Eastern Europe."[41] Johnson also promoted cultural exchanges with the Soviets, and on June 1, 1964, the two countries signed a Consular Convention in Moscow. Throughout his campaign for the presidency in 1964, Johnson affirmed himself as the "peace candidate" against the strident anticommunism of his Republican rival, Barry Goldwater, who had suggested giving NATO's supreme commander the authority to use nuclear weapons.[42] "Control of nuclear weapons," Johnson responded, "is one of the gravest of all responsibilities of the Commander-in-Chief, the President of the United States." There is no doubt that the weight of this responsibility weighed heavily on Johnson from the moment he became president.[43]

Although rarely acknowledged, Johnson could be extraordinarily eloquent in his convictions about the nuclear danger. Throughout the 1964 campaign, he made it plain that he rejected all notions of "limited nuclear war" or any delegation of the responsibility to use nuclear weapons. In one of his most powerful speeches during the campaign, Johnson told a Detroit audience in September, "Modern weapons are not like any other. In the first nuclear exchange, 100 million Americans and more than 100 million Russians would all be dead. And when it was all over, our great cities would be in ashes, our fields would be barren, our industry would be destroyed, and our American dreams would have vanished. As long as I am president I will bend every effort to make sure that day never comes."[44]

Latent in his early approach to the Soviet Union was a pattern he would follow throughout his presidency. Although Johnson was strongly anticommunist, he did not challenge the legitimacy of the

Soviet Union or its role as America's rival superpower. The potential for mutual nuclear destruction meant that the ideological crusading of the 1950s, along with Dulles's talk of the "rollback" of the Soviet empire in Eastern Europe, were practices that were simply too dangerous. One of his first steps as president was to lower the rhetorical temperature of the Cold War, avoiding phrases such as "captive nations" and "ruthless totalitarians."[45] Johnson came to conceive of the United States and the Soviet Union as the "two eldest children in a large family . . . with the responsibility for keeping peace and order in the family." But the younger children were now too old and independent to take orders, so the two nations had to fulfill their role by other methods, including setting a good example in their own relations, working to create "an environment of peace," and trying to settle conflicts where they broke out, or avoiding involvement in them.[46]

As important as the goal of lessening tensions with the Soviets was to Johnson, the president still hedged his bets, largely for domestic political reasons, in the harshly anticommunist atmosphere of the early 1960s. Bridge building toward Eastern Europe was portrayed not only as a way toward peace but also as a way of weakening the Soviet empire.[47] Goldwater had made it clear after Johnson's State of the Union address that he would make Johnson's policy of "unilateral disarmament" toward the Soviet Union a campaign issue.[48] Goldwater's assault clearly affected Johnson's interest in an early summit meeting with Soviet leader Nikita Khrushchev. Johnson had decided, National Security Advisor McGeorge Bundy told the Soviet ambassador Anatoly Dobrynin, that he could not leave the country for "any but the most urgent of meetings." In having Bundy deliver this message to Ambassador Dobrynin, Johnson revealed that his own doubts about his domestic legitimacy—and perhaps also about his foreign policy ability—were not far from the surface. In his talk with Dobrynin, Bundy emphasized the president's concern that there would be "real difficulties in domestic terms" if he left the country without a new vice president in place. (Until the Twenty-fifth Amendment was ratified in February 1967, there was no provision for the appointment of a new vice president, and presidential succession went first to the speaker of the House and then to the president pro tempore of the Senate, in this case, respectively, John McCormack of Massachusetts and Carl Hayden of Oklahoma. Though Johnson often exaggerated, the sight of the aged McCormack, his potential successor—then seventy-three years old—was not a reassuring one.) Bundy also told Dobrynin that since Johnson had already turned down a proposed meeting with de Gaulle in Martinique, holding a summit with the Soviets might place him in an awkward position with the French. (That Johnson put the two meetings, with de Gaulle and with the Soviets, into the same category is revealing as well of the state of U.S.-French relations.) Finally, Johnson had Bundy emphasize the importance the president placed on finishing Kennedy's domestic program—the tax bill and civil rights— and the need for him to be present "to maintain a sense of urgency" and "pressure upon the Congress." Unspoken in this litany of excuses was Johnson's sense that the Republicans would criticize him for weakness toward the Soviet Union, and that a summit without a substantive agreement—and there were no matters as significant as the partial test ban treaty that was in the works—could damage him politically.[49]

Although for domestic reasons Johnson proceeded cautiously, the overall direction of his efforts was clear to European leaders. They quickly recognized Johnson's "peace policy," seeing it as very much in line with the policy that Kennedy had initiated. British prime minister Douglas-Home found during his February 1964 visit that "the Americans [were] as anxious as we to promote a further relaxation of international tension and we were agreed on the need to maintain the momentum of discussions with the Soviet Union."[50] The British also recognized the obstacles that Johnson faced, especially the powerful force of domestic anticommunism. They regarded Johnson's policies as an effort designed to "educate American opinion to new ideas by discrediting the simplistic 'total victory' school of thought and propagating more sophisticated and positive ones."[51] But while the British were, as one recent study puts it, "dedicated to detente," and the French, in the person of de Gaulle, had already declared that the Cold War was over and that Europe needed to break free of its respective "blocs," the Germans presented a much different problem.[52] Their country and former capital city remained divided, and German issues were at the heart of the Cold War. From the American perspective, German foreign policy was in the grip of rigid and legalistic approaches such as the Hallstein Doctrine, which compelled a break in diplomatic relations with nations that recognized communist East Germany.[53] For this reason Johnson demonstrated a determination early in his presidency to "push" West German politics in the direction of detente, albeit gently and carefully.[54]

During their first summit meeting in December 1963, amid the informal confines of the LBJ Ranch, the president told Chancellor Erhard that the United States was "going down the road to peace, with or without others," and asked the chancellor to be more flexible toward the Soviet Union.[55] Johnson praised the Christmas pass program, which allowed thousands of West Germans to visit relatives in East Berlin. (For Erhard, who told LBJ that the Christmas pass program "has dynamite in it even though it looks harmless," Johnson's praise could only help his political rival, the Social Democratic mayor of Berlin, Willy Brandt, who had initiated the program.)[56] At one point in the talks Johnson complained that during the "last 16 or 17 years" he had had numerous conversations with Dr. Adenauer, who always told him that "you had to be careful, that you couldn't trust the Russians," which Johnson knew very well already. But he also didn't want the world to think that only the Russians wanted peace. "We could be firm without being stubborn," Johnson emphasized. In

Visit of Chancellor Ludwig Erhard, December 1963, to the LBJ Ranch. Johnson and Erhard started off well together, despite Johnson's insistence that Erhard be more flexible in his dealings with East Germany and the Soviet Union. (LBJ Library; photo by Yoichi Okamoto)

Johnson's view, a policy of detente was the best approach to German reunification and progress with the Soviets.[57] Johnson even associated his efforts on arms control with the German issue, telling Erhard, "There is no doubt in my mind . . . that . . . a slowing down in the arms race is more likely to achieve a free and reunified Germany, than an uncontrolled arms competition which strengthens those elements in Eastern Europe determined to resist change and perpetuate the present division of your country."[58]

Johnson also made it clear, in both words and actions, that he had a more conciliatory view of the Russians than the Germans did and was willing to set an example with his own careful response to confrontations in Germany. In late January LBJ rejected taking retaliatory action when the Soviets shot down an American plane that had strayed into East German territory, killing the three Americans on board. He told Walker Stone, a sympathetic editor, "They got in the wrong territory and they had no business there," and said that the Russians had acted like the United States would have: "You may not be sleeping with my wife, but if I catch you with your britches down and you're coming out of her bedroom, and she's in bed, God I might do something bad."[59] After another incident in March, Johnson directed as much anger toward American military officials in Germany as toward the Soviets, and he took steps to reduce the possibility of further incidents.[60] Johnson also touched on other sensitive issues, as when he told Germans that he sympathized with the Russians' concern about Germany and their fear of German reunification. In April 1964 Johnson gave an interview to a German magazine in which he said that the Germans needed to consider the "Russian point of view" on a question like German reunification, a perspective that made some influential West Germans extremely defensive. As one put it, "In what concrete ways" could the Russians be induced to "release 17 million Germans from slavery?"[61] But despite this angry reaction, German officials were gradually coming to the realization that the United States was seriously interested in defusing the Cold War in Europe. It was a message the Americans continued to repeat. As Secretary of State Rusk told the U.S. ambassador to West Germany, George McGhee, "An improvement in relations between the Federal Republic and the Soviet Union is a very desirable goal and something which, within the limits of our resources, we should continue discreetly to work for."[62]

Spurred on by LBJ, Erhard and his foreign minister, Gerhard Schröder, began to step cautiously in this direction. The Germans called their own approach the "policy of movement," and it was aimed at reducing the suspicions about West Germany that still existed, and in fact had not dissipated greatly, in Eastern Europe. Bonn emphasized trade agreements, and in 1963 and 1964, the Germans successfully established trade missions in Poland, Hungary, Romania, and Bulgaria. However, even though it appeared that the Germans were following the American lead, their emphasis on "movement" was designed to contrast with any notion of the acceptance of the status quo in Eastern Europe, and the German Foreign Ministry remained adamant in its adherence to the Hallstein Doctrine and the isolation of East Germany.[63]

German initiatives were also encouraged in part by Nikita Khrushchev, the mercurial Soviet leader who in many respects resembled LBJ in his direct and earthy manner. In March 1964 Khrushchev indicated his willingness to visit West Germany to discuss the prospects of improving relations. The Soviets also made a deal with the Krupp firm, one of the more infamous names from the war years, to purchase a chemical herbicide plant. These gestures complicated Soviet relations with East Germany, and as a concession to his East German comrades, Khrushchev finally agreed to sign the long-anticipated Treaty of Friendship and Cooperation with the German Democratic Republic. However, the treaty had lost the significance it had before the Berlin Wall stabilized Germany's division, and it gave only a modest boost to the East German leadership. Indeed, just a few days after the treaty was signed, Erhard announced that the Soviet premier would visit West Germany in 1965.

Hopes for a significant breakthrough were soon dashed, however. Khrushchev had accumulated a significant number of enemies during his volatile years as premier, and they now came together to plot his ouster. Recent research in Soviet archives demonstrates that Khrushchev's interest in a rapprochement with West Germany played an important role in his downfall.[64] A report drafted by his opponents specifically criticized the visit Khrushchev's son-in-law, Alexei Adzhubei, made to Bonn in July 1964, arguing that it "created an impression that the Soviet Union was prepared, in the interest of improving relations with the FRG, to make some concessions to the militarists at

the expense of the GDR and People's Poland. This produced justi-
fiable discontent among East German and Polish comrades who have
bluntly declared that they do not understand why the Soviet Prime
Minister was going to visit West Germany at a time when there was a
wave of revanchism there and when German militarists were openly
threatening the security of the GDR, Poland, and Czechoslovakia."[65]
In October 1964 Khrushchev's enemies struck, deposing him from
office. His successors, party chairman Leonid Brezhnev and Premier
Alexei Kosygin, rejected the invitation to visit Bonn.[66] Erhard came
up empty in his hopes for an early breakthrough with the man who
had once threatened to bury the West.

The Johnson Foreign Policy Style

If John Kennedy loved the diplomacy and drama of foreign policy
more than the contentiousness of domestic issues, Lyndon Johnson's
passion lay in dealing with the problems of Americans.[67] Within days
of Kennedy's death, Johnson used the national mourning for Kennedy, and the resulting change in the political environment, as a
means of breaking the logjam in Congress that had frustrated most of
Kennedy's legislative program.[68] Johnson's State of the Union address
in January 1964, during which he declared an unconditional "war on
poverty," was the first in more than a decade that was devoted primarily to domestic affairs. In May 1964, in an address at the University of Michigan, Johnson outlined his vision of a "Great Society," a
program of social and economic reforms designed to promote full
employment and civil rights for African Americans and other minori-
ties, and to expand the role of government in guaranteeing adequate
health care, education, and housing for all Americans. Johnson
sought, as his assistant Joseph Califano has noted, "to mount a social
revolution" in civil rights and the expansion of the welfare state.[69]

Even many of Johnson's foreign policy advisers recognized that

America's domestic problems required the kind of leadership Johnson exercised.[70] Secretary of State Dean Rusk argued that tackling such issues as civil rights was a "fundamental prerequisite" for strengthening the American voice abroad.[71] Johnson wanted his foreign policy to serve his domestic objectives, and he believed that a policy of peace and easing tensions would allow him to undertake such wide-ranging domestic reforms. Even Johnson's later critics saw this connection, believing that domestic reform would allow for a more congenial and pacific foreign policy. Despite his segregationist past, Senator J. William Fulbright, the influential chair of the Senate Foreign Relations Committee, came to support much of the Great Society reform program from a conviction that "if his country were ever to pursue a policy of reason, restraint, and understanding abroad, it must do so at home as well."[72]

Johnson's shift from Kennedy's priorities highlights the larger issue of the relationship between domestic and foreign policy in 1960s America. It is clear, as Philip Geyelin wrote in one of the first studies of Johnson's foreign policy, that "not since Roosevelt, or perhaps ever, have foreign politics been integrated so inextricably into the processes of domestic politics."[73] Johnson's approach was hardly that of a naive provincial. A politician's politician, he recognized that the response of other nations to American initiatives would be conditioned, if not determined, largely by their domestic politics, and that the domestic situation of both allies and enemies needed to be taken into consideration. Perhaps even more important, Johnson thoroughly understood that American domestic politics constrained or limited U.S. foreign policy. Eric Goldman was correct that as a "man of the Hill, . . . no modern President has shown so intense a concern with maintaining broad approval for his foreign policies in the House and Senate."[74] Johnson was never passive in his attempts to persuade Congress what to think, and his attentiveness to congressional opinion was a characteristic of his approach to foreign policy. He also, to some extent, brought the analogy of the Senate into his dealings with other leaders. He was, as McGeorge Bundy called him, "a very majority leader President," who often sought to deal with his alliance partners as he had the Senate committee chairmen whose votes or support he had needed to put across legislation, and who had also needed his help in arranging legislation and patronage for their political benefit. Johnson was willing to be attentive and to try to understand their problems and the limits they faced, so long as they did the same for him. It was a skill that would ultimately serve him well in managing the politics of the alliance.[75]

However, at the beginning of his presidency, with his time-consuming attention to domestic affairs, critics argued that Johnson was failing in foreign policy.[76] In late January 1964 newspaper articles appeared depicting Johnson "as disorganized and disengaged in foreign affairs."[77] The president reacted angrily, telling sympathetic reporters, "I've had 117 meetings and 188 conversations" dealing with foreign policy, and attributed the criticism to disgruntled "Kennedy people."[78] Yet there was truth in the criticism.[79] Early crises over Panama, Cuba, Cyprus, and Vietnam had put the administration into a reactive style, with Johnson moving between issues without any of the sense of command or control he displayed in domestic affairs. Johnson's defense of his approach, citing the numbers of meetings and conversations he had had dealing with the subject, reflected a narrow and blinkered perspective on foreign policy. In the telephone tapes from this early period, Johnson's demeanor and tone change when the subject moves into foreign policy, and he does not display the intellectual engagement and quickness that characterize his approach to domestic politics.[80] Foreign leaders also came away with the impression that Johnson lacked "his predecessor's grasp of detail in foreign affairs" and that he was devoting his attention to domestic policies and politics, with one of his central aims being his reelection in 1964.[81] After meeting Johnson at Kennedy's funeral, de Gaulle assessed him as a parochial American politician, remarking that he was a "cowboy-radical" and a "sergeant who's been crowned."[82] In another comment to a Paris journalist, de Gaulle sarcastically remarked, "I rather like Johnson. He doesn't even take the trouble to pretend he's thinking."[83] The influential German politician Kurt Birrenbach came away from a visit to the United States in early 1964 with the impression that Johnson was a man of *"Innenpolitik,"* who, unlike Wilson, Roosevelt, and Kennedy, "did not speak the language of Europe" and was unlikely to emerge the leader of the Western alliance, a position that Birrenbach feared would be filled by de Gaulle.[84] British diplomats were also critical of Johnson, with Prime Minister Douglas-Home telling his assistant after meeting Johnson that "this man knows nothing of foreign policy."[85] British diplomats thought they might use this to their advantage, as when the thorny issue of British trade with Cuba arose. Oliver Wright, Douglas-Home's private secretary, advised that "as President Johnson's strength is domestic politics not international affairs, it might be best to answer him on his own ground" and stress British opinion in favor of such trade.[86] When LBJ reacted harshly to Douglas-Home's White House press conference in which he defended British trade with Castro's Cuba, the British foreign secretary correctly interpreted Johnson's primary motivation as domestic politics: "The President is most anxious not to bring anything to a head in foreign policy which would be disagreeable or which would upset his electoral chances."[87]

Though both superficial and excessively critical, these European impressions contained an element of truth. For Johnson, the 1964 election was crucial, as it would give him the political legitimacy to pursue his domestic visions. Johnson sought as large a mandate as possible, recognizing the strength of the opposition to his domestic objectives. From such a perspective, foreign policy issues, although important, were clearly secondary to him, and as other historians have noted, he put off key decisions on Vietnam until his electoral mandate was secure.[88] Even detente with the Soviets was in part a domestic issue, as the public acclaim for the Limited Test Ban Treaty had convinced Johnson of the popularity of the "peace issue." Goldwater's suggestion that the NATO supreme commander should have authority to use nuclear weapons only solidified Johnson's determination to emphasize the nuclear issue. When Attorney General Robert Kennedy told Johnson that the election would hinge on domestic issues because "there's not a crisis like the Berlin Wall or Cuba," Johnson disagreed and, referring indirectly to the popularity of the Limited Test Ban Treaty, replied, "A mother is pretty worried if she thinks her child is drinking contaminated milk or that maybe she's going to have a baby with two heads."[89]

When he first took office, Johnson was less certain of his touch in foreign policy, more insecure about his judgment, and more inclined to rely on his advisers and experts. Unlike Kennedy, Johnson disliked meeting with foreign diplomats, and Bundy had to plead with the president to spend an hour a week doing so.[90] Although he enjoyed the informal personal diplomacy of the Erhard visit, he avoided meeting with his rival for Western leadership, President de Gaulle of France. De Gaulle had embarrassed Johnson by denying that he had agreed to another visit to Washington after Kennedy's funeral after Johnson had already announced that he had. (De Gaulle told an aide that he had disliked Johnson's premature announcement of the visit and that he was not eager "to lick the boots of the Americans.")[91] However, the French president subsequently offered to meet with Johnson when he visited Mexico or the French island of Martinique. Despite a strong push from Dean Rusk, Johnson refused to go, citing his pledge not to leave the United States while "Congress is in session and it's an election year." Worried that the Republicans would "say that the alliance is cracking up, and Johnson refused to meet de Gaulle, creating division in the Alliance, and Johnson's bungling everything," LBJ sought the reassurance of Richard Russell and Senate majority leader Mike Mansfield. Though comforted by their support, Johnson's dislike for such summit diplomacy is clear in his lament, "If I start going to one place, I'll have to go meet others."[92] And Johnson knew that despite his vaunted desire—and capacity—to "reason together" with opponents, it was highly unlikely that that would work with de Gaulle. U.S. ambassador to France Charles Bohlen advised LBJ that de Gaulle "prefers a certain amount of friction" in his relationship with Washington, and that he himself was strongly against a meeting with de Gaulle, as "there would appear to be no subjects that could be profitably discussed."[93] After the French president decided to recognize communist China—a move Johnson would have liked to make, but which was politically impossible for him—Johnson agreed fully with his confidant Russell that "we've really got no control over their foreign policy."[94]

Johnson's reasons for not meeting with de Gaulle were transparent, but his judgment of the French leader's motivations was on the mark. Although some historians have strongly criticized LBJ for not taking seriously de Gaulle's proposals for the "neutralization" of Vietnam, they often fail to see the degree to which de Gaulle's critique was embedded in a larger effort to both project renewed French power and undermine and weaken U.S. influence in Europe and around the world.[95] As *Time* magazine editorialized in July 1964, "From NATO to the U.N., Latin America to Red China, there is hardly an issue or an area in world politics on which France has not taken a stance at variance with U.S. policy."[96] De Gaulle even moved into the realm of symbolic politics when he refused to attend the ceremonies commemorating the twentieth anniversary of the Allied landings in Normandy.[97] This slight hit a sensitive nerve in U.S. domestic opinion, and made it difficult not to regard de Gaulle and his criticisms as simply anti-American. Almost instinctively—and perhaps surprisingly, given his own reputation as an insecure man who sought constant approval—Johnson recognized that attempts to win the general's favor were doomed to disappointment, and that the key was to avoid additional damage to the alliance from a nasty public debate that might force other allies to choose between Paris and Washington.[98]

At times Johnson sounded peevish and self-pitying when he discussed foreign policy issues. Stung by a visit from British prime minister Douglas-Home, who announced on the steps of the White House that Britain would be selling buses to Castro's Cuba, Johnson told his economic adviser Walter Heller, "I am not an isolationist and I don't want a fortress America but I am being driven to it more and more every day." LBJ went on to say that "the trouble is . . . everybody just treats us as like we all used to treat our mother. They impose on us. We just know that she's sweet and good and wonderful and she is going to be kind to us and she'll always know that we came out of her womb and we belong to her and every damned one of them talk to me that way . . . I just talk to 113 nations and they just screw us to death."[99] But this type of neo-isolationist rant falls more into the category of blowing off steam, a characteristic Johnson shared with his predecessor Harry Truman, who often wrote vivid letters full of invective that he never mailed. Johnson's real anger with Douglas-Home stemmed from the prime minister's refusal to recognize that the Cuban issue for LBJ was primarily a matter of domestic politics, in which Britain's desire to sell a few buses was not as important as giving the appearance of at least *trying* to cooperate with the American blockade. As Johnson explained to Heller, the British had actually reduced their trade with Cuba considerably over the past few years, and Johnson urged Douglas-Home to stress that point when he met with reporters.[100] Instead, Douglas-Home chose to emphasize the defiance of the U.S. embargo and recent sale of buses, and to do so on the steps of the White House. To LBJ, such an approach showed little appreciation of the American domestic situation and smacked of political campaigning in Washington. He never forgot it, and was still complaining about it long after the Conservatives were defeated in

Visit of Prime Minister Alec Douglas-Home, February 1964. Johnson complained to his advisers that Douglas-Home stressed his defiance of the U.S. embargo of Cuba rather than emphasizing Britain's positive cooperation with other aspects of U.S. foreign policy. (LBJ Library; photo by Cecil Stoughton)

October. As one diplomat once put it, "Compared to LBJ, elephants suffered from amnesia."[101]

The Grand Design and the Kennedy Round

Johnson's style may have been very different, but in the wake of Kennedy's death he had pledged to continue his predecessor's policies. For Europe, this suggested the attempt to make a reality of the "Grand Design." The Grand Design was not Kennedy's own phrase—it was used by George Ball in his speeches promoting U.S.-European cooperation, and then it became the title of journalist Joseph Kraft's book about Kennedy's Atlantic policies.[102] Although Kennedy's personal approach to the Grand Design was more pragmatic, in the hands of "ardent Europeanists" like Ball and others in the State Department, it came to stand for a "firm and ideological commitment to the Atlantic Community." Its three main components, as one recent study suggested, were "a loose Atlantic community based on NATO in the political and defense areas, a sweeping round of Atlantic tariff reductions in the economic sphere, and the MLF (Multilateral Force) in the nuclear realm."[103] As one recent study has argued, the Grand Design was supposed to counter the influence and efforts of de Gaulle to create what Washington perceived would be an independent "Third Force" and a "Western Europe under French domination."[104]

During Kennedy's administration, the Grand Design's central legislative achievement came in the Trade Expansion Act (TEA) of 1962. Kennedy hoped that some of the international economic problems that the United States faced—primarily a continuing gold outflow caused by the U.S. balance of payments deficit—could be resolved by expanding U.S. exports to the rapidly growing market of Western Europe.[105] The White House told Congress that the TEA would help the sluggish American economy as well: "Our efforts to expand our economy will be importantly affected by our ability to expand our exports, and particularly upon the ability of our farmers and businessmen to sell to the Common Market."[106] Kennedy and his advisers advertised the TEA as legislation designed to promote a broad program of trade liberalization within the West that would "benefit substantially every state . . . every segment of the American economy, and every basic objective of our domestic and foreign policy."[107] The Atlantic partnership would spur economic development in the Third World and thereby contain communism as well, making the TEA much more than a simple economic measure.

As was often the case during the Cold War, the rhetoric was overheated. Kennedy argued, for example, that the TEA could well affect "the unity of the West, the course of the Cold War, and the growth of our nation for a generation or more to come."[108] Still, the passage of the TEA in October 1962 was an important achievement, stamping Kennedy as "the American president who established the most liberal trade legislation of the twentieth century."[109] It gave the president authority to reduce tariffs by as much as 50 percent to promote foreign trade, up to 100 percent in trade with the Common Market. The problem was that to achieve the bill's passage, the Kennedy administration had made numerous promises to Congress, not the least of which were the creation of a new executive office, the special trade representative, and a commitment to hard bargaining with the Common Market over agricultural trade, which had been excluded from the previously completed agreement, known as the Dillon Round. Christian Herter, a former secretary of state, became the first special trade representative (STR), and he was committed to adopting a "linear" approach to the reduction of tariffs that would involve across-the-board reductions more sweeping for the Common Market than for the United States.[110]

The negotiations to implement the "Kennedy Round" did not progress quickly during 1963, and they degenerated into something of a media joke with the outbreak of the so-called chicken war over American exports of poultry to West Germany. Although Kennedy himself made light of the conflict—Sorenson recalls him asking in mock horror: "Is the Grand Alliance going to founder over chickens?"[111]—the president began to have doubts about dealing with the European Community over economic issues. He thought that the trade negotiations were pulling the alliance apart rather than bringing it together, and he knew that more serious conflicts were on the horizon. He wondered out loud whether "we had not made a mistake in encouraging the creation of a Common Market in the beginning," and that it was "probably fortunate for us that Britain had not gotten into it." Although he had pushed hard for the TEA, Kennedy now told his negotiators that "he saw no reason, either for industrial or agricultural products, why we should have a 'Kennedy Round' if it was not going to benefit the United States."[112]

Kennedy's heretical thoughts ran up against a powerful institutional momentum to support European integration and more liberalized trade. However, they also reveal the complicated economic legacy Johnson faced when he became president, a legacy of contradictory commitments and promises. On an ideological and personal level, LBJ was committed to free trade as part of his larger commitment to economic growth on both the international and domestic level. Protectionist pressures were strong, particularly on such issues as textiles and steel, but Johnson wanted to hold to a policy he identified with Roosevelt.[113] Johnson shared the traditional southern view that high tariffs were designed by wealthy northern interests to keep the South in bondage to high-priced domestic goods.[114] Whatever the roots of Johnson's beliefs, Barry Goldwater's own adamant opposition to the TEA and his support for protectionist policies made Johnson's views seem even more in line with the established wisdom and gospel of American foreign policy.[115]

Trade issues were not prominent during the first year of the Johnson presidency. The Kennedy Round remained stalled by internal disagreements within the Common Market, where France and Germany fought over the proper level of price supports for grain. On this issue the French, whose grain producers were more efficient, wanted a lower price than Germany and insisted that the EEC settle the issue before the Kennedy Round bargaining got under way in a serious fashion. For his part, Erhard feared that a compromise with the French would damage his party's standing with German farmers, an important constituency of the Christian Democrats. The disagreement made clear the degree to which the EEC's Common Agricultural Policy (CAP), when it was finally agreed upon, would be a major stumbling block to any deal in the Kennedy Round that included agriculture. An economist from MIT, Francis Bator, McGeorge Bundy's newly appointed deputy for economic issues, warned the president in July that the United States might eventually have to settle for a bad deal in agriculture to get the type of industrial agreement that would be in the American interest.[116] Herter had taken a hard line with Erhard during his June visit to Washington, telling him that the failure of the Europeans to reach a "unified grains price decision" should not prevent negotiations, and that continued delay could put the Kennedy Round "in serious jeopardy."[117] Washington also wanted to see a price determined that would assure "the maintenance of grain imports" from the United States.[118] As the November deadline approached for the United States to table its offer on industrial tariffs, it became clear that there would be no resolution of the rules by which the negotiations would proceed on agricultural products. Herter wanted to dig in his heels on the issue, and stories circulated that the Kennedy Round itself was "approaching its greatest crisis to date" and that the dispute with the EEC could "wreck the negotiations altogether."[119]

With the presidential election in mind, George Ball recognized that "we had to avoid a crisis this week." In a series of meetings, Ball and Bundy joined forces to bring Herter around to their view that the United States needed to go ahead with its industrial offers and avoid giving the French the chance to "pin the blame on our rigidity" for a collapse of the talks. Bundy feared that if America took the risk of killing the Kennedy Round by standing on its insistence that agriculture be covered, this was likely to be counterproductive, for the EEC would "take unilateral action to cut back imports of U.S. farm products."[120] When the Department of Agriculture's representative, Charles Murphy, objected and wondered "how firm the United States would be" in fighting for agriculture in the negotiations, Herter echoed his complaint, adding that in his judgment "agriculture should be brought in soon" and "everyone should be clear on this." Bundy deflected this criticism by saying that "only the President" could make the basic decision about the role of agriculture in the negotiations, but that he could do so later in the process.[121] Despite the possible domestic political costs, Johnson decided to accept his advisers' judgment and go ahead with an American offer on industrial goods alone.

A month later the Europeans reached their own bargain on grain support prices, midway between the German and French positions, but still some 60 percent above world prices. The State Department had urged the Germans to compromise and was quick to take some credit for the agreement in talks with the French.[122] However, this triumph for European integration did not have unanimous support within the American government. Those in the Department of Agriculture were likely "to come down hard against the decision as a serious threat to U.S. agricultural exports," but in Bator's view, they overstated their case. Bator now argued that technological improvements in European agriculture were likely to reduce American exports in any event, and that we simply "[did] not have the bargaining power to make the Common Market import $325 million of grain a year beyond its needs." Beyond the technical questions of price supports and export levels, Bator pointed out that the German agreement on a grain price strengthened their hand in negotiations with the French and was "a clear gain in terms of Atlantic politics." The Germans were now in a much better position to "stand up to French buffeting in cooperating with us on NATO matters" and in taking the lead "in working for a large industrial tariff cut," in which they shared the American interest. Bator conceded that all of this was "bitter medicine" for the Agriculture Department, which might now try to force Herter to "dig in his heels," but Bator warned LBJ that "the danger in that is that we may paint ourselves into a corner and lose the chance for a really profitable deal on industry without making a nickel for agriculture."[123]

Johnson's decision to move ahead on the Kennedy Round without agriculture was one aspect of his careful retreat from the exaggerated expectations of the Grand Design. As with many other aspects of the Kennedy inheritance he received, Johnson faced difficult decisions in moving away from the rhetoric of his predecessor, and in making tough choices about what policies truly promoted the American interest. In this case the president recognized that the political costs of pushing hard on agriculture against what was likely to be a stone wall of European opposition, buttressed by the French, were simply not worth the expenditure of American prestige and influence. The United States had a larger interest in continuing its support for the process of European integration, even if it exacted short-term costs for some American interests. The Kennedy Round was not the only area of Atlantic politics in which Johnson would have to make such choices.

The Multilateral Force

Along with the Kennedy Round of trade negotiations, the Multilateral Force (MLF) was another component of the Grand Design. Despite Kennedy's own deep ambivalence about the project, the State Department bureaucracy, in the person of such figures as Undersecretary of State George Ball, NATO Representative Thomas Finletter, Deputy Assistant Secretary of State Robert Schaetzel, and the chair of the Policy Planning Council, Walt Rostow, remained focused on the MLF proposal as the priority in relations within the Western alliance. Designed to head off Germany's interest in having its own national nuclear force, and to give Germany a role in the decision to use nuclear weapons, the MLF concept had changed considerably since it first emerged late in the Eisenhower administration.[124] The basic idea of the MLF was that the United States would provide some of its nuclear arsenal to the North Atlantic alliance, thereby reinforcing the commitment that Europeans, especially the Germans, relied on—namely, that their security against a possible Soviet attack was guaranteed by the nuclear weapons. Though he had his own doubts about the MLF, Kennedy continued to support the MLF after his 1963 European trip and allowed the planning to proceed, primarily because of his concern about a future German interest in nuclear weapons.[125] Indeed, only two weeks before the assassination, Vice President Johnson spoke for the administration and endorsed the idea, calling the MLF "a first step toward a greater European voice in nuclear matters."[126] By early 1964, the MLF proposal involved the creation of a "fleet of surface warships, armed with Polaris missiles, owned, controlled, and manned jointly by a number of NATO nations."[127] After Kennedy's death, State Department supporters of the MLF, sometimes referred to as the "theologians" because of their passionate desire to use the MLF to push their ideal goal of a politically unified Europe, wanted Johnson to renew his earlier commitment and put pressure on the Europeans to act. At a meeting with the president on April 10, 1964, George Ball argued that the MLF would "give Germans a legitimate role in the defense of the Alliance, but on a leash." Thomas Finletter, the U.S. ambassador to NATO, reported that the Europeans had the impression Johnson wasn't interested in the project. He argued that the "U.S. had to stop being diffident about the MLF."[128] The only major reservations about the MLF came from William Foster, head of the Arms Control and Disarmament Agency, who worried that the MLF would damage the chance for a disarmament or nonproliferation treaty.[129]

Johnson took up the challenge that Finletter presented. The president was most interested in the argument that Germany would have to be treated as an equal with regard to nuclear weapons. In characteristic language, Johnson told his advisers, "The Germans have gone off the reservation twice in our lifetimes, and we've got to make sure that doesn't happen again, that they don't go berserk."[130] Rostow reinforced Johnson's fears when, with characteristic exaggeration, he told LBJ, "If the multilateral solution is shot down now, as it was in 1932, the swing to the Right is all too likely to repeat itself."[131] Johnson set a year-end deadline for signing a treaty, and in a speech to newspaper editors in April 1964 announced, "We support the establishment of a multilateral nuclear force composed of those nations that wish to participate."[132] This support for the establishment of the MLF was coupled with a decision to stop secret undertakings, begun in the Kennedy administration, to work out some type of compromise with the French about supporting their role as a nuclear power. National Security Action Memorandum 294 affirmed that "it continues to be in this government's interest not to contribute to or assist in the development of a French nuclear warhead capability or a French national strategic nuclear delivery capability."[133] The victory of the MLF theologians seemed complete.

Johnson later commented that he made his decision in April because "I thought Kennedy was for it, and it was mine to carry on, and I thought Congress was for it."[134] But although at the time Johnson thought the MLF could "satisfy the pride and self-respect of the Europeans," he also "warned against trying to shove the project down the throats of potential participants."[135] In a more important qualification to his decision, Johnson also told his advisers that while they "work on the Atlantic nuclear problem, we keep Soviet interests in mind."[136]

Johnson's deadline brought the MLF to the center of American diplomacy toward Europe, and ambassadors were urged to press their host countries for approval. The U.S.S. *Claude V. Ricketts,* a vessel with a mixed crew from eight nations, set sail in the Mediterranean to prove that the MLF was a workable proposition militarily. The

United States Information Agency was instructed to attempt to dispel the impression that the MLF was a bilateral U.S.-German arrangement.[137] (Thus it proved highly embarrassing to the administration when German ambassador Wilhelm Grewe arrived in October 1964 with a proposal from Chancellor Erhard to proceed with the MLF on a bilateral basis.)[138] But while pressure from the United States elicited more support for the proposal, it also served to motivate the opposition, especially the French.[139] As the deadline approached, French attacks on the "two horned and apparently powerless body" of MLF increased, with the prediction of a "very serious situation" if the MLF was approved.[140] To the French, a German share in the MLF would diminish the significance of the distinction that France was a nuclear power and Germany was not. With the Americans retaining their veto over the firing of the nuclear weapons, the MLF was, in de Gaulle's words, "an American naval foreign legion."[141] The French believed that German participation would only confirm American hegemony over Europe, and in private de Gaulle asserted that the success of the MLF would signal "the end of Europe," with a Germany totally subservient to American policy.[142] Dismissive of Erhard, the French sought to influence the German Gaullists within the CDU by linking their opposition to the MLF with the ongoing negotiations over the grain price issue within the Common Market.[143]

The French were not alone in their objections. The Soviets also stepped up their criticism, repeating their attack on the idea of giving the German "revanchists" nuclear weapons and contending that the MLF would doom a nuclear nonproliferation treaty.[144] The U.S. ambassador in Moscow, Foy Kohler, believed the Russians were "genuinely concerned that MLF will only hasten the day when the FRG becomes a nuclear power."[145] Soviet concerns about the MLF and any possibility of a German "finger on the nuclear trigger" intensified after Khrushchev's downfall in October. Gromyko emphasized repeatedly the Soviet belief that the MLF posed a "great danger" and would encourage "provocations" by the Germans.[146] On November 15, 1964, the Soviets released a statement condemning the MLF and stating that it was completely incompatible with a nuclear non-proliferation agreement.[147]

After President Johnson's landslide victory in November 1964, a conference was arranged with the new British prime minister, Harold Wilson, whose Labour Party held only a two-seat margin in the House of Commons. Although he had moderated his opposition to an independent British nuclear deterrent, Wilson remained skeptical of the MLF. In the weeks before Wilson's visit, McGeorge Bundy established a special committee, comprised of himself, Ball, Rusk, and McNamara, to work out a negotiating position. Bundy was particularly interested in evaluating the European prospects for the MLF, and he suspected that the picture being presented by MLF advocates—"who are determined to make the Europeans do what is good for them"—was seriously flawed.[148] As new information came in, Johnson's own doubts about the project grew. The president had just won an election against Barry Goldwater in which the nuclear question was one of the important issues. (In the Johnson campaign's famous "Daisy" ad on television—in which a young girl picked the petals from a daisy as a nuclear countdown commenced and a bomb exploded—LBJ in effect accused his opponent of being trigger-happy with nuclear weapons.) Although Johnson had officially maintained his support for the MLF, the Chinese nuclear test in October 1964 had led him to warn against "the fearful possibility of nuclear spread."[149] Now he was struck by the assessment that German support for the MLF was lukewarm and that one of the reasons Germany did support it was because "it also believes that we want it very badly."[150] After a trip to Germany, the Harvard professor Henry Kissinger took issue with Rostow and told Bundy that "it is simply wrong to allege that the future orientation of the Federal Republic depends on pushing through the MLF."[151] Even George Ball, an MLF supporter, reported that Erhard's political party was badly divided over the MLF, with its Gaullist wing bitterly attacking the idea.[152]

In keeping with his approach to all politics, domestic and foreign, Johnson now began to canvass the Senate, where he found little support for the MLF proposal. Conservatives disliked any sharing of the nuclear trigger, while liberals feared the MLF "would further imperil the prospects for arms control and divide the NATO alliance, all without adding to the security of the United States."[153] The need to conduct a "great effort of political education" in order to secure passage of the MLF sobered Johnson to the dangers the MLF posed to his political power.[154] With historical analogies in mind, LBJ decided he neither wanted to be a Woodrow Wilson, trying to push a League of Nations on a hostile Senate, nor a Franklin Roosevelt, squandering his electoral landslide in a Supreme Court–packing plan.[155]

Prime Minister Wilson arrived in the United States with a compromise proposal—an Atlantic Nuclear Force (ANF), which replaced the mixed-manned ships with various national components, thereby preserving British ownership of its V-Bomber and Polaris fleets. The prime minister might have been prepared to deal on the MLF, but Johnson decided that there was no good reason to press a fragile Labour government with an unpopular idea. Bundy convinced him that President Kennedy had had the same doubts about the MLF.[156] "If Europe isn't for it," LBJ told a small group of advisers, "then the hell with it." Reminded of the argument that America was already committed to the MLF, and that the United States had to save face, Johnson dismissed the concern with one of his favorite sayings: "While you're trying to save face, you'll lose your ass."[157]

Johnson made it clear to the British that his major concern with the nuclear sharing issue was the proper treatment of Germany as an equal member of the West, in large measure to ensure against any renewed German instability or aggression: "The object was to keep the Germans with us and keep their hand off the trigger."[158] Johnson was so graphic in his picture of the German "danger"—telling Wilson that there was a boy in short pants in Germany today who could, if the West handled things badly, grow up to be another Hitler—that Wilson later told his cabinet that he had "been surprised at the intensity of the President's anti-German feelings; this was much worse than anything on Labour's back-benches. Indeed in the President's own mind, the MLF was not least a form of anti-German insurance."[159] That Wilson was not far from the mark is indicated by Johnson's subsequent remark to Soviet foreign minister Gromyko, that "we did not have in mind to give the Germans nuclear technology or to encourage nuclear aspirations in any other way." The United States was trying to prevent Germany from seeking an independent nuclear capability, "because we could see what happened in China."[160] Johnson's comparison of Germany with China—the Soviet Union's own two-front dilemma—is particularly revealing of his thinking and underlying goals. With Johnson's decision, American pressure for the MLF came to an end, and although Johnson told the British and Germans that they were welcome to devise their own solution, the MLF lost its centrality in America's NATO policy.[161]

By the end of 1964, the Johnson administration had withdrawn Washington's commitment from controversial and politically charged proposals in the Grand Design. The movement had been far from smooth, and it reflected the largely reactive character of the administration's foreign policy, as well as its own focus on domestic affairs and the 1964 election. Yet although Johnson was criticized for abandoning the more idealistic and visionary aspects in Kennedy's rhetoric about interdependence, in each case it is clear that there was substantial continuity with the major objectives of his predecessor. Although his successful European trip obscured the fact, the direction of Kennedy's policies had been away from his State Department's Grand Design. To the extent that the Grand Design was supposed to counter de Gaulle's influence in Europe, Kennedy had not brought himself yet to repudiate it. However, in the months before he died, Kennedy had begun to express doubts about the overwhelming emphasis on Europe in U.S. policy. He told the Belgian leader Paul Henri Spaak in May 1963 that "the whole debate about an atomic force in Europe . . . is really useless, because Berlin is secure, and Europe as a whole is well protected. What really matters at this point is the rest of the world."[162] During a time in which the global interests of the United States would assert themselves more forcefully, Johnson sought to manage the problems of the Atlantic alliance in a way that preserved the vital elements of cooperation between the allies as he moved the alliance toward a policy of detente and peaceful coexistence with its determined ideological foe. That process would not be an easy one, especially as events in Southeast Asia portended a new confrontation.

2

Policy in the Shadows

January 1965 was a high-water mark for the Johnson presidency. *Newsweek* commented that Lyndon Johnson stood at "a pinnacle of power that no American had reached before," presiding over "the mightiest nation in history at a time when that nation is prosperous, calm, and . . . generally sure of purpose."[1] Although the situation in South Vietnam continued to worsen, Johnson hoped that no other foreign problems would interfere with his determination to confront two of the central—and connected—issues of his presidency: the problems of race and poverty in America. He wanted to place domestic issues at the center of his attention during the year, believing that his window of opportunity for enacting important legislation would remain open only until the midterm elections in November 1966.

Despite his domestic priorities, Johnson recognized that in the nuclear age, no American president could ever ignore foreign policy. The fall of Nikita Khrushchev in October 1964 raised questions about which direction the new Soviet leaders would take. With the Sino-Soviet relationship continuing to deteriorate, the possibility for change in dealing with the communist world was certainly there.[2] China's revolutionary rhetoric and espousal of "People's Wars of Liberation" made the Soviet Union appear as the voice of reason and restraint, and encouraged those Americans who sought better relations with the Russians. LBJ hoped for "new breakthroughs," and in his State of the Union address, he renewed his call for "bridge building" with the communist world, including the Soviet Union with Eastern Europe in his proposal for a significant expansion of East-West trade.[3] He publicly expressed the hope that the new Soviet leaders would visit the United States, and behind the scenes his advisers were exploring the possibility for a summit conference.[4]

Western Europe seemed to be in less urgent need of the president's attention. The removal of the MLF as an American priority convinced Johnson that relations with Western Europe, especially France, could become better than they had been in years. There was, however, a fundamental asymmetry between the secure Johnson electoral mandate and the political situation in Europe. With elections coming up later in the year in both France and Germany, and with Harold Wilson's Labour government clinging to a razor-thin majority in Britain, European leaders were in a cautious mood. The possibility for dramatic initiatives, even if the United States had wanted to propose them, was extremely limited. In this atmosphere, the Johnson administration "allowed the situation to drift, on the theory that Europe was basically sound and not much was needed to be done."[5]

Although 1965 proved to be the year of Johnson's most dramatic legislative successes for the Great Society—notably Voting Rights Act, Medicare, and the Aid to Education Act—foreign policy appeared to be LBJ's Achilles' heel.[6] By the end of the year critics were accusing the administration of forfeiting the strong American position in Europe and losing important opportunities for negotiations with the Soviet Union. Johnson's decision to begin the bombing of North Vietnam in February, followed by the deployment of combat troops, dominated both the headlines and the working hours of American officials throughout 1965. Soviet premier Alexei Kosygin's presence in Hanoi during the first bombing raids in February embarrassed the Russians and stiffened their determination to assist the North Vietnamese. A prospective meeting between Johnson and the Soviet leaders was an early casualty of this escalation of the war, with the Soviets citing "the obvious contradiction" between the desire for talks and the bombing of North Vietnam.[7] European criticism of the war in Vietnam also increased, along with the perception that in Washington European issues had receded into the background and America was now focused solely on developments in Asia. Yet this perception obscured the progress made by the Johnson administration during 1965 on a number of foreign policy fronts, including the nuclear question, and hid from public attention as well some important policy initiatives, especially dealing with international economic questions. But it accurately reflected the degree to which almost all the foreign policy of the Johnson administration would soon be associated in the public's mind with the war in Southeast Asia.

The Nuclear Planning Group and Nuclear Nonproliferation

When the dust began to settle after the December 1964 meeting with Prime Minister Wilson, when Johnson ended American pressure for the MLF, McGeorge Bundy praised LBJ in a manner certain to gain the president's attention. He compared LBJ's performance at the Wilson meetings with that of his predecessor, telling him that "this was without doubt the most productive and useful two days that we have had in foreign affairs since President Kennedy went to Berlin." Bundy was responding to a Johnson demand to justify the time he spent meeting with the British prime minister—Johnson still had to be convinced of the value of such bilateral meetings, a sign of both his continuing unease in foreign affairs and his suspicion, which he often voiced, that "Britain is not that important anymore." To Bundy, Johnson's determination to put "the ball back in the European court" was the "major achievement" of the Wilson meeting, and it established the president as "the firm but patient leader of the Alliance." Although Bundy's praise might appear excessive, the national security adviser was simply acknowledging that Johnson's personal involvement in the MLF issue, after a year of domestic political campaigning in which he had taken little direct role in alliance issues, had proved the key to resolving the matter. Bundy promised the president that he would make it his "business to make sure the state of the play is before you at every stage and that every significant decision is signaled as far ahead of time as possible."[8]

As pleased as Bundy was with the outcome of the MLF issue, there was the inevitable fallout within the alliance. News reports of the NATO meeting in December 1964 described the U.S. withdrawal of pressure for the MLF as "the year's most spectacular rug-pulling operation" and a "victory for de Gaulle."[9] The German foreign minister, Gerhard Schröder, who had strongly supported the MLF, was "at a loss as to how next to proceed" in the wake of the American decision. The Germans had "almost no confidence" that the British would negotiate an acceptable MLF or ANF without U.S. pressure.[10] Complicating matters further were German concerns that the United States was weakening in its support for reunification, despite a Johnson speech in favor of it at Georgetown University in December and an added reference to the issue in the State of the Union. With German elections set for the fall, Rusk predicted that the administration would be "dealing with a feverish friend during the next several months" and noted "a serious conflict between German electoral politics and sober international realities."[11] The president was less charitable and reacted angrily to a message from Ambassador McGhee in Bonn that suggested that recent events had contributed to a "crisis of confidence" in U.S.-German relations. As Bundy told McGhee, in an understated but firm tone, "The President does not now find it agreeable to have repeated and renewed German questions about the firmness of his purpose or the direction of his policy."[12]

Rusk's assessment was correct—the German mood was "feverish" and reactions went over the edge. Privately German leaders lamented the "successes of world communism" and wanted the Americans to support a new plan for reunification.[13] In the public arena, the German tabloid *Bild-Zeitung* ran the headline, "SHOWDOWN WITH THE US—NO NEGOTIATIONS WITH MOSCOW OVER REUNIFICATION IN 1965!" and dramatized this U.S.-German tension.[14] Walt Rostow, then chair of the Policy Planning Council in the State Department, traveled to Bonn in March and reported that he found great discouragement among German officials, who believed Erhard to be offering only weak leadership and the United States to be absent.[15] Kurt Birrenbach, the influential CDU leader with such important American contacts as former high commissioner John J. McCloy, knew that many in the East Coast foreign policy establishment regretted the "laissez-faire policy" of the Johnson administration toward Europe.[16] After a trip to the United States, Birrenbach bemoaned the "trend toward disintegration in the alliance," occasioned by Johnson's "peace strategy" toward the Soviet Union. He also observed the loss of the American "fascination" with European unification, a development he blamed squarely on de Gaulle. Although critical of the United States, Birrenbach reminded German leaders that the Americans were monitoring the German electoral campaign, as well as such debates within Germany as the extension of the statute of limitations clause for Nazi war criminals.[17] (After meeting with Birrenbach, Dean Acheson wrote his friend Noel Annan that his office had become a "wailing wall" for German visitors, and that "a good many of the cracks in Weimar are appearing in Bonn.")[18] Though American leaders rarely spoke of the Nazi past publicly, Birrenbach recognized that Germany still needed to prove itself a reliable and democratic partner within the West.[19]

To deal with the Germans, whose concern about equal treatment within the West had stimulated the original moves toward the MLF, the Johnson administration now contemplated alternatives. It quickly became apparent that the British were not serious in their ANF proposal. Former foreign secretary Patrick Gordon-Walker, who had been defeated in a by-election, revealed during a Washington visit in early 1965 that he had little hope of reaching an agreement with the Germans and, with "a certain overtone of sarcasm and flipness," said the United States "had killed and buried not only the MLF but the ANF" with its position of not intervening in the negotiations.[20] Bundy now argued that with the "growing conviction" that MLF/ANF was "never going to be the right step for the necessary number of nations all at the same time," the United States needed to give "close thought to other possibilities for nuclear coordination within the Alliance which may be more modest but which are also more likely to happen."[21] Bundy mentioned that he had forwarded this thought to both George Ball and Robert McNamara, and it was the latter who would provide what would become known as the "software solution," the Nuclear Planning Group (NPG).

Years later McNamara recalled, "If I could do things differently, I would have introduced the Nuclear Planning Group much earlier than I did as a means to draw the Europeans into nuclear affairs." The NPG, McNamara added, only developed "after it looked like the MLF would fail."[22] In fact, such consultative arrangements had been discussed at the Athens meeting of the NATO council in May 1962, but there had been little response. Indeed, the neglect of this idea tended to convince some of the non-nuclear members of NATO, especially the Germans, that they "would not gain sure access to nuclear planning until they had actual co-ownership in a nuclear force."[23] London had also suggested various consultative arrangements, and Dennis Healey, Britain's defense minister, had proposed one during the December 1964 Washington meetings. But it was only with the clear indication that the British and Germans were unlikely to find an area of agreement that McNamara returned to some form of consultation, making his case at the May 1965 NATO defense ministers' meeting. Although McNamara emphasized that his proposal was "additional to whatever action may be taken re ANF/MLF proposals," the Germans were hesitant, fearing correctly that the committee might be a substitute for the MLF.[24] But they agreed to participate, and planning for what would become the NPG proceeded throughout the remainder of the year, with the first meeting scheduled for November.

The NPG proved to be one-half of the policy to replace the MLF; the other was the drive toward a Nuclear Nonproliferation Treaty (NPT), which began in earnest in 1965. The catalyst for reviving American interest in the project was China's test of a nuclear weapon in October 1964. In response, Johnson had appointed a committee chaired by Roswell Gilpatric, former deputy secretary of defense, to examine the issue of nuclear proliferation and "explore the widest range of measures that the United States might undertake in conjunction with other governments or by itself."[25] The committee concluded, not without considerable debate over the MLF issue, that "the spread of nuclear weapons poses an increasingly grave threat to the security of the United States," and that the United States should "intensify [its] efforts for a non-proliferation agreement," not waiting or depending on "the resolution of any issues relating to an Atlantic nuclear force, however helpful such a resolution might be."[26] Before forwarding the report to the president, Bundy cautioned LBJ that there were still "real doubts" about its recommendations among the president's advisers, including Secretary of State Rusk. At the ceremony presenting the report to Johnson, Rusk said the report was "as explosive as a nuclear weapon and that its premature disclosure could start the ball rolling in an undesirable manner." He added that the United States could "have an agreement on nonproliferation by 6 P.M.—it was then about 2 P.M.—if we would abandon the MLF." Rusk thought that the Russians would immediately embrace a nonproliferation treaty if it meant a ban on Germany's developing its nuclear potential. For that reason Johnson ordered the committee's report kept secret, even to the point of denying that a written report existed.[27]

Although one recent study has argued simply that Johnson "rejected" the Gilpatric report, and Glenn Seaborg, chairman of the Atomic Energy Commission, came to believe the "time and conscientious effort of distinguished private citizens and a superbly qualified government staff" were "to a large extent wasted," these conclusions are incorrect.[28] Seaborg himself acknowledged that "much of what the committee recommended would, within three years, become national policy."[29] The real issues for President Johnson were timing, balance, and correctly playing the game of alliance politics. Joseph Califano, one of Johnson's most perceptive assistants, described Johnson's decisionmaking style in a manner that captures the way he played the political game, both domestically and in foreign policy: "Johnson continued to consult and ferret out opposing views even after he'd made up his mind but before he revealed his thinking, because he didn't want to be surprised by any opposition, fail to muster all possible support, or miss any opportunity to overwhelm or undermine an opponent he could not persuade. He was a political and intellectual baker, kneading with those enormous hands until every aspect of the proposal was explored; once confident of that, he would put the bread in the oven."[30]

Johnson faced difficult choices on the question of nuclear sharing. Although his own instincts and desires argued for moving ahead with nonproliferation as a part of his overall effort toward detente, he recognized that abandoning a five-year-old policy supported by the last two of his predecessors would exact heavy political costs, especially in alliance relationships.[31] Germany was the most important U.S. ally in

Western Europe, and Johnson recognized that its pro-Western—and pro-American—orientation had been one of the most important achievements of post-1945 American diplomacy. Germany was also in an era of political transition, with its first change in government and a bitter split within the leading party between pro-United States Atlanticists and pro-French Gaullists. Altering the U.S.-German relationship might be necessary for larger national interests like detente and nonproliferation, but it needed to be done in a manner that maintained the health of the Atlantic alliance and the Western orientation of Germany.

Johnson proceeded cautiously. While Vietnam may have taken his attention away from the conflict between nonproliferation and nuclear sharing, there were other important factors, including the upcoming German elections, that figured into Johnson's calculations. As it happened, a combination of alliance politics and domestic politics within the United States accelerated matters. Early in June 1965 the British presented to NATO a draft nonproliferation treaty that allowed existing nuclear states to keep their veto power over any future nuclear collective force. This insistence on the maintenance of the veto collided with the continued German desire for at least the appearance of real multilateralism in nuclear decisionmaking and made it clear that the British priority was nonproliferation, not some form of nuclear sharing as embodied in the ANF.[32] The British position further isolated the Germans and increased pressure on the Erhard government to come up with an acceptable alternative or abandon the project.

On the domestic side, Senator Robert Kennedy, Johnson's most disliked and feared political rival, made his maiden speech to the Senate on June 23, 1965, and in a revealing insight into the relative significance of foreign policy issues at the time, ignored Vietnam and made a strong plea for a nuclear nonproliferation treaty and indirectly criticized Johnson for not having done "all we can" to obtain a treaty.[33] (As early as spring 1964, Kennedy told an interviewer that he believed that even with the eventual Limited Test Ban Treaty, President Kennedy's "greatest disappointment" in 1962 and 1963 had been that the United States "hadn't been able to get any [nonproliferation] agreement.")[34] Parts of Kennedy's speech revealed that Roswell Gilpatric, a close friend of the Kennedy family, had served as a critical adviser.[35] After telling Bundy that he recognized that Kennedy "wants to do a little needling" and "develop a little independent stance," Johnson also insisted that Kennedy's speech could be "helpful to us."[36] Previous accounts have argued that Johnson decided to eliminate references to "halting the nuclear spread" in a speech for the ceremonies commemorating the twentieth anniversary of the UN, because, as he told advisers, "I don't want one word in there that looks like I'm copying Bobby Kennedy."[37] Although Johnson himself argued that a "birthday party" was no place to "announce what [our] program is going to be in the year 2000," he had other reasons outside of his rivalry with Kennedy to hold off on nonproliferation.[38] He left the reference to nonproliferation out of the speech, but on June 28 ordered the U.S. Arms Control and Disarmament Agency (ACDA) to submit to him a new program to stop the spread of nuclear weapons.[39] On July 1, 1965, the Gilpatric report was leaked to the *New York Times* and received immediate attention.[40] Only a few days later, in an article appearing in the influential journal *Foreign Affairs*, William Foster, the director of the ACDA, argued that nonproliferation should take priority over any alliance arrangements on nuclear weapons, a position that he had been secretly advancing within the government for some time. Foster even acknowledged that this position might lead to some "erosion" in NATO.[41]

Although Foster's position was represented as the viewpoint of the ACDA and not of the administration as a whole, the timing of the article lends weight to the argument that the administration was seeking to move opinion in the direction of a nonproliferation agreement.

It is not surprising that Johnson was annoyed by Kennedy's speech and the resultant publicity, especially the front-page coverage in the *New York Times.* Johnson was always angry when, as Bundy put it, he was deprived of "control over what happened next," especially in this case by Kennedy.[42] However, in the world of alliance politics, where domestic pressure is one of the key elements in forcing bargains and compromises, LBJ used Kennedy's speech and its aftermath to further the impression that he was under growing political pressure to adopt a more aggressive stance toward negotiating a nonproliferation treaty.

The German ambassador in Washington, Heinrich Knappstein, was quick to pick up these signals. He told Bonn that the debate in the United States was moving in a clear direction against German interests and went immediately to see Secretary of State Rusk, who assured him emphatically that "there will be no nonproliferation treaty without MLF."[43] Knappstein even tried to present the German case to Kennedy, whom he found willing to give him only as little time to present his case as politeness to an ambassador required.[44] A possible nonproliferation treaty even became an issue of controversy during the election campaign in Germany, when the fiery Bavarian leader and Gaullist Franz Josef Strauss attacked the possibility of such a treaty as a new "Versailles" that could produce another "Führer."[45] In a much more moderate reaction to Kennedy's speech, Foreign Minister Schröder, who was the most politically committed to the MLF of Erhard's advisers, told a German newspaper that Bonn would agree to a nonproliferation agreement only after some form of MLF/ANF was in existence. Later in the month Schröder told Rusk that there was a direct connection, in his view, between a nonproliferation treaty and the reunification of Germany: "The Soviets have an overriding interest in respect to Germany and that is the denuclearization of our country. We have an overriding interest in respect to the Soviet Union: namely the reunification of Germany." The questions, Schröder insisted, had to remain connected.[46]

This was, of course, a connection that many in Washington no longer wanted to make. Rusk told Knappstein that "we did not accept the need to link non-proliferation, MLF, and reunification."[47] But with the elections in Germany in September, the growing certainty of a crisis with France in NATO, financial instability in Britain, and the escalation of the war in Vietnam, the Johnson administration stepped back from a direct confrontation with the Germans. Debate continued within the State Department, where a study by Martin Hillenbrand on the "Nuclear Problems of the Alliance" concluded that the "ANF/MLF approach is incompatible with certain of our major objectives."[48] Assistant Secretary John Leddy rejected the study's equation of "consultative" solutions like McNamara's proposed NPG with the "meaningful responsibility" of nuclear hardware in an ANF/MLF arrangement.[49] NSC deputy Bator drew together the various opinions within the bureaucracy and made his own pitch to the president against any type of "hardware" solution. He insisted that any attempt to use nuclear arrangements as a "bargaining chip" for reunification would backfire and increase suspicions of Germany in Eastern Europe and the Soviet Union: "The only tolerably safe path to unification is one which involves lessening rather than intensifying fear of Germany in Eastern Europe."[50] However, the State Department, after a visit by Leddy to Germany, hardened its own view supporting the "creation of a collective nuclear weapons system within NATO [which] is in the long-term national interest."[51]

In the midst of this internal American debate—and despite the chill in official relations with the Soviets brought on by Vietnam— McGeorge Bundy held "the most candid and cordial conversation of our three-year acquaintance" with Soviet ambassador Anatoly Dobrynin. Queried by Bundy about the Soviet position on MLF/ANF, Dobrynin responded that it would be easier for the Soviet Union to comment on U.S. policy "if it knew exactly what that policy is." Bundy emphasized to Dobrynin Johnson's oft-stated position that "we should approach the problem of Atlantic nuclear defense with a full awareness of the concerns of the Soviet Government," but that so long as the Soviet Union appeared opposed "to all arrangements, it would be hard for anyone in the government to believe the choice we made would have any effect on our relations with the Soviet Union." Dobrynin appealed for a "private" indication of U.S. policy, and told Bundy that the Soviet expression of concern over Germany and nuclear weapons was "not merely another example of Soviet hostility toward NATO." NATO was not a "Soviet favorite," Dobrynin added, but the "problem of nuclear proliferation and Germany was far different and much more serious." Bundy assured him that the United States shared his concerns about Germany, and then stated, in unusually strong terms, that "there was no one in USG who had the smallest intention of allowing the Germans to have national control of nuclear weapons, and no one who would support the Germans in any effort to use any German nuclear role as an instrument of pressure against the Soviet Union." In reporting the conversation to the president, Bundy was uncharacteristically enthusiastic, concluding that there was the "opportunity for a real Johnson breakthrough here." If LBJ and Erhard could reach an agreement that no new weapons system of the MLF/ANF variety was necessary, he said, "the way might be open toward a nonproliferation treaty and toward a new collective arrangement for command control and consultation in NATO."[52]

With Bundy's thinking foremost in his mind, Johnson approached two December meetings, one with Harold Wilson and the other with Ludwig Erhard. Beyond the problems of alliance politics, Johnson himself had recently undergone gallbladder surgery, and the news related to Vietnam was grim: the battle in the Ia Drang Valley made it clear that the United States faced a North Vietnamese enemy that could inflict significant American casualties.[53] Secretary McNamara now predicted a larger war, and he warned Johnson that even with a major increase in U.S. deployments, and a casualty rate reaching one thousand per month, "the odds are even that we will be faced in early 1967 with a 'no decision' at an even higher level."[54] Johnson came under considerable pressure to escalate the war dramatically and also to declare a national emergency. Treasury Secretary Fowler pushed Johnson to adopt a "war tax" to help with the deteriorating balance of payments. Resisting such pressures took its toll on Johnson, and he decided in December to opt for a bombing pause.[55] But ironically enough, his meetings with the British and German leaders actually served to further LBJ's goal of a nonproliferation treaty.

The Wilson meeting was a surprising success, in part because of Wilson's own care in dealing with LBJ. Given Wilson's earlier criticism of Johnson's handling of the war, British foreign secretary Michael Stewart warned the prime minister not to forget to "acknowledge the troubles besetting the United States as well" and to recognize that "you are making the visit at a time when the president is reported not wholly to have recovered his strength and good humour. You might hit him on a bad day."[56] Both men compartmentalized the issues they addressed at their meeting. Wilson adroitly handled Johnson's lectures on Vietnam and the president's pointed question about what the British had learned about German sentiment on nuclear matters. Though rather disingenuously, the prime minister reaffirmed British commitment to an Atlantic Nuclear Force, saying the British "would put their submarines in if the Americans would put submarines in, and then the Germans could pay for a part in the undertaking." Wilson confessed to LBJ that he thought it all "a bit unreal," and the description he gave was hardly something likely to excite German interest, but Johnson chose not to press him on the issue. Wilson said he hoped that the Germans might be satisfied with the type of consultation arrangements that McNamara had suggested— the Nuclear Planning Group—on which a preliminary meeting had been held in November.[57]

Unfortunately, when Erhard arrived in Washington it became clear that the Germans were not prepared to give up on proposals for nuclear sharing. Acting as the chancellor's informal foreign policy adviser, Kurt Birrenbach had traveled to the United States the month before and thereafter had warned Erhard that "if the German side at the December meetings did not put forth a clear statement of its position on nuclear matters, there existed the danger that the pressure of public opinion in the U.S. in connection with the forces in the Senate and the efforts of other NATO partners, especially Britain, would lead the president to accept the wording of the NPT."[58] Birrenbach added that without a strong expression of German views, the Americans might be inclined to go along with the Soviets in order to get their help with Vietnam. He encouraged the chancellor to state that "we do not ask for a new weapons system, but we have to say quite clearly that until now no better system has been proposed to us than the MLF. The ANF proposal contains interesting as well as negative elements."[59] And if Birrenbach's reports were insufficient to move the Erhard government to action, Erhard also heard from two representatives of the East Coast foreign policy establishment, John McCloy and Dean Acheson. McCloy told Erhard that Germany must insist on its equality within the Western alliance, and that it would be a "grosse Dummheit" (great blunder) to give up this policy and allow the Soviet Union to advance its objectives through a nonproliferation treaty.[60] Acheson echoed the sentiment, encouraging the chancellor to make no concessions in respect to a nonproliferation treaty: "For the future of humanity the most important thing was for the United States, Great Britain and the Federal Republic to work closely together within NATO."[61] In effect, the chancellor's position became part of an internal American struggle by those who resisted the Johnson administration's priority of nuclear arms control and easing relations with the Soviet Union over devotion to NATO and the Germans. The result was that the chancellor arrived in Washington with a prepared paper that dismissed purely consultative arrangements and made a strong plea for the establishment of a "collective nuclear force, a force that would be jointly owned and financed by the participating countries." However, the chancellor's paper made it clear that the Germans no longer contemplated "the creation of a new weapons system," a critical point for Johnson. The German willingness to forgo a new weapons system opened up important possibilities in the pursuit of a nonproliferation agreement with the Soviets.[62]

Johnson did not press the nuclear issue at this meeting. He had a different agenda for his talks with Erhard and was prepared to take the chancellor's paper and once again try to put the ball back into the European playing field.[63] After his meeting with Erhard, Johnson told Wilson that the chancellor had come down "squarely on the side of a 'hardware solution.'" Since "what is essential is keeping a stable and healthy Germany" on the side of the West, it was necessary to review the German proposals and make "a serious effort" to respond. Johnson believed that the German proposal was similar enough to the British ANF to warrant another attempt by the British to negotiate an arrangement with the Germans.[64] Johnson followed up this direct approach to Wilson by instructing David Bruce, the U.S. ambassador to Britain, to "hold the PM's feet to the fire" on his willingness to negotiate on the ANF. However, even after such a strong admonition, Johnson rejected Bruce's suggestion that he "make a hard issue of this question." He continued to remind Wilson of the importance of keeping the German perspective in mind, writing him a strong note before the prime minister's trip to Moscow in February: "We must not let the Soviet Union use this most important issue [of nonproliferation] to undermine German confidence in our willingness to treat their nuclear problem seriously and constructively." However, Johnson's reluctance to use U.S. pressure on Britain is revealing: as important as LBJ believed it was to "keep the Germans with us so that they will not cut loose and become dangerous again," he recognized that the strength of the British opposition to nuclear sharing with the Germans made an agreement on a plan highly unlikely. In the interim period, he would seek to steer the alliance through this conflict of priorities until a decisive opportunity arose to take the next step toward a nonproliferation treaty.

The International Economy: Sterling, Gold, and the Balance of Payments

Lyndon Johnson's presidency is rarely thought of in terms of the international economy, and then only in terms of the inflation caused by the Vietnam War.[65] The domestic economy was clearly an important issue for him, and not just because of the 1964 election. As one recent study has demonstrated, both Kennedy and Johnson believed in "growth liberalism," an interpenetration of growth economics and liberal politics that defined great enterprises of public life in the 1960s, such as the space program, the War on Poverty, and the Vietnam War.[66] Johnson believed in the extraordinary potential of the American economy: "Hell, we've barely begun to solve our problems. And we can do it all. We've got the wherewithal."[67] However, that did not mean that Johnson took the economy for granted. Johnson spent, as Joseph Califano points out, "more time on economic matters than on any other subject" during his presidency, since he considered "a robust, noninflationary economy" critical to his Great Society.[68] As another study put it, Johnson "made full use of the presidency in pursuit of his policy goals, and exercised continuing leadership in the development and management of macroeconomic policies."[69] In the same way that Johnson related domestic and foreign policy, his concern over the health and vibrancy of the domestic economy required that he confront the concerns of the international economy as well.

Johnson's presidency witnessed considerable ferment over the future of the international economy, and the president faced important decisions on the future of the Bretton Woods system.

John Kennedy felt hamstrung by the international economy, especially vis-à-vis the ongoing problem of the U.S. balance of payments deficit. The speculation against the dollar that had accompanied his election in 1960, and his pledge to maintain its value and "determination to do whatever had to be done to make certain that . . . the dollar is sound" remained central themes of his presidency. Early on he recognized that he would not be able to use monetary policy, especially lowering interest rates, to "get America moving again," because of his fear of aggravating the balance of payments deficit. Indeed, he often remarked—and not in jest—that the two things that scared him most were nuclear war and the payments deficit.[70] Despite his stirring Cold War rhetoric of bearing any burden, and the advocacy of a "flexible response" strategy in Europe, Kennedy continually considered drastic cutbacks in U.S. forces overseas, particularly in Europe, primarily because of the balance of payments deficit and the drain of gold from the United States.[71] Congress shared his sentiments, at least so far as the unpopular foreign aid program was concerned. In 1963, strong congressional opposition to foreign aid, encouraged in part by the deficit problem, resulted in a reduction of the president's requested amount by a record 34 percent.[72] Kennedy sought to respond to the crisis in a number of ways. The Trade Expansion Act was one element of Kennedy's strategy for dealing with the balance of payments, as was his insistence that West Germany "offset" with military purchases from the United States the approximate cost of the stationing of U.S. forces in its territory. However, by the end of 1963 U.S. gold reserves stood at $15.6 billion, down from $22.9 billion after World War II, with the largest losses occurring after 1958.[73]

Kennedy knew that many of his advisers questioned his obsessive attention to the balance of payments issue, but he told them, "I know everyone thinks I worry about this too much . . . but if there's ever a run on the bank, and I have to devalue the dollar or bring home our troops, as the British did, I'm the one who will take the heat. Besides it's a club that De Gaulle and all the others hang over my head. Any time there's a crisis or a quarrel, they can cash in all their dollars and where are we?"[74] To Kennedy, preserving the Bretton Woods system of fixed exchange rates and the dollar's connection to gold was a matter of U.S. power and independence, as important as America's actual military presence abroad.[75] It was also, not surprisingly, a matter of his own political stature as the undisputed leader of the Western alliance, a position with domestic political implications as well.

Although it would later become clear that Johnson viewed the issue differently from Kennedy, when he became president LBJ affirmed that America's dollar would remain as "good as gold" and continued to seek to reduce the payments deficit. Even though the overall American economy was improving, and the president already had in mind his own plans for a massive expansion of the American welfare state, the political realities of the mid-1960s—both international and domestic—required that Johnson publicly and repeatedly affirm the need to reduce the balance of payments deficit and maintain the value of the dollar. In March 1964 Johnson pledged to place greater emphasis on self-help and private investment instead of foreign aid, and asked for approximately $1 billion less for such assistance than Kennedy had a year earlier.[76] During his December 1963 and June 1964 meetings with Erhard, Johnson made sure that the German chancellor knew how important continuing offset payments were to the United States, explicitly underlining the connection between the presence of the six U.S. divisions in Germany and the German purchase of American weapons.[77] Johnson signed into law in September 1964 Kennedy's proposed interest equalization tax, which was designed to stem the flow of U.S. capital abroad by increasing the cost to foreign borrowers of raising money in the United States.[78] For a time the problem seemed to dissipate. The balance of payments deficit declined over the course of 1964, with gold losses 60 percent less than the previous year and almost 90 percent less than the annual average for 1958 to 1960.[79] The United States still faced difficulties, however. "An acceleration in the gold outflow" in the last quarter of 1964 worried the Treasury Department enough to lead to its advocacy of additional restrictive measures. Bundy, however, cautioned Johnson not to overreact to the treasury's gloom about the subject, invoking the authority of Johnson's hero-president: "It is much better to defend the dollar, as we are now doing, than to have to show the bankers who is boss, but it is worth remembering that Franklin Roosevelt did not weaken his eventual place in history by his refusal to let gold be his master."[80]

The defense of the dollar also involved a large dose of alliance politics, especially in regard to U.S.-British relations. The British pound sterling was the other major reserve currency alongside the dollar, and it remained a symbol of Britain's continuing, if diminished, role as a global power. Along with those Americans who wanted British participation in defense and strategic questions, there were American officials with financial responsibilities who worried that if sterling succumbed to speculation and was devalued, the dollar would face a similar onslaught and the same fate. During the Kennedy administration, the pound sterling had been a component of the various schemes of the U.S. Treasury and the Federal Reserve Bank of New York to defend the value of the dollar. In 1962 the Fed set up a series of "swap arrangements" with the Bank of England to enable the bank to obtain short-term credit in the event of a crisis, and in 1963 it increased the swap line from $50 million to $500 million.[81] It was, as one recent study suggests, "clear recognition that the fortunes of the pound and the dollar had become effectively intertwined."[82]

Intertwined, yes; identical, not quite. American officials, especially those in the Treasury who enjoyed close contacts with their counterparts in the British Exchequer, did see the connections between the two currencies, but others had different priorities. The Defense Department—and especially Secretary of Defense McNamara—was particularly concerned to see the British maintain their commitments east of the Suez Canal. Rusk shared this view, but he also wanted the British Army of the Rhine to maintain its presence in Germany. His undersecretary, George Ball, who had increasing responsibility for European issues as Rusk was consumed with Vietnam, stressed the need for Britain to enter the Common Market and was hostile to the maintenance of Britain's nuclear deterrent.[83] The president's own assessment of the British economy was defined less clearly, although he acknowledged shortly after taking office that "almost everywhere in the world our interests and concerns are intertwined." LBJ was concerned with how Britain might help in promoting his foreign and domestic objectives, but he was also concerned to prevent, as he saw them, "ineffective" British economic policies from impairing his pursuit of the Great Society and domestic reform.[84] What linked the variety of administration perspectives was a general sense that a strong Britain—with a stable British currency—was important to U.S. foreign policy goals. Johnson himself was more skeptical and less willing to sacrifice American objectives than some of his advisers, whose pro-British sentiments he acknowledged by describing them to Wilson as "men with the temperament of Rhodes Scholars, dangerously sympathetic to the UK."[85]

During 1964, American Treasury officials nervously watched the British economy, concerned that the Conservatives' "dash for growth," an economic expansion policy, might yield an election victory but an economic disaster for sterling.[86] The Tories did make up considerable ground before the October election, and the election proved one of the closest in modern British history. However, after the Labour Party's narrow victory, economic reality set in. The new chancellor of the Exchequer, James Callaghan, discovered that the balance of payments deficit was almost twice what Labour had expected, raising the specter of a run on the pound and the possibility of devaluation.[87] Harold Wilson, however, was determined not to begin his time in office with a devaluation that he believed would gravely damage Anglo-American relations. Wilson, who had visited Johnson earlier in the year when he was still the opposition leader and was trying to overcome the mistrust of some Americans because they saw him as being too far to the left and "somewhat of a trimmer,"[88] now wanted to make the "special relationship" with the United States the "cornerstone" of his foreign policy.[89] Although there were domestic politics involved—Labour had devalued the pound in 1949 and Wilson did not want the party to suffer from that opprobrium again —foreign policy considerations, especially relations with the United States, played a significant role in his decision.[90] To bolster the British economy, Wilson initially resorted to the use of a 15 percent surcharge on imports, and Johnson applauded his decision not to seek higher interest rates a week before the U.S. election.[91] (Johnson had failed earlier in the year to persuade Douglas-Home not to put up the rates—Johnson always remained, from both his populist leanings and his concerns for financing the Great Society, an advocate of cheap money.)[92] After the U.S. election, when the situation with sterling reached crisis proportions, Wilson found himself forced to raise interest rates. When that step did not halt the crisis, the United States used its influence with other European countries, particularly West Germany, to arrange a multilateral $3 billion loan to secure the exchange rate of sterling.[93] Wilson recognized that the United States played a critical role in the rescue of the pound, calling in the U.S. ambassador, David Bruce, to tell him that "he was most grateful for all the support he had received from the President and the whole U.S. administration." Wilson went on, in his own hyperbolic manner, to tell Bruce that "we had looked down into the abyss over the past week, much as President Kennedy had in the nuclear context at the time of Cuba; now was the time to give some serious thought to putting the international financial and economic arrangements of the West on a more sensible basis."[94]

Though it was the multilateral force that made the headlines, Wilson's December 1964 meetings with LBJ also concerned the economic problems facing both countries. LBJ made clear his displeasure with Wilson's economic policies and the "troubles" they had given the president in his own budgeting process. Johnson also warned that the crisis "was in no sense over," and he conceded "that problems for the pound would also be problems for the dollar."[95] Wilson, fearing the domestic fallout from any report that he had discussed his government's economic plans with the Americans in such intimate detail, announced dramatically at the beginning of their session that this "meeting had never taken place." The British prime minister tried to rouse the group by declaring that they "were partners in guarding the two great reserve currencies of the world, which prospered or suffered together." But he still faced stiff lectures from the U.S. Treasury secretary Douglas Dillon and the Federal Reserve Board chairman William McChesney Martin about the deficiencies of British economic policies. Martin, for one, left no doubt that the United States expected within the next few months the announcement of an effective incomes policy as well as steps to promote exports. Martin added to the gloom by portraying the dollar's situation as being "as delicately placed as sterling" because of its own liabilities, and then he engaged in a debate with Secretary of Defense McNamara about what further cutbacks could be made in the American budget. Johnson closed the meeting by urging the experts on both sides to closely consult and coordinate their policies.[96]

The first sterling crisis of Johnson's presidency brought into focus two issues concerning the international economy and alliance politics that would preoccupy American policymakers during 1965. The first issue was structural problems in the Bretton Woods system, problems that were certain to be repeated. With its fixed exchange rates and dollar-gold link, the Bretton Woods system had imposed a healthy order on the world monetary system for almost twenty years, allowing the revival of multilateral trading and capital movements, and providing the framework for the revival of the European and Japanese economies. In its very structure, the system symbolized the overwhelming relative power of the United States in 1945, when America accounted for more than half of the world's economy. However, the very revival of European and Japanese strength that had been a priority of the United States in the Marshall Plan also created a diffusion of economic power that challenged American dominance and the special position of the dollar within the system.

The French had long disputed the special position of the dollar within the Bretton Woods system, and they had originally sought some other means to promote international liquidity than the dollar. Now in February 1965 de Gaulle changed the direction of French policy as part of his larger struggle against what he called "American hegemony."[97] The French leader proclaimed his own interest in returning to the gold standard as a basis for settling international payments, and announced his decision to exchange dollars for gold. The resulting drain on America's gold reserves threatened the stability of the entire system.[98] The United States had become the world's banker, but now one of its clients starting a run on the bank. The irony was that if the United States stopped pumping its dollars into the world's monetary system—by ending its balance of payments deficit—the resulting shortfall in liquidity would stall the growth of international trade and limit global economic development. These concerns forced the Johnson administration to consider initiating dramatic reforms in the world's monetary order that would allow for a move away from some of the rigidities and structural flaws in Bretton Woods—and, not coincidentally, keep the French from wielding a "club," as JFK had called it, over American policies.

The second aspect of the crisis was more directly connected to U.S.-British relations, and Rusk emphasized it at the December meetings. "The United Kingdom," Rusk told the group, "fulfilled a strategic function in many parts of the world which the United States could not attempt; and because they could do this, with relatively small forces, the value of their contribution extended beyond the immediate local impact—in particular it had a kind of 'multiplier' effect by enabling the greater power of the United States to be deployed in areas which might otherwise be largely inaccessible to it."[99] This multiplier effect occurred most acutely in the geographically huge region "east of Suez," where the United States desperately wanted to maintain a British presence. American leaders were coming to recognize that the pound's weakness threatened to present them with another crisis like that which had precipitated the Truman Doctrine in 1947 —a British withdrawal due to economic weakness that would leave a dangerous power vacuum. Already feeling overextended themselves, American leaders were certain, as McNamara put it, that the "Congress of the U.S. and the people of the U.S. would not tolerate a situation in which the U.S. was the sole world policeman."[100] Although Wilson had made it clear that the British would not directly assist the United States in Vietnam, his country's role in Malaysia, where Britain helped defend that country against the increasingly pro-Chinese government of Prime Minister Sukarno of Indonesia, was of great importance to America.[101] With the growing American involvement in Vietnam, a British withdrawal would be perceived as a foreign policy calamity to be avoided under any circumstances. Knowing that Wilson's government was seeking to restrict defense expenditures and review its commitments, the United States sought to influence the process. It was not only the value of the dollar at risk—America's entire strategic position was threatened by British weakness.

To deal with the structural problems of Bretton Woods, the administration contemplated a major new initiative. Earlier in 1964 the United States had proposed a 50 percent increase in the quotas of the

International Monetary Fund as a way of dealing with periodic balance of payments crises and increasing international reserves. Led by the French, the European finance ministers resisted this idea, seeing it as a ploy by the United States to print its way out of its deficit, and approved only a 25 percent increase.[102] In a memo to the president discussing this, Bator noted that the decision was "more mouse than elephant," a clear reflection of short-term thinking about the need to increase international liquidity. But Bator argued that the United States would acquire the "whip hand" to push for reform as its balance of payments situation improved.[103] After the November 1964 election, Johnson's Task Force on Foreign Economic Policy also recommended seeking "two essential improvements in the international monetary system: first a more orderly process of reserve creation; and second, a more automatic mechanism for making international credit available to countries in balance of payments difficulties, on terms that correspond to the realities of the adjustment process."[104] (The second point corresponded to the wish to find a better means of dealing with the problem of sterling as well as reforming the overall system.) The general belief was that the balance of payments problem was not as serious an issue and was coming under control. In February 1965 Johnson outlined a ten-point balance of payments program that was largely voluntary in nature—"moral suasion" was the term used—seeking the cooperation of U.S. business in restricting investment abroad and encouraging travelers to stay home and "see the U.S.A."[105] Johnson explicitly rejected a policy of tighter money and higher interest rates, in large measure because of his desire to see the domestic economy become more robust and to provide the economic wherewithal for Great Society programs.[106] His continuing optimism was matched by reality, as the payments deficit for 1965 dropped to $1.3 billion, the smallest since 1957.[107]

In this atmosphere, the prospect of employing Bator's "whip hand" led the Johnson administration to create a high-level interdepart-

mental study group, the Deming group, whose aim was to develop
and recommend "a comprehensive U.S. position and negotiating
strategy designed to achieve substantial improvement in international
monetary arrangements."[108] McGeorge Bundy sold the idea, the
brainchild of Bator and the Undersecretary for Monetary Affairs
Frederick Deming, to LBJ by assuring him that it was "carefully
drawn so as to commit you to nothing and yet [would] force a broad-
gauged study of the problem as a whole."[109] Bator and Deming's proposal reflected the fact that there had been an important change in
economic thinking within the government. Now the "idea that a reserve currency standard is inherently unstable," an idea associated
with the economist Robert Triffin, had become a dominant para-
digm.[110] Triffin had defined the dilemma created by the Bretton
Woods system: "The more the reserve-currency country (United
States or Britain) builds up its liabilities or pays out its reserves . . .
the less confidence foreign depositors will have in its ability to redeem
these commitments, and hence the greater danger of panic. . . . On
the other hand, [if the reserve-currency country balances its pay-
ments] . . . world liquidity would fall short of rising world needs. The
result could be deflation by deficit countries, competitive deprecia-
tions, and controls on trade and capital."[111] The implication of the
"Triffin dilemma" was that there should be some other way, more
centralized and controlled, to increase international reserves to sustain the growth in international trade. Triffin himself wanted to create something akin to a "Federal Reserve bank of the world," by
transforming the International Monetary Fund (IMF) and giving it
the power to create new reserves.[112] In proposing to create what
amounted to a world central bank, with its infringement on state sovereignty, Triffin's idea went well beyond the politically possible. However, the dilemma Triffin defined was one that had contributed to an
increasing consensus in favor of some type of reform. Given the re-
current problems with sterling, the British had supported the creation

of a new reserve asset at the IMF meeting in 1962.[113] Even the French had initially proposed at the 1963 and 1964 IMF meetings the CRU, or composite reserve unit, a form of reserve creation that was tied to the amount of gold each government held and that would bar central banks from additional accumulation of dollars. However, de Gaulle's February 1965 endorsement of what most believed to be the anachronistic gold standard undercut the position of his finance minister and the idea of the CRU. The French government now backtracked, opposing attempts to create additional liquidity. It seemed that the French believed that the "existing monetary system would inevitably decay and that [French] interests would best be served if they waited for the moment of collapse, when they could bring forward proposals for a new system."[114]

Given the French position, the timing for a U.S. initiative was auspicious, with the new secretary of the Treasury, Henry Fowler, willing to entertain proposals well beyond those his successors would consider. Fowler knew that reforming a system sanctified by precedent and involving "powerful nationalistic passions" would be a very difficult struggle: "Blood will be spilled on the floor," he said at a press conference before his first trip to Europe to begin consultations.[115] Announced in July 1965, Johnson's memorandum authorizing such "forward planning in international finance" provided an opportunity to assemble an American proposal for reform that could take advantage of the current strength of the U.S. economy and balance of payments in 1965. It also took particular note of the ongoing crisis with sterling, which it defined as a "major foreign policy concern."[116]

This concern mounted throughout the first half of 1965. The $3 billion rescue of sterling at the end of 1964 bought time, and encouraged a greater activism among Johnson administration officials concerning British internal policies, especially the prospective budget of the Wilson government. Despite warnings from the U.S. embassy in London about the tradition of budget secrecy, Johnson dispatched his

Visit of Prime Minister Harold Wilson, April 1965. Despite his complaints about Wilson's criticism of his Vietnam policies, LBJ cooperated successfully with the prime minister to maintain the value of the pound sterling and keep a British presence in Europe and the Far East. (LBJ Library; photo by Yoichi Okamoto)

director of the Bureau of the Budget, Kermit Gordon, to London to insist on a tough budget.[117] Bundy informed the British that the reason for the American interest was the "necessary relation between any attack on sterling and the strength of the dollar."[118]

Reassured by Gordon's report that the British were taking the necessary steps to secure sterling's value, Johnson received Wilson in April 1965 at the White House, offering praise for the "toughness of the decisions in a number of directions."[119] (Showing a willingness to compartmentalize his approach to policies, Johnson's lavish praise for Wilson and his government came despite his intense anger over British criticism of his Vietnam policies, especially the decision to begin regular bombing of North Vietnam in February.)[120] In a further meeting with Treasury Secretary Fowler, Wilson received assurances that the United States would continue to support sterling.[121] Wilson's government, after its shaky start and with its slim majority, seemed to be firmly in the saddle.

The pause in concern over sterling's value now found Americans coming to terms with the implications of the British Defense Review, which the Wilson government had initiated earlier in the year. During talks between Secretary of Defense McNamara and Defense Minister Dennis Healey, McNamara expressed surprise and outrage that the British were considering reducing their military commitments east of Suez. McNamara tried to invoke the "interdependence" of the United States and Britain, only to have Healey sharply rebuke him, saying that "in light of recent events [in Vietnam and the Dominican Republic] there could be little confidence in interdependence, and the upshot might be that His Majesty's Government would prefer to drop commitments rather than continue to play a part in meeting them in conjunction with the USA." After Dean Rusk expressed his own hope that the British would maintain their position east of Suez, Foreign Secretary Michael Stewart warned him that "we might well have to stop spreading the butter so thin," and that "an overextended military position based on a shaky pound was not a source of strength or confidence." Stewart assured Rusk that the British would not "chuck everything" without "proper consideration," but the Americans had now been duly warned of the connection between Britain's economic woes and its security commitments.[122]

In late June 1965 Chancellor of the Exchequer James Callaghan planned a visit to the United States to secure "from President Johnson . . . an announcement that the US Government would give full support to maintaining the position of sterling."[123] Callaghan had a very pleasant meeting with Johnson, who deliberately avoided detailed discussion of specific points and simply stressed that the United States and Britain should "keep together" on financial questions.[124] Ambassador Bruce, who was present at the meeting, noted that LBJ was in a storytelling mood, recounting wartime experiences in Australia—which reminded him of Texas—and that Johnson "gave the feeling he was seven feet tall, ready to uncoil like a snake, a combination of Rodin's *Le Penseur,* a Texas ranger, and Laurence Olivier."[125] Johnson's behavior was quite deliberate, since the American assessment of the British economy was far more negative than it had been only a few months earlier. The United States believed that the British had "cut the meat too thin" and that there was little likelihood of any sudden improvement in Britain's export performance.[126] In meeting with officials from the Federal Reserve Bank, Callaghan was told that they believed the British economy was "overheated," that the government's incomes policy was not "credible."[127] The Americans pushed for tougher deflationary measures, indicating a willingness to reciprocate by participating with the Europeans in a multilateral, long-term loan for the U.K. This was not the response that Callaghan had anticipated, and he said "frankly" that "he could not carry the present level of foreign exchange expenditure on defense and did not intend to do so. It affected the whole U.K. economy and the ability of Britain and 56 million British people to survive as a viable economic community and a sound ally."[128]

Despite his good meeting with LBJ, Callaghan was shaken by his trip to Washington. He returned to London convinced of the need to act decisively in order to gain American assistance. The one place where he found a sympathetic ear was in the White House, where NSC deputy Francis Bator made it clear that, "provided the United Kingdom economic plan was credible and the Americans were assured there would be no unilateral reduction of our defense commitments, White House officials would feel able to recommend to the president that he should authorize short-term financial help for the United Kingdom if this was required."[129] As David Bruce noted in his diary: "The whole affair transcends monetary problems; it is essentially political."[130] However, the question of what would constitute a "credible" British policy, and what the United States would want in return, remained open, ultimately to be based on a presidential decision.

When the balance of payments figures were released in mid-July, reflecting an accelerating British deficit, the stage was set for another run on sterling. Devaluation was now a serious option within Wilson's government, supported by George Brown, the first secretary of state. Brown believed that another U.S. rescue of the pound would involve "politico-military commitments," which he was "not willing to underwrite."[131] Wilson, however, strongly resisted devaluation, in large measure because of the damage it would do to his standing as an ally of the United States. Instead of the wage-price freeze the Americans were demanding, Wilson announced that new social welfare programs would be postponed along with other restrictions on government spending. The prime minister then called in Ambassador Bruce and told him that he wanted to fly to Washington to discuss "Defense, Economics, and Politics at the highest levels."[132]

Wilson's desire for a summit underscored the seriousness of the crisis. In Washington, George Ball, who was in the process of losing his own fight against a further escalation of the war in Vietnam, saw the British situation in the most dire terms. He feared that a "substantial devaluation of sterling" might lead to "monetary infighting through floating rates, threats of countervailing duties, the suspension of gold purchases and sales, and the ensuing collapse of the IMF and Kennedy Round . . . and would shatter the free world political and defense system that is already seriously strained." Ball wanted the United States to insist that the British not devalue or withdraw from their commitments, and in return the United States would "offer necessary financial assistance ourselves, and necessary help in rounding up funds from Europe."[133] Ball's fears were echoed in a transatlantic phone call from NSC adviser Bundy and Wilson's principal private secretary, Derek Mitchell. Bundy told Mitchell that "the most knowledgeable and most sympathetic and least banker-like people" within the Johnson administration did not think the British had gone far enough, particularly in dealing with wage increases. Mitchell retorted that this was as far as a Labour government could go and asked Bundy what the American reaction would be if the British government were "forced over the edge" into devaluation. Bundy, perhaps stunned by the blunt question, replied, "Don't," and then added that if the worst happened, the United States and Britain could work together so that the British would "only fall half way down the precipice." Bundy told Mitchell that Washington considered devaluation "unthinkable" and something that might have horrendous consequences for the international stability.[134] Secretary of the Treasury Fowler was even more graphic in discussing the "terrible consequences" of a British decision to devalue: "Devaluation on a modest scale would be useless, while on a drastic scale it would be like lighting a match to find a gold piece in a barn stocked with kerosene."[135]

On July 30 and 31, 1965, the British cabinet secretary, Burke Trend, one of Wilson's closest advisers, paid a quiet visit to Washington. Trend's intensive discussions with White House and cabinet officials amounted to an attempt to coordinate the American and British government's global policies, and in particular to maintain a British presence east of Suez at the very moment America was expanding its war in Southeast Asia. The two days of talks covered a wide range of issues, with the Americans pressing the British to follow more stringent economic policies to prevent devaluation and maintain their global commitments. Although the Americans insinuated a general link between their support for sterling and British defense policies, they stayed away from any direct connection to Vietnam. Before the talks, McGeorge Bundy suggested to LBJ that "a British Brigade in Vietnam would be worth a billion dollars at the moment of truth for Sterling."[136] When other Johnson advisers, like George Ball, reacted by arguing that that would make "mercenaries" of British soldiers, Bundy told Ball that if the British "really want to do business with Lyndon Johnson they have to take into account his basic problems . . . they must not be under the illusion [that] they can . . . make a money deal without our getting certain satisfaction on some political points."[137] LBJ, who understood Wilson's views and his domestic political position far better than his NSC adviser, simply told him, "[Wilson] won't do anything on Vietnam—his peace people won't let him."[138] And when Bundy reported to LBJ the results of his talks with Trend, he stated, "In accordance with your instructions, I kept the two subjects of the pound sterling and Vietnam completely separate."[139]

As sterling's situation continued to deteriorate in the first week of August, Bundy reported to the president that if Wilson were faced with imminent devaluation, he would "try to come over here and dump the problem in your lap, no matter what stage of agreement or disagreement the two governments may be at."[140] Bundy wanted to avoid such a British approach, and assured the president he would not be seeing Wilson without further consultation, especially since the prime minister had left for his annual holiday in the Scilly Isles. Bundy also noted that Johnson's advisers remained of the opinion that any rescue operation had to be multilateral, as "it would be better to let Sterling go than for us to take on its defense without a major foreign contribution."[141]

Johnson was angry about the British situation, telling World Bank president Eugene Black that the British were "laughing at us," knowing the Americans wouldn't allow a devaluation. "They've got us by the yin yang," he told Black, knowing as they did that the Americans feared the effects of a possible British devaluation on the dollar.[142] Like "a reckless boy writing bad checks" on his father's bank account, was the analogy Johnson used with Federal Reserve chairman William McChesney Martin, who told Johnson that the president of the Bank of England, Rowley Cromer, was "absolutely disgusted" with the Labour government and Harold Wilson.[143] That same evening, August 5, Johnson summoned Francis Bator, Bundy's deputy for international economic issues, to brief him on the possible consequences of sterling devaluation. Bator encountered a pajama-clad LBJ, who told him that Fed chairman Martin and his British counterpart, Crowley, both opposed any bailout of the Wilson government. Johnson angrily asked Bator how the British government had come to believe that the United States would rescue the pound. Bator's rejoinder that the president's friendliness and cordiality to Callaghan had created that impression did not receive a response. Bator went on to provide the president with an analysis of the consequences of devaluation, arguing that it might prove "inconvenient" for the United States, but that it would not be a calamity. This view affected Johnson's ongoing approach to the crisis, as he remained far more calm than his advisers while continuing to push them to think about alternatives, and he proved reluctant to act until every last possibility was explored.[144]

As Britain's economic crisis unfolded in August, the United States continued to urge a wage-price freeze but also took the initiative in recruiting European support for a rescue operation. Bator made the case that only if Wilson himself made "an absolute objective of $2.80" (that is, maintaining the exchange rate of $2.80 to the pound) would the United States be in a position to dictate terms to the prime minister. Bator did not think this a likely scenario, but he underestimated Wilson's desire to avoid devaluation.[145] The Americans backed away from their insistence on a wage-price freeze and settled for a policy that had the Wilson government place the Price and Incomes Board on a statutory basis, in effect placing a legal ceiling on further wage increases, "an enormously difficult step for a Labour government." In return Secretary of State Fowler organized an international credit totaling $925 million in support of sterling, including $400 million from the United States. Despite this contribution, and true to his own cautious approach, the president was careful not to insist on—and Wilson did not give him—an explicit "deal" on any larger political or defense issue.

Much of the historical literature, led by the work of British historian Clive Ponting, argues that there was such a deal involved in the British decision to maintain its military commitments east of Suez and the financial assistance proffered by the United States.[146] However, the evidence indicates that the arrangement was more in the nature of a classic "gentleman's agreement" than an explicit bargain. In September, as the specifics of the sterling package were being finalized, Rusk, one of the administration's strongest Anglophiles, cabled Ball in London and insisted that he tell Wilson that the "[United States] is undertaking [a] present short-term support operation for sterling . . . on [the] explicit assumption that [the] UK will not in [the] interim unilaterally disengage from existing commitments."[147] Although Ball told Wilson that the "United Kingdom was the only nation apart from the United States which was doing serious things" and stressed the importance that the United States placed on Britain's global role, his meetings did not result in any formal understanding of a link between the two issues.[148] Wilson agreed to "consult" with the Americans during the Defense Review, but Ball himself stressed that American assistance was not conditioned on any specific quid pro quo by the British government. Indeed, Wilson used the meeting with Ball and Fowler to emphasize his own support for the British position east of Suez but also to warn that he didn't want the Americans to "corral the United Kingdom into Europe," a none-too-veiled reference to the more expensive British Army on the Rhine (BAOR), the British presence in Europe. Wilson also underlined his own view that "the integration of the sterling and dollar was bound to come and should be the long-term objective of joint policies."[149] Neither Ball nor Fowler echoed this sentiment.

As the most recent and definitive study of the sterling crisis makes clear, "By the end of August 1965, the Johnson Administration had achieved its main objectives."[150] The United States did not gain an immediate wage-price freeze, but Wilson had publicly pledged to curb the wage demands of the unions, something that most American officials thought he would refuse to do. During a meeting between Treasury and White House advisers to review the British plans, Bator noted that "they [the Labour government] really have gone pretty far" and that he was doubtful "whether any Tory govt. could or would go further." Bator went on to tell the president that Harold Wilson had "staked his political life on getting Parliament to adopt a more ambitious wage-price policy (short of outright controls) than any major Western country has tried except during war or postwar recovery."[151] The United States had also made it easier for Wilson to stay east of the Suez longer than might have been the case otherwise, without taking on the specific—and potentially costly—commitment to sustain that presence. At relatively little cost, the Johnson government avoided a major international financial crisis at the same time as the escalation of the war in Vietnam, a crisis that might have exacerbated the politics of both Vietnam and LBJ's real love, his Great Society.

The Impact of Vietnam

The sterling crisis, occurring roughly simultaneously with the Johnson administration's decision to escalate the war in Vietnam, offers an insight into the impact of the war on American foreign policy. Certainly the war had an impact on efforts to improve U.S.-Soviet relations, as Moscow undertook to aid its ally, North Vietnam, and thereby meet "Chinese accusations of 'betrayal' of the interests of socialism."[152] Along with any prospect of a U.S.-Soviet summit meeting, another direct casualty of the escalation of the war was Johnson's East-West trade bill. Early in the year the president had appointed a special committee to explore the idea of expanding trade with the Soviet Union and Eastern Europe. The Miller committee, composed of representatives from business, labor, and academia, advocated an expansion of trade, primarily as a way "to influence the internal evolution and external behavior of Communist countries."[153] However, trade with the East, especially after the escalation of the war in Vietnam, was widely regarded as "trade with the enemy." Johnson chose to table the East-West trade bill rather than bring it to a vote.[154]

The impact of Vietnam on relations with the European allies is less clear. Eminent journalist Walter Lippmann, who broke with Johnson over Vietnam, reported from Europe in June 1965 that "there has been a spectacular decline in respect for United States foreign policy." Lippmann, who enjoyed good connections with Gaullists in France, identified the doubts as brought on by "President Johnson's expansion of the war in Vietnam and by his massive intervention in the Dominican Republic."[155] His assessment stood in stark contrast to the views expressed by some diplomats only a few weeks earlier. *Newsweek* had reported that "the Continent is intrigued—and in many instances reassured—by LBJ the man."[156] Although the success of the Dominican intervention in bringing about elections and the subsequent quick withdrawal of U.S. forces soon put the issue on the back burner of concerns, Vietnam's increasing importance for the rest of 1965, especially after the July decisions, made it a major source of European discontent with the United States. Public demonstrations in Europe during this period were still relatively small-scale affairs, drawing small crowds and maintaining a relatively civil atmosphere.[157] The deterioration of support for the United States was most apparent in France, where Johnson was considered by almost a third of the population as the "most dangerous threat" to peace, only slightly behind China's Mao Tse-tung. (This connection between LBJ and Mao is not accidental. The French fear, which they continually expressed to foreign counterparts, including the East Europeans, was that the American escalation in Vietnam would lead to a direct U.S.-

China war.)[158] With the French government strongly opposed to U.S. policy and the French media encouraged to present the war in the same light, French public opinion became the most anti-American in Europe. The Vietnam War contributed to the popular support that sustained de Gaulle's increasingly anti-NATO and anti-U.S. stance. As elections approached in France at the end of the year, running against American hegemony was a central part of de Gaulle's electoral appeal.

With the British, the impact of Vietnam was more complex. It was certainly an important issue for Wilson. He had criticized the American position before coming to power, and he was steadfast in rejecting any direct British involvement in the conflict. His great hope was to be a mediator, both in the larger interest of world peace and in his own political interest to appear to be an important figure on the world stage. After the February 1965 attack on the American barracks at Pleiku, and Johnson's decision to bomb North Vietnam, Wilson called Johnson directly, hoping to come to Washington for direct consultations, much as Clement Attlee had done at the height of the Korean conflict. Johnson reacted with unconcealed anger, believing that the prime minister, like his predecessor on Cuba, was posturing for domestic consumption.[159] He told Wilson that "if one of us jumps across the Atlantic every time there is a critical situation, next week I shall be flying over when Sukarno jumps on you and I will be giving you advice . . . Why don't you run Malaysia and let me run Vietnam?"[160] Although the conversation ended with assurances of British support, Wilson maintained his doubts about U.S. policy. As he told Ambassador Bruce, there "was a real danger of the moral authority of the United States diminishing very sharply," and he saw an analogy with the "moral isolation" of the British position in the Suez crisis of 1956.[161]

Despite Wilson's genuine concern about the conflict, the actual impact of Vietnam on U.S.-British relations and policy is difficult to ascertain. The United States did not use its considerable financial leverage to coerce the British into even a token commitment to South Vietnam. In part, the British support for Malaysia in its "confrontation" with a Chinese-supported Indonesia allowed Britain to argue that it was already playing a critical role in the free world's defense of Southeast Asia against Beijing's expansionism.[162] Johnson recognized that Wilson faced a difficult position with the left wing of his party, and at times he was reminded by his advisers that Wilson's general support for the U.S. position in the conflict was not an easy position to maintain within the left-leaning parliamentary Labour Party.[163] The British government's own survey of elite opinion in the country at the end of 1965 found a division of views of the conflict shaped by political preference, with Labour Party members seeing the conflict as a civil war that could be settled by a U.S. withdrawal, and Conservative elites perceiving the conflict as a part of Chinese communist expansionism. What was interesting was the degree to which both sides favored the government's policy of noninvolvement and support for negotiations. Britain's popular concerns were focused on its political role in Europe, and Vietnam, while important, was not an overriding issue for either the public or for the Wilson government.[164]

Although some authors have argued that the Vietnam War was a "dominating factor" and a primary source of contention between the United States and West Germany, the evidence does not support this claim.[165] The Vietnam War was "a secondary factor that had some influence on more important factors of contention" between the two countries, but other factors, primarily Johnson's pursuit of detente, were far more significant issues.[166] Erhard remained firmly in support of the American position in Vietnam, even adopting Johnson's formula that "US actions in Vietnam meant to the Germans that they could rely on the US. This is what formed the close link between South Vietnam and Berlin."[167] Although George Ball, himself a skeptic about U.S. policy, tried to argue that Erhard "was telling us [about

Vietnam] what he believed we would like to hear," Erhard and his advisers told unsympathetic French leaders the same thing.[168] Erhard even continued his support for the U.S. position in Vietnam after he left office.[169] German public support in 1965 for the United States was the strongest of any European country. In February 1965 only 9 percent of Germans blamed the United States for the escalation of the war, and that summer more than half thought the United States was justified in its intervention.[170] The significant problem for the United States, in terms of its political impact, was criticism from the strongly anticommunist retired chancellor Konrad Adenauer, who told American visitors that "Vietnam was a disaster" and that "Europe was the decisive area and we were instead getting sucked deeper into the morass in South East Asia."[171] This was the worry that was foremost in the mind of German policymakers, as they tried to keep the United States as engaged as possible in their own concerns in Europe. As Ambassador George McGhee summarized the German interests, "They didn't want us to capitulate in Viet Nam, because that would decrease our credibility in Western Europe. On the other hand, they didn't want us to get too deeply involved so that we wasted our resources there, because they thought Europe [was] the most important."[172]

The war had its impact on U.S.-German relations in two distinct but interrelated ways. The first was the U.S. request, under the "More Flags" campaign, for a tangible German contribution to the effort in South Vietnam. With memories of Nazi-era and wartime destruction less than twenty years old, most German leaders understood the political impossibility of providing German soldiers for the Vietnam war effort. Most American officials had no illusions, either, about actual German soldiers, but they hoped for as much nonmilitary assistance for South Vietnam as they could get. In June 1964, Johnson asked Erhard for help in South Vietnam, and the chancellor replied that "Germany stood ready to do all that could be done economically, politically and financially."[173] Erhard was slow to fulfill this promise—German personnel in Vietnam numbered just twelve at the end of 1964.[174] Johnson's efforts in 1965 to launch a Southeast Asian Development Program, the heart of an April 1965 speech at Johns Hopkins University, also called for European contributions. Again Erhard assured Johnson "that he believed that this was the right way to come to grips with the problems," but the Federal Republic pledged only $30 million, not the $75 million the administration sought.[175] The German reluctance to aid the American effort with any substantial contribution became an increasing irritant in the relationship.

The second way in which the Vietnam War had an impact on U.S.-German relations concerned the offset policy and the American balance of payments. The escalation of the war, announced by Johnson in July, soon had its impact on the American balance of payments deficit. Bator reported to the president in October that "if we take no action, the deficit during the second half of 1965 is likely to be appreciably larger than during the first six months."[176] Johnson considered imposing mandatory restrictions on capital investment abroad, but decided instead to tighten the application of the voluntary program. Johnson worried that serious balance of payments deficits might force him to adopt a "commander-in-chief" tactic with the problem: the call for sacrifice because of Vietnam would encourage those who wanted him to escalate the war in Vietnam even further. Any help Johnson could get on the balance of payments deficit became a priority, in his thinking, and German purchases of U.S. military items, the offset agreements, were an obvious target. In particular, Secretary of the Treasury Henry Fowler wanted Bator to "crank this in" to the next meeting between LBJ and the German leader.[177]

During the December 1965 meetings between Erhard and Johnson, Germany's poor response in terms of aid in Vietnam, together with the offset payments, led to one of the most dramatic examples of the "Johnson treatment" of a European leader. Even Lady Bird John-

son could sense it was coming. After listening to Erhard say at a
White House dinner that when he considered U.S. sacrifices in defense of the "free world in Vietnam I feel ashamed, because what we
can contribute is very modest compared with what you do," Mrs.
Johnson wrote in her diary, "I am sure before he gets out of town
Lyndon will ask him in as forceful a manner as possible how much
more they can contribute."[178] Johnson—who once told his speech
writer Richard Goodwin, "There's only one way to deal with the Germans. You keep patting them on the head and then every once in a
while you kick them in the balls"—clearly had decided to deliver one
of his kicks.[179] According to the sparse American record of the talks,
Johnson asked Erhard to issue "instructions to his Finance and Defense Ministers to meet fully the terms of the Offset Agreement," and
for "the deployment of a German medical company and construc-
tion battalion to South Vietnam." Erhard was evasive in his answers
to both demands, telling Johnson that he "intended to stand by our
agreements" but that he must find the "ways and means." "I can't say
when I can pay [since] I [have] to balance my budget," McGhee recorded the chancellor as saying. On assistance to the Vietnam effort,
Erhard acknowledged the German "moral obligation" to help, but
referred to "certain legal difficulties" with sending labor battalions.[180]
Johnson was clearly irritated by Erhard's answers. According to
McGhee, whose memoir account of the meeting is the fullest, Johnson's "tall, rangy figure towered over the comparatively small figure
of the chancellor. Gesticulating and speaking in a strong, strident
voice, Johnson alternately wheedled and threatened." Professing his
shock at Johnson's approach, McGhee quotes the president as telling
Erhard, "Now we're going to find out who our friends are," recounting all the United States had done for Germany, and saying that now
was the time for Germany to pay America back.[181] According to the
German memorandum of the conversation, Johnson said, "If I can
get legislation to put 200,000 more men in Vietnam, surely the

Visit of Chancellor Ludwig Erhard (left), December 1965. Although there are smiles in this picture, LBJ used this visit to pressure the German chancellor for stronger support for American policy in Vietnam. (LBJ Library; photo by Yoichi Okamoto)

Chancellor can get two battalions to Vietnam. If we are going to be partners, we better find out right now."[182] The United States badly needed the help and public support of its allies, Johnson told the chancellor, and he expected Germany to take the lead.

McGhee believed that Johnson had "greatly overplayed his hand" and even frightened the chancellor with his outburst.[183] But the fact is that Johnson's "kick" did lead to action by Bonn and an announcement on January 12, 1966, that the German hospital ship S.S. *Helgoland* would be dispatched to South Vietnam. Over the next several years German aid to South Vietnam averaged $7.5 million annually.[184] The list of German aid projects for South Vietnam grew and included additional medical aid, refugee camps, and even reformatories for street children in Saigon. Although Erhard did agree to "honor" the offset agreement, that issue remained a much more significant problem than the relatively small amounts of German assistance to South Vietnam. Together with the actions of French president de Gaulle, the offset issue would contribute to a series of crises in the coming year that threatened to unravel the NATO alliance and stamp Lyndon Johnson's presidency as a disaster in its policy toward Europe.

3

The French Challenge

It was characteristic of Lyndon Johnson's caution and penchant for secrecy that he would wait until the last possible moment before making a decision. The British ambassador Patrick Dean lamented the constant difficulty of figuring out "which way the president is likely to jump on any particular matter."[1] Johnson's assistants recognized his prolonged search for consensus before acting, "his fixation with keeping his options open on any new policy venture until he had every political stone turned and set in place."[2] Critics, including former secretary of state Dean Acheson, were exasperated by Johnson's penchant for "endlessly reconsidering decisions."[3] However, along with Johnson's innate caution went his extraordinary talent for using a crisis or perceived crisis as an opportunity to move forward with long-stalled initiatives. The most dramatic evidence of Johnson's skill in this regard was his use of Kennedy's assassination, and the national trauma it created, to push through the tax cut of 1964 and the civil rights bill. Similarly, despite his initial doubts about getting another civil rights bill passed in 1965, Johnson used the outbreak of violence in Selma, Alabama, in March to propose one of the most consequential laws in U.S. history, the Voting Rights Act.

For European policy, Johnson had not needed these "crisis skills" during the first two years of his presidency, for the situation had been relatively quiet, and his only major decision was a negative one, the postponement of the MLF deadline. However, in March 1966 President Charles de Gaulle's announcement that France would withdraw from NATO's integrated command put NATO in "a situation in which the survival and future course of the Alliance were in jeopardy."[4] Later in the year, the collapse of Ludwig Erhard's government in Germany, another sterling crisis in Britain, and moves by the U.S. Senate to withdraw American forces from Europe created a "crisis of credibility" in Europe.[5] These challenges, confronted in the midst of the war in Southeast Asia and severe racial disturbances at home, would severely test Johnson's plans for moving American foreign policy toward detente and a reduction of the danger of nuclear war.

The French Withdrawal from NATO

Despite Johnson's hopes that U.S.-French relations might improve in 1965, the year had seen continuing conflict. De Gaulle's attack on the dollar in February 1965 was only the beginning. The escalation of the war in Vietnam and U.S. intervention in the Dominican Republic were extremely unpopular in France, with de Gaulle himself attacking the United States as the "greatest danger in the world today to peace."[6] Almost two-thirds of the French had "no confidence in the wisdom of U.S. leadership," and more than half preferred a neutral course in international affairs.[7] A minor flap ensued in July 1965 when an American plane was discovered to have photographed a secret French nuclear installation at Pierrelatte. The result was National Security Action Memorandum 336, dictating that all agencies of the U.S. government "take special measures to prevent U.S. activities in France which could needlessly embarrass United States relations with France."[8] U.S. refusals to issue export licenses for any computers that might assist the French nuclear weapons program further aggravated relations. The French argued that some of the computers were ordered for civilian purposes, and some French officials argued the American refusal was contrary to the spirit of the North Atlantic treaty.[9]

By the end of the year, de Gaulle was quoted by one diplomat as saying, "I will not rest until the last American soldier has left Europe."[10] Johnson relaxed his strict verbal restraint and remarked informally at a White House luncheon that de Gaulle was "a grouchy old grandfather grumbling by the stove," who had to be tolerated "as long as he stayed in the house." He also likened the general to "a train that scatters people walking on the track. But as soon as the train has passed I am back again with my friend Erhard, walking arm in arm down the track."[11] Johnson's dismissal of de Gaulle's influence infuriated the general, confirming his own belief that the crude Texan was not fit to lead the alliance. To de Gaulle, Johnson was just an ordinary politician, comparable to Henri Queuille, one of the bland leaders of France's weak and unstable Fourth Republic.[12] He was a slave to American public opinion who had to hold a news conference "every two days." The general agreed with his friend and frequent visitor former chancellor Adenauer, that Johnson was incapable of the vision needed to guide the Western countries, and that Europe must acquire its own voice. It was "absolutely intolerable" that Europe was dependent on such a country and its "accidental president."[13]

Adenauer's own desire that de Gaulle lead Europe was compromised by Gaullist policies that contributed to France's isolation. In the early-morning hours of July 1, 1965, French officials staged a walkout from the Council of Ministers, the decisionmaking body of the European Economic Community, leaving an "empty chair" in the council. At issue in the empty chair crisis was the financing of the EEC's farm support programs, but the breakdown had as much to do with de Gaulle's resistance to any strengthening of "supranationalism" in Europe and his attempts to secure his dominance over the other

Visit of Foreign Minister Maurice Couve de Murville of France, October 1966. The French did not respond as well to the Johnson treatment as some of the other allies. (LBJ Library; photo by Yoichi Okamoto)

five countries in the community.[14] France wanted the other EEC countries to pick up a larger portion of the farm subsidies that greatly benefited French farmers. However, the other EEC countries demanded, in return for the funding, expanded authority for the EEC in both budgetary and political matters. France refused, determined to "freeze everything as it was" rather than add to the authority of the EEC's decisionmaking institutions.[15] France's boycott effectively paralyzed the EEC and the Kennedy Round negotiations, and American diplomats forecast that the crisis was "likely to last through [the] year with the end result of De Gaulle getting about what he wants."[16] And he did. After de Gaulle's reelection in January 1966, the French boycott was ended with the so-called Luxembourg Compromise, which allowed for a "member state of the European Council to invoke the need for a unanimous vote if its vital interests were at stake."[17] France had put the brakes on the process of European integration.

With the NATO treaty up for renewal in 1969, and with de Gaulle's ongoing attacks on the current structure of the alliance, American officials knew that the French would soon act in some way against the treaty. By the summer of 1965 the State Department was assuming that "since France was likely to require that all integrated commands and combat forces not under French command be removed from France, the United States should consult at once with its other allies to make the necessary transfers in an orderly fashion."[18] That August the White House instructed the State Department, the Pentagon, the CIA, and the U.S. Information Agency, as well as the Atomic Energy Commission, to undertake the necessary studies with a view toward coping with an expected French withdrawal.[19] One result was an October 1965 State Department paper entitled "France and NATO," in which the department took a hardline approach, threatening that "the United States would withdraw [NATO's military] protection from France" if the country "ceased to participate constructively in the Alliance." At a meeting to consider this issue, Johnson's White House advisers, led by McGeorge Bundy, objected strongly. Bundy called the State Department paper an "empty threat" and argued with an air of resignation that the United States "might as well face the fact" that the French assumed they had American protection regardless of what Washington might leak to the newspapers.[20] With an eye to the upcoming French elections in December, George Ball fired back that the threat of withdrawing military protection was one of the few actions Washington could take that might affect the French people. McNamara jumped into the argument as well, stressing that a France that did not contribute troops or support facilities was not entitled to U.S. protection. He also raised the issues of Congress and the problems the administration would face if

France should cease to participate constructively in the organization and activities of the alliance. Ambassador David Bruce intervened in the debate to suggest a compromise formulation that papered over this division within the administration, simply asserting that "the U.S. security commitment given in Article V [of the NATO treaty] will obviously have to be re-examined by the President, so far as it relates to France."[21]

This argument between White House staffers and the representatives of the State and Defense Departments reflected the different priorities and agendas of each group. The State Department was determined to protect that pillar of American diplomacy, the NATO alliance, and to punish the French for undermining it. State was also afraid of the example that the French might set, especially with the Germans. Secretary of State Dean Rusk reprimanded the U.S. ambassador in Germany, George McGhee, for taking a position that Rusk felt encouraged good relations between the French and the Germans "at any cost." In language similar to that which he used when discussing the communist world, Rusk told McGhee that "the present French leadership responds to firmness and exploits any whisper of weakness . . . We should not display any lack of confidence in our own positions or any willingness to compromise them in the interests of transient amity between France and Germany—and this applies to nuclear and offset arrangements, as well as other elements of policy."[22] Rusk's angry statement reveals that the conflict with France had escalated to the point that some American officials were willing to put aside the U.S. policy of promoting Franco-German reconciliation; some even hoped they could "go over de Gaulle's head" and appeal to the French public for its support.

McNamara's position, and that of the Defense Department, was more complicated. On the one hand, he complained that the Gaullist challenge would "force us to adjust to a peacetime arrangement which would endanger our wartime capability" and weaken the policy of "flexible response." But the actual U.S. commitment to flexible response was minimal, and it was already affected by the demands of Vietnam and the sense of a reduced threat in Europe.[23] De Gaulle's defiant position opened up backdoor opportunities for the Defense secretary to reduce the conventional American military presence in Europe. In talks with the British, McNamara had already complained bitterly of the "inadequate German force contribution" and the need for a substantial increase. McNamara felt stymied by what he saw as a German overreaction "if we withdraw a battalion," and yet the Germans were unwilling to face up to their responsibilities and provide the necessary manpower and funding for an effective military defense of their country.[24] He saw that de Gaulle's behavior might create opportunities for a reduction in the U.S. troop presence in Europe, an objective McNamara increasingly championed, especially as offset negotiations with the Germans became more difficult, congressional pressure intensified, and the Vietnam commitment escalated.

Bundy recognized that President Johnson was "determined that France should not be allowed to push the U.S. around," but that Johnson would "want to play the large cards with France himself; particularly he will want to control what is said to the French and when." Johnson was aware that his cabinet secretaries did want him to draw a much tougher line with the French, since de Gaulle's behavior complicated their relations with other allies as well as with the all-important Congress. Nevertheless Johnson wanted to maintain his own grip on policy, so that he could connect his response to the French with other American priorities. Bundy hinted at one of these priorities in the meeting, when he discussed the possibility of trilateral arrangements with the Germans and British that might help move them forward on the "nuclear problem." By this he meant not only the increasingly unlikely MLF or ANF, but the possibility of connecting U.S. responses to movement with the Soviets on nonproliferation, an objective that had risen in the list of U.S. priorities and that could serve as an effective response to de Gaulle's own East-West initiatives.[25]

De Gaulle's electoral victory in January 1966, along with the resolution of the EEC crisis and the failure of Johnson's thirty-seven-day bombing pause to prevent renewed escalation of the war in Vietnam, provided the opportunity for de Gaulle's decision to move against NATO.[26] British diplomats speculated that "he may increasingly become an old man in a hurry" with a "determination to change the European scene in some marked way before he leaves."[27] De Gaulle publicly expressed the fear that a U.S.-dominated NATO would drag Europe into conflicts like Vietnam, and that he believed Johnson might soon involve the United States in a war with China.[28] Although de Gaulle's move was planned well in advance, media speculation at the time focused on the French president's conviction that "the Cold War with Russia is over and that the NATO defensive alliance is therefore not only obsolete but, worse, an impediment to a permanent entente between West and East Europe." The timing of de Gaulle's remarks may be significant, as he made them shortly before his trip to Moscow in June 1966. De Gaulle had carefully observed what he believed to be important changes in the situation of the Soviet Union. The bitterness of the Sino-Soviet dispute and the emergence of a Chinese nuclear threat to Russia, the increasing calls for greater independence among the Eastern European states, and America's distraction in Vietnam highlighted an opportunity to de Gaulle. The French leader believed that the Soviets might be willing to return to their pre-1914 role and their "natural affinity" for France in the creation of a new European security system. Such a new system would marginalize the role of the United States in Europe—something de Gaulle predicted would happen in any event—and might even allow for the eventual peaceful reunification of Germany within a Europe controlled by this new Franco-Russian entente. In such a fashion, de Gaulle's vision of a Europe "from the Atlantic to the

Urals" could be conceivable.[29] Although his ultimate objectives remain subject to debate—de Gaulle himself may not have known how far he wanted to push the concept of France's "independence"[30]—de Gaulle did envision a transformation of Europe, perhaps replacing NATO with a series of bilateral arrangements.[31] In August 1967 de Gaulle proclaimed, "France, in leaving the system of blocs, has perhaps given the signal of a general evolution toward international detente," words indicative of the general's strong desire to cast off the burden of NATO.[32]

On March 7, 1966, Maurice Couve de Murville, the French foreign minister, handed Charles Bohlen, the American ambassador in Paris, a handwritten letter from President de Gaulle to President Johnson. During their long and tense meeting discussing the letter, Bohlen eventually got Couve to admit that the letter constituted a "denunciation" of existing agreements between the United States and France rather than any bid for further negotiations. Bohlen raised the issue of America's commitment to France's security under Article V and warned Couve that, in his view, the "French move looked very much like a step in the direction of neutrality."[33] Bohlen had long been an advocate of restraint in dealing with de Gaulle, having stressed that the president should keep a low profile and stay out of de Gaulle's line of fire. Earlier he had counseled patience, convinced that most of the French did not agree with de Gaulle: "It should always be borne in mind that de Gaulle cannot have many more years in power, and the present indications are that a very large portion of the objectionable features of current French policy would disappear with his departure from power."[34] However, having long predicted that the general "would not take France out of NATO," he now felt de Gaulle had gone one step too far.[35] Long worried that LBJ did not possess the same ability of President Kennedy to appreciate "the complexity of the General,"[36] Bohlen now launched into the advocacy of a tough new policy toward France, a policy designed to separate de Gaulle

Johnson and his senior advisers—(left to right) Francis Bator, Walt Rostow, Dean Acheson, David Bruce, George Ball, Dean Rusk, and Robert McNamara—meet on the NATO Crisis, May 1966. Johnson rejected the advice of his "Wise Men" to undertake a tough policy toward French president Charles de Gaulle. (LBJ Library; photo by Yoichi Okamoto)

from both the French public and the majority of the French civil service, whom Bohlen believed did not share the general's antagonism toward the United States.[37] He told LBJ that the French withdrawal had radically changed the situation, amounting to a "complete destruction . . . of the entire NATO organization and cooperative defense efforts." To accept de Gaulle's move with equanimity would, in Bohlen's words, "have a chilling effect upon the opposition in France" and lead to a "panic" in French public opinion.[38]

In fact, the French move was much more ambiguous than Bohlen had presented. De Gaulle's letter began with the assurance that France would remain an active member of the Western alliance, "determined even as today to fight at the side of her allies in case one of them will be the object of unprovoked aggression." However, France was now determined "to recover the entire exercise of her sovereignty over her territory," a sovereignty that was "impaired" by the presence of foreign military forces and her participation in "integrated" commands.[39] French diplomats told the British that the move was linked to de Gaulle's desire to promote detente, that "only if the East saw the Western defense effort relaxing, would they realize they could afford to relax their own."[40] De Gaulle's trip to Moscow lent credence to this interpretation, and American diplomats speculated on a revival of the Franco-Russian alliance, with a new version of French neutrality.[41] De Gaulle's distinction between France's treaty obligations and the peacetime organizational arrangements of the alliance presented the Americans with a dilemma that had not been fully anticipated. Indeed, Couve had told Bohlen that "we could interpret [the] French step as we wished," and that de Gaulle's deliberate ambiguity was one of his political tactics.[42] (Bator described de Gaulle to LBJ as a "lightweight jujitsu artist whose leverage comes from others' exertions.")[43] In Johnson's initial reply to the general, he refrained from taking any immediate action, noting only that the letter raised "grave questions regarding the whole relationship between the responsibilities and benefits of the Alliance."[44]

In preparing a full response to the de Gaulle letter, Johnson's NSC deputy Francis Bator was guilty of considerable understatement when he suggested to LBJ that "your advisers may disagree." Was there a distinction between the treaty and the organization? Bator put forth a strong case for not pressing the issue yet. He appealed to Johnson's common sense: "It is a fact of geography that a U.S. threat to deprive France of our protection is at best barely credible and at worst, just plain silly. It is like threatening to abandon Kentucky in the face of a land attack by Canada. It is hard to do unless one is prepared to throw in Ohio. If we are going to defend the Germans against the Russians, we cannot help but defend France too."[45] Bator also stressed that de Gaulle's move had the potential to put the United States in the middle of a Franco-German dispute over NATO and the presence of French forces in Germany. The Germans would "as usual look to us for guidance" in any response to de Gaulle, and Bator urged Johnson to approach the issue cautiously. The real problem, as he stressed to LBJ, was "as always . . . not France but Germany—and the more we agitate the alliance the more we may bring this potentially divisive issue to the fore."[46]

On the other side of the issue there were powerful emotions at work. After de Gaulle told him that every American soldier must leave France, Dean Rusk replied, "Does that include the dead Americans in military cemeteries as well?"[47] (Bill Mauldin, a noted political cartoonist of the time, captured the same sentiment by drawing de Gaulle standing in a cemetery of white crosses and proclaiming, "Why do you Americans stay where you're not wanted?")[48] Resentment toward France was a widely held sentiment among Americans, and it had the potential to inflame the issue beyond any calm resolution. (Not only Americans expressed this sentiment—Canadian prime minister Lester Pearson later told Johnson that he had said the same thing Rusk had to de Gaulle.)[49] Within the Senate, Henry Jackson was determined to use his Governmental Operation Committee to hold hearings to "mobilize enough public sentiment on behalf of a renewed commitment to NATO to persuade the president to respond to de Gaulle more aggressively."[50] The State Department reaction also reflected this indignation, urging what one critic called a "clarion call to propaganda battle."[51] It wanted to push an accelerated program of integration in NATO, in effect arguing that the best way to stop de Gaulle was to beef up the alliance—make it "more integrated rather than less."[52] On this point, Rusk and Ball received support from Bohlen. Although State took the lead in proposing a tougher policy, it could count on the support of Defense and Treasury, as well as the senior "Wise Men," like Dean Acheson and John McCloy, whom

Johnson brought in for advice on the issue. (Johnson appointed Acheson to chair the committee to determine a response.) The State Department, however, was determined to use the interlude created by McGeorge Bundy's departure at the end of February and before Walt Rostow's succession as national security adviser to reassert its own role in determining the direction of American foreign policy. There was, as Francis Bator remembered, "just a bit of 'who is this Texan fellow to tell us about high diplomacy' in the air" and a determination to be free of the "meddling" of the White House staff.[53]

Johnson resisted this move, determined to retain control of foreign policy decisions. Historians have generally not given Johnson credit for resisting the temptation to exploit the French action for his own short-term political gains.[54] Polls at the time demonstrated that an overwhelming majority of Americans disapproved of de Gaulle's action, and Johnson, in the midst of his own declining approval rate in the polls and dealing with the ongoing crisis in South Vietnam, could have chosen to exploit the French issue as a welcome diversion, a chance to rally Americans against the ungrateful, patronizing, and insulting French.[55] Even Johnson's critics, such as Senator Fulbright, who had just put the administration through highly publicized hearings to debate Vietnam policy, supported Johnson in his confrontation with de Gaulle. Fulbright acknowledged that de Gaulle might have a point about reorganizing NATO, but said that "the worst thing about General de Gaulle is the offensive way he puts everything. He looks to me often as if he intentionally wishes to be insulting."[56]

Johnson chose not to arouse passions with a public attack on de Gaulle. In characteristic language, he told George Ball, a dove on Vietnam but one of the administration's hawks in dealing with the general, that he didn't want to get into a "pissing match with de Gaulle," which "would serve to build de Gaulle up and to build France up."[57] Johnson worried that a public argument with de Gaulle would blur the issue of responsibility, and that it was important, for the domestic politics of the other allies, that Paris be perceived as the party to blame. Connected to this belief was Johnson's reading of American domestic politics. Johnson was concerned that the American public's resentment of Europeans, already present because of Europe's failure to aid the United States in Vietnam, could easily get out of hand and affect public support for NATO. Despite the advice of men who knew Europe far more thoroughly and intimately than he did, Johnson refused to give the French leader the confrontation he wanted. He played—or, more correctly, *assumed*—the role of statesman, determined to rally the alliance behind his leadership to regroup and reform NATO for the new challenge of detente. At the same time, he continued to hold an olive branch out to the French, as shown in the last line of his reply to de Gaulle's letter: "As our old friend and ally her place will await France whenever she decides to resume her leading role."[58] In response to Ball's argument that de Gaulle had "repudiated a solemn agreement," Johnson now insisted that he saw "no benefit to ourselves or to our allies in debating the position of the French government," and that "our task is to rebuild NATO outside of France as promptly, economically, and effectively as possible."[59] Although not always successful, Johnson now sought to restrain his advisers from criticizing de Gaulle or French policy.[60] And in one of his most famous remarks, the president told McNamara, "When a man asks you to leave his house, you don't argue; you get your hat and go."[61]

Although Johnson asserted a line of restraint in response to de Gaulle, this approach was still subject to implementation by members of his administration who did not share his views. This became clear as allied diplomats confronted the many questions raised by the French withdrawal, including allied overflights of French territory, the continued transportation of oil across France, and reentry rights for NATO forces into France in the event of war. With Johnson's strong urging, NATO forces withdrew from France ahead of schedule, but many of these other matters were subject to prolonged talks. One of the stickiest—and most important—issues was the question of French troops stationed in Germany. Consisting of air and army units comprising approximately 76,000 personnel, these forces posed less of a military question than a political one, deeply intertwined with alliance politics.[62] The French government made it clear that although these forces would no longer come under NATO command, France would leave the forces in Germany if the German government wanted them. The German government now faced a dilemma: if it insisted that French troops could remain only if they were committed to NATO, it would precipitate a French withdrawal and cause a major setback in Franco-German relations, with important domestic political consequences. The Gaullists in the Christian Democratic Party, led by Franz Josef Strauss and former chancellor Konrad Adenauer, would vigorously protest such a move, and they could mobilize significant public support. In a note of significant understatement, the American ambassador in Bonn, George McGhee, reported that "if the present confrontation results in a withdrawal of French forces . . . German public opinion will not react with exhilaration." Indeed McGhee suggested that such a clear failure in the attempt to "build Europe" would lead the Germans to a renewed focus on "the other elusive goal of German foreign policy—reunification," a game in which, McGhee commented, the "key cards are held by the other side."[63] However, if Germany agreed to seek a new arrangement with the French, that would seem to reward de Gaulle's nationalism, and it would raise questions about a special status for France that would be particularly irritating to Washington. Other allies could demand their own special arrangements, further fragmenting the alliance and creating political difficulties for Washington. But the most significant point was that de Gaulle's policy forced the Germans to choose between Paris and Washington, a choice no German leader wanted to make.

On this issue, most of Johnson's advisers were of one mind. Privately, Acheson told the British that he wanted the Germans to take a "firm line" on the issue and that the departure of the French troops would be "no great loss."[64] At a meeting on April 4 between Rusk, McNamara, Ball, and Acheson, they decided that the United States "should fully support" the Germans if they took a hard line toward the French and their troops in Germany, "and do nothing to dissuade them." If the Germans decided to try to negotiate an agreement with de Gaulle about the troops, the "U.S. should urge them to incorporate in these new arrangements effective safeguards assuring their use in accordance with NATO requirements and an adequate quid pro quo giving to other allies in Germany facilities in France such as transit and overflight rights."[65] These conditions were designed to be unacceptable to the French and thus call their bluff. They were the basis of the instructions given to John J. McCloy, the president's special envoy, as he prepared for talks with Chancellor Erhard a week later.

Johnson was at his ranch when the State Department finished drafting the instructions for McCloy. Ball sent them to the president, with the note that they "[would] constitute Mr. McCloy's instructions."[66] When Bator saw Ball's message, he objected to what he perceived as pressure on the Germans to take a hard line. He believed that such pressure would both complicate Erhard's position in German politics and go against Johnson's own clear preference for a muted response to de Gaulle's challenge. He feared that "if under U.S. pressure, German-French negotiations fail, and French Divisions withdraw, Germans will join other Europeans in blaming us for resulting grave damage to German-French relations." The desire to avoid choosing between Paris and Washington, Bator warned, is "still at the center of German politics." Bator also worried that if the French troops were forced out in the face of "U.S. inspired conditions" the result would "tie our hands on a variety of related issues," including any U.S. desire for troop reductions or agreements with the Soviets. Bator immediately cabled LBJ at his ranch, asking him to change McCloy's instructions. Bator urged a less conditional American approach, offering the Germans support for *whatever* they decided to do about the French troops.[67] Johnson, who was on vacation and "wanted to focus on his cows," did not look at Bator's message until later in the week, after McCloy's first meeting with German foreign minister Schröder. McCloy delivered the tough message to Schröder, who appreciated the American approach as a weapon he would use against the Gaullists in his own party. However, after Johnson read Bator's message, he immediately told Dean Rusk that he agreed with Bator and that the secretary should change McCloy's instructions. Johnson wanted the Germans to know, as McCloy subsequently told Chancellor Erhard, that the "United States should support any position taken by the FRG that recognized the seriousness of the situation and provided an adequate response to the French. The FRG must itself decide the position it wishes to occupy in Europe. We are not thinking of forcing the FRG toward any policy or decision."[68]

Erhard appreciated the American position, seemingly oblivious to the softening in the U.S. attitude toward de Gaulle. Accompanied to the Bonn meeting by the more stridently Atlanticist Schröder, Erhard took a very hard line against de Gaulle, at one point even comparing the general's violation of "solemn agreements" with Hitler's behavior "at the time of the Munich crisis in 1938." He thought that the Americans and Germans had de Gaulle in a "difficult position," from which he was almost certain to "suffer a defeat." He even asked McCloy in a serious tone what the United States would do if the French refused to leave Germany. Schröder laughingly suggested cutting off their electricity and water, and then alluded to the possibility that de Gaulle would call on his "fifth column" in Germany. The reference to the Gaullists in his own party led Erhard to dismiss their importance, and the subject was dropped. Erhard had only recently become the chair of his party, finally forcing the ninety-year old

Adenauer into retirement. He was confident—and as subsequent events would show, overconfident—about his leadership.

In truth, the French held the trump card on this issue, as their soldiers in Germany possessed a symbolic value that gave them great importance to German leaders. Erhard was forced to conclude that the political importance of the French troops outweighed any other considerations. After a major electoral defeat in North Rhine–Westphalia in July 1966, Erhard decided to appease the Gaullists in his party, telling de Gaulle that the French troops were welcome under almost any arrangements.[69] France was allowed to keep its troops in Germany on its own terms, free, as Lawrence Kaplan notes, "from alliance obligations and free, for that matter, to leave whether or not the Germans or Americans wished them to go."[70]

Johnson's "soft" treatment of de Gaulle aroused the fury of his advisers, notably Dean Acheson. Acheson and McCloy had planned the tough approach to the Germans over the issue of the French troops in the hope that it "would have been clear notice to France and the French Army that de Gaulle's attack on NATO has failed." Both were convinced that the United States could appeal to the French over the head of de Gaulle, a conviction based more on their personal devotion to "their" alliance than a careful reading of French politics. Privately, the former secretary of state constantly condemned the "irresolution" and "feeble councils" of the Johnson administration that had allowed de Gaulle to "squeak through" the trap they had laid for him.[71] At a Washington dinner party, Acheson, his discretion eroded by strong martinis, told Bator, "You made the greatest imperial power the world has ever seen kiss de Gaulle's arse."[72] Acheson's fury was not confined to the White House staffer but exploded directly at LBJ during a meeting in May 1966. The president, "primed" to object to an Acheson draft on negotiations with France, suspecting the sabotage of his policy toward de Gaulle, launched into what David Bruce considered a "wholly intemperate attack" on his anti–de Gaulle advis-

ers. Johnson's criticism, in Bruce's words, ignited "the Acheson powder magazine," and the former secretary of state raised his voice
against the president. As Bruce put it, the "fat sizzled in the fire for
quite a time." The president continued to insist that everyone in the
administration remain "scrupulously polite in references to the General," and on this point his advisers found him unyielding.[73]

As with the MLF, Johnson's refusal to make NATO the overwhelming priority of U.S. foreign policy brought him into conflict as
much, if not more, with the traditional U.S. foreign policy establishment as with other Atlantic leaders. However, this portrait of conflict
between Johnson and his advisers over France is only one part of the
picture. The other part is the recognition by Johnson and his aides
that the French move created an opportunity to solve many alliance-
related issues, from adopting the flexible response doctrine to nuclear
sharing to the need to revitalize the alliance and move it toward detente with the Soviet Union. Johnson insisted, a position given institutional weight in National Security Action Memorandum 345, that
in the wake of the French action, the important thing was to "develop
. . . proposals which would bind the Atlantic nations closer together;
support, as best we can, the long-term movement towards unity in
Western Europe; and explore the possibilities for easing East-West
tensions."[74] Acheson himself, despite his occasional outbursts, played
a vital role in this process, agreeing to chair the special committee to
deal with the response to de Gaulle and the future of the alliance.[75] As
the direction of the president's thinking became clear to Acheson, the
former secretary of state finally abandoned the "cabal" of "theologians" who had supported the MLF and agreed to work toward a
"sensible package (with no ownership) which might be workable in
London and on the Hill, as well as in Bonn."[76] The Acheson committee's recommendations focused on "emphasizing, clarifying and implementing NATO's political function" and in particular in organiz-
ing the West's approach toward a detente with Eastern Europe. The

Dean Acheson (left) and David Bruce, May 19, 1966. At this meeting Acheson exploded in anger at the president and his policies toward de Gaulle's France. (LBJ Library; photo by Yoichi Okamoto)

committee acknowledged the danger of "leaving the field of East-West relations" to General de Gaulle, and it proposed a more positive policy toward improving the "Central European environment." One step would be a presidential speech outlining a new policy for NATO and new initiatives in East-West relations, reviving the "bridge-building" that Johnson had spoken of two years earlier. However, despite giving weight to the progress toward detente, the committee still reflected the traditional eastern establishment view, identified strongly with Acheson, Ball, and McCloy, that urged that "at every stage in policy making and execution scrupulous attention must be paid to German interests and sensitivities."[77]

Despite his interest in improving East-West relations, Johnson certainly shared this view. De Gaulle's move had contributed to Johnson's sense, as he often told Bator, of the importance of being "nice to the Germans."[78] Although Johnson himself had been responsible for "pulling the plug" on the U.S. push for the MLF, the de Gaulle challenge renewed his sensitivity to the continuing German interest in some type of nuclear sharing. To Johnson, de Gaulle's example was always less important in itself than in what it might mean if it contributed to an increasing German nationalism, one of the few dangers that could lead to a superpower confrontation. The president knew that his administration had already gone far down the path toward a "software solution" using the Nuclear Planning Group in NATO to give Germany a sense of participation in nuclear decisionmaking. Nevertheless he had tried to be sensitive to Erhard's political problems and had kept open the possibility of a "hardware solution" if the Germans and British could agree on an acceptable formula. LBJ pleaded with British prime minister Wilson not to "leave the Germans under the impression that we have shifted our views just when they were moving towards us," noting Erhard's December 1965 proposals and the continuing expressions of interest by the Germans. Johnson wanted the British to give the appearance of having seriously considered the Germans' proposal and to avoid pressing them to accept any "nuclear solution that [Erhard] might consider at variance with the concept of equality."[79] Johnson made it clear to Wilson that, in his view, "we cannot risk the danger of a rudderless Germany in the heart of Europe."[80]

At the same time, the president was increasingly aware that his closest advisers were seeing a strong positive gain from closing off the hardware solution to the problem of nuclear sharing. After LBJ reaffirmed his point to Bator about "the importance of the Germans finding a place in the sun," his NSC deputy prepared a detailed memorandum arguing strongly that a hardware solution was not the way to proceed. Bator easily dismissed the British-proposed Atlantic

Nuclear Force, noting that "in essence, the scheme would give the Germans the privilege of paying perhaps large amounts of money for essentially non-voting stock in a club which would hold title to a very small fraction of the strategic forces available to the Alliance." In a point certain to gain Johnson's attention, Bator added that "during the course of Congressional testimony and debate," these limits on German "ownership" would be broadcast loud and clear, and would be certain to have their impact on German public opinion. In answering Schröder's point about using the MLF/ANF as a bargaining chip for reunification, Bator stressed, in language echoing Johnson's discussions with Erhard, that "the only tolerably safe path to unification is one which involves lessening fear of Germany in Eastern Europe and the Soviet Union." Schröder himself had taken a series of "small steps" in this regard, trying to open up trade with Eastern Europe and insisting that Germany did not represent a danger to those countries. In pushing for McNamara's Nuclear Planning Group as the software solution to the German demands, Bator urged Johnson to treat the German chancellor the same way as the British prime minister on nuclear policy: with "intelligence, consultation, programming and disarmament." Among the advantages of such an approach would be avoiding any "*unnecessary*" damage to the prospects of an agreement on nonproliferation, although Bator stressed, for political reasons, that the Nuclear Planning Group "be justified in terms of the welfare of the Atlantic Alliance, *not* as a bargain with the Russians over non-proliferation" (emphasis in the original). In what would be a relatively prophetic note toward the end of his "devil's advocate" paper, Bator argued that the Germans should take the "hardest" step "unilaterally to renounce collective as well as national ownership of nuclear weapons, and to justify this as an essential step toward nonproliferation, world-wide arms control, a European settlement, and unification." Bator thought that "making a virtue out of non-nuclear status" would powerfully contribute to reducing the fear of Germany in Europe, and wrote, "If there is any hope for movement towards unification, such a renunciation strategy is it."[81]

Although Bator's memo had little immediate effect, it served to reinforce Johnson's essentially political approach to the German demand for nuclear sharing. He stressed again to Wilson that he, LBJ, perceived the issue not in terms of any "particular solution" but believed that what was at stake was "a political question of the deepest moment: Germany's relations with the West. In the context of the present crisis, the pressures on the Germans it has already generated, and the likelihood that those pressures will increase as French diplomatic maneuvers add further confusion, we must all keep together."[82] True to his own sense of where the power lay, Johnson was determined to reform NATO on a trilateral basis, and finding out if the British and Germans could work out anything on nuclear sharing was his first priority. The British continued to resist, concerned, as Wilson told Johnson, by the "Soviets' obsession with the prospect of Germany obtaining access to nuclear weapons."[83] However, the British were also worried that the Americans would try to force them to get rid of their own nuclear weapons in the interest of "equality" with the Germans. British ambassador Patrick Dean argued that "we must go on making clear to the Americans that because the Germans feel a sense of nuclear nakedness, it is not in the long run going to solve anything for Britain to undress as well."[84]

Despite the opportunity that Johnson afforded him, Erhard did not pursue the issue with the British during his talks with Wilson in May 1966. Wilson told Ambassador Bruce that Erhard "had few ideas about foreign policy, and changed his mind all the time." Bruce agreed, and told Wilson that the president had expected some type of follow-up on the nuclear issue, and that that had been his reason for encouraging Wilson to act. But Erhard did not respond, paralyzed by the political divisions within his government and political party.

Bruce found himself agreeing with Wilson that "whatever one might think of Adenauer, his judgment of Erhard was almost certainly right."[85] Indeed, at their meetings in May, the issue that dominated the discussions was not nuclear sharing but the question of offset payments for the British army in Germany. Nuclear sharing, Wilson wrote LBJ, was "a secondary issue," and the British prime minister added, "it is wise to leave it there for the time being."[86]

The Offset Crisis and the Downfall of the Erhard Government

In the summer of 1966 it became increasingly clear that Germany would not meet the terms of the offset agreement it had made with the United States in 1965. Under the offset arrangements, West Germany was to purchase American military hardware for its forces, the Bundeswehr, in an amount equal to the approximate balance of payments loss that the United States experienced in deploying its forces in Germany. Offset agreements had been in place since 1961 and were efficient, if unpopular, reminders of the hated "occupation costs" of an earlier era.[87] However, in mid-1966 Germany experienced its first economic slowdown in almost two decades. As a recent study makes clear, the economic conditions in West Germany that produced the crisis were not particularly severe, especially in comparison with subsequent decades. The German gross domestic product sank by only 0.1 percent, with unemployment rising to 2.1 percent in 1967 and investment stagnating.[88] However, some sectors of the economy, particularly those in the Ruhr, such as mining and steel producing, were harder hit, helping to produce a significant electoral defeat in July 1966 for Erhard's CDU in Germany's largest state, Nordrhein-Westfalen. Erhard's government had also complicated the economic situation by greatly expanding public expenditures in 1965, appeasing a multitude of interest groups and ensuring the

CDU's electoral victory in September 1965. With the lag in tax revenue from the economic slowdown, Erhard now faced serious budgetary problems in a political environment in which deficit spending was simply an unacceptable choice.[89] As the economy threatened to overheat in 1965, the German central bank, the Bundesbank, pursued an increasingly restrictive credit policy, slowing economic activity and increasing the budget deficit. Though the economic slowdown was modest, its psychological impact on a country that had seen sustained and impressive growth since 1949 was powerful, even feeding the growth of a right-wing, neo-Nazi party, the Nationaldemokratische Partei Deutschlands (NPD), the National Democratic Party, which experienced modest success in several *Länder* (regional) elections. With Erhard's claim to legitimacy resting on his reputation as an economic wizard, the economic crisis fueled challenges from within his "political family." Franz Josef Strauss attacked from the Gaullist wing, and Rainer Barzel, chairman of the party in the Bundestag, put forth new proposals for German unification as a way to undermine Erhard.[90] The chancellor found himself under constant attack, standing at only a 30 percent approval rating in July 1966, down 14 points from April. Along with achieving a success in foreign policy, Erhard needed to make decisive cuts in his budget, with the most likely target being defense expenditures and the offset payments.

Offset payments had become an increasing political liability for the German government, because they were associated in the public's mind with a series of crashes of American F-104G Starfighter jets, which were the cornerstone of the new German air force. Sixty-six planes (in a fleet of 700) had crashed between 1960 and 1966, with 10 going down in the first half of 1966, and thirty-eight pilots had been killed. These tragedies fed the impression that the United States was selling unreliable and unnecessary military equipment to the Germans.[91] Secretary of Defense McNamara became a hated symbol of this policy in Germany, with his frequent public lectures on the German need to purchase more, and his outspoken threat to reduce American forces in Germany if the offset payments were not fulfilled. The defense secretary's belief that offset payments were linked to American troop levels was widely shared within the American government, especially in the Treasury Department, but McNamara's frequent and forceful reiteration of the point, especially during a meeting with the German defense minister, Kai-Uwe von Hassell, in June 1966, made him the focus of German displeasure, and headlines such as "McNamara's Heavy Hand" were increasingly common in German newspapers.[92]

On July 5, 1966, Erhard sent LBJ a letter that seemed to combine nuclear sharing and offset payments into one set of issues as the agenda for their next meeting. Erhard praised the nonproliferation negotiations in Geneva but said again, in what was a relatively "soft" manner, that "the possibility must not be excluded of building up in the future a joint integrated force among those partners of the NATO alliance who are prepared to do so." On offset payments, he assured the president that he wanted to find a solution "acceptable also to the United States," but wanted consideration "given to payments and services other than the mere purchase of weapons and military equipment." Most important for Erhard was his wish that the offset payments not be linked with "the question of the future presence in Germany of U.S. troops," a connection that Germans saw as an implicit threat to their security, since it placed the presence of U.S. troops on the same level as occupation costs.

The Erhard letter posed a number of difficult and complicated questions for U.S. policy, and Johnson took the advice offered by his staff to delay his reply, pending some internal discussion of American priorities. At the same time, the British were facing new economic problems, including a sterling crisis that would complicate the offset issue. During Wilson's meeting with Erhard in May 1966, the British prime minister and his chancellor of the exchequer, James Callaghan, had pressed Erhard for more offset payments to Britain. Bonn had been offsetting about 55 million pounds out of a British expenditure of 94 million pounds. The BAOR presence in Germany was roughly 55,000 men, and the British wanted to reduce it to a number that matched whatever amount Bonn was willing to provide in offset payments.[93] Callaghan told Erhard that Britain's "margin between success and failure on the economic front was too small to permit us to separate our foreign policy from economic considerations" and that the "BAOR would only be maintained if the problem were solved."[94] Erhard resisted the demand, but he did agree to set up an Anglo-German study commission to address the issue. However, it rapidly became clear that the German negotiators "did not have any authority to agree to a direct budgetary contribution for offset," and Callaghan grew increasingly angry, asking the British cabinet to give the Germans an "ultimatum" that "we should withdraw troops from Germany if our costs are not fully met."[95] The foreign minister, Michael Stewart, strongly advised against such a step, noting, "We are in no position to hold such language to an ally and we should do ourselves great damage by doing so," and insisting that withdrawal must be done in terms of alliance procedures "and after proper consultation with our allies, especially the United States."[96] Although Wilson agreed with Stewart procedurally, the cabinet decided that without 100 percent offset, it would reduce the size of the BAOR. Shortly thereafter, Britain informed NATO of its intention to withdraw forces.

This determination grew stronger as Britain's economic dilemma worsened. Despite an impressive electoral victory in March 1966, the Wilson government still faced problems managing the economy. In mid-May, the National Union of Seamen, frustrated by the limits on wage increases, voted to strike. The strike inflicted immediate damage on British trade, as export goods piled up in the ports. Wilson refused to back down, fearing that the government's prices and incomes policy was at stake. However, investors began to sell sterling, uncertain of the ability of the Labour government to hold the line. As the strike dragged on, sterling was buffeted by wave after wave of speculation. Even the end of the strike in late June did not bring relief, and by the first week in July sterling stood at its lowest level in almost twenty months. Wilson finally put up the bank rate by 1 percent on July 14, but it was clear this would not be enough to save sterling. U.S. Treasury officials called Britain "the sick man of Europe," believing that its dependency on the United States had kept its leaders from addressing its problems and that Britain was "a spendthrift headed for bankruptcy."[97]

The sterling crisis coincided with the planning for a visit by Prime Minister Wilson to Washington in July. The atmosphere surrounding the visit was not helped by Wilson's decision to "disassociate" himself in Parliament in early June from the American decision to bomb oil refineries and other targets near the cities of Hanoi and Haiphong. Johnson questioned why Wilson would support his Vietnam policy when he had a small majority, but "when Wilson had a really big majority, he felt it necessary to disassociate himself much more than before from American action."[98] Nevertheless, despite his irritation over Wilson's criticism, Johnson continued to compartmentalize the Vietnam issue and did not allow it to spill over into alliance debates—despite worries of White House staffers that it would.[99] Preparations for the prime minister's visit went ahead, amid anxious concerns about the future of sterling. Bator prepared an assessment for Johnson entitled, "The Pound, the Dollar and What We Want from Harold Wilson," outlining the various—and occasionally contradictory—U.S. objectives with respect to Great Britain. He described again McNamara's insistence that Britain remain east of Suez, even if it might lead to cuts in the BAOR. He noted George Ball's conviction that Britain must make every effort to enter the Common

Market, a policy that militated against cuts in its presence in Germany. Bator described Treasury Secretary Fowler's views, pointing out that he wanted to tell the British that while the U.S. would not offer a bailout, the British "must not under any circumstances devalue." Both Bator and Fowler wanted "a thorough review of our priorities and our general bargaining position vis-à-vis the U.K.," and "since German offset is involved, this would also involve a look at financial (and therefore political) relations with the Germans."[100]

The American deliberations were strongly affected by Wilson's decision on July 20 to impose a six-month wage-price freeze in combination with government spending cuts of some 500 million pounds and an increase in indirect taxation. The tough measures, more stringent than any in postwar British history, prompted a positive American reaction and a new willingness by the Federal Reserve to help sterling maintain its exchange rate. Wilson's decisions also contributed to a much more positive atmosphere for his meetings with LBJ, in which he emphasized to the president his own determination "to show the world that Britain meant business."[101] Although the American role in "encouraging" Wilson to deal with his economic problems was not as intrusive as in the previous year, it is still apparent that Wilson had weighed the potential American reaction in his considerations.[102] Wilson's refusal to devalue, despite substantial support for such a step within his cabinet, reflected his conviction that this would seriously damage Anglo-American relations and his own international standing. He also saw his determination to keep British forces east of Suez as another gesture to the Americans, although he was careful to make no guarantees against a possible future cutback. The result of his efforts made for a successful meeting with Johnson, even though Wilson clearly exaggerated in claiming that he had secured unconditional support for sterling.[103] Bator praised Wilson "as a very good bet for us," and he encouraged the president to show his support in as public a fashion as possible.[104] Privately, British diplomats reported that the president still assessed Britain "in terms of performance alone," and that his attitude was one of "reserve and puzzlement rather than bad temper and resentment." "Insofar as we fail to come up to his expectations," Patrick Dean reported to London, "he will relegate us to a lower position in his league table of reliable and useful Allies and leave it to us to work our passage back into favour by concrete actions."[105] Whatever reservations Johnson had, he went overboard publicly in his attempt to show American approval for the economic course Wilson had taken, even comparing Wilson's leadership with Churchill's during the war. The "corny" rhetoric, as David Bruce referred to it, may well have been intended to "demonstrate to the markets his approval and confidence in the British government's economic policy."[106] It also infuriated some of the more left-wing members of Wilson's cabinet, who believed, as Barbara Castle wrote in her diary, that "whatever the economic cost, Harold cannot now renege on Johnson."[107]

The United States' success with Britain and the sterling crisis directly affected the offset question and U.S. relations with the Erhard government. The British were determined to save 100 million pounds in overseas expenditures, and with Wilson's promise not to cut back east of Suez, the BAOR looked like the prime target. Wilson was determined to achieve either full offset of British costs in Germany or to withdraw a large element of the BAOR. The British actions increased pressure on the United States to do likewise, especially in an atmosphere in which the U.S. Senate, restive because of Vietnam, was increasingly exerting its influence. Earlier in the year the Fulbright hearings had raised serious questions about the course of the Vietnam War. On European policy, the Senate had passed the Pastore Resolution, which called for a nuclear nonproliferation treaty to be the priority of U.S. policy. Now, in August 1966, the Senate Democratic leader, Mike Mansfield, put forward his own nonbinding "Mansfield Resolution," cosponsored by twelve other senators, calling for a substantial reduction in U.S. forces in Europe. Although Mansfield drew substantial support from those concerned about the Vietnam commitment and the balance of payments drain, he offered the resolution because "he felt there were clear indications that fundamental changes had taken place and that the continued presence of so many American troops in Europe 20 years after the war was beginning to grate on the nerves of Germans and Europeans outside of government."[108] With Johnson's own popularity having declined to the 40-percent level, and with protests against the Vietnam War continuing to increase, this sign of disaffection within his own party on European policy was potentially devastating to Johnson. He called Senator Russell Long of Louisiana and told him that "this thing y'all did yesterday really murdered us on NATO." He told Long that he had "had a war with the British for two weeks now," asking them not to make their cutbacks until their action could be coordinated with any American withdrawals, and to "take into account what the French are doing, and that we satisfy the Germans that we are just not pulling out completely so they don't start a complete rearmament or blow up." He sympathized with that "poor devil" Erhard, who was down in the polls because he had supported the United States, and wanted to help him. At the same time he was intrigued by the possibility, which he mentioned to Long, that the Russians might be interested in mutual troop withdrawals from Europe. But with the Senate acting as it had, Johnson's position in any negotiations with the Russians was compromised. "Now, I'm just an old Johnson City boy, but when I'm playing bridge and I show the other fellow my whole hand, I can't make a very good deal with him."[109]

Johnson worried that the British actions, along with the Mansfield resolution, de Gaulle's withdrawal, and the German economic difficulties, would set in motion a process of "unravelling in NATO which could easily get out of hand." As he told a sympathetic Long, he didn't believe the Russian threat to Europe had disappeared: "I'm not one of these folks that's just sucked in by the Russians. I don't believe in the Fulbright, Mansfield, Symington whole goddamned theory, that it's all over there . . . I think those sons of bitches want to eat us any day they can."[110] In more diplomatic language, Johnson told Harold Wilson that "while I would not think it likely that our Russian friends will develop itchy fingers, one cannot rule it out. In any case, it would be foolish to run down our assets vis-à-vis Moscow without some quid-pro-quo."[111]

The solution Johnson came to favor during the summer of 1966 was a tripartite consideration of "this entire range of issues: force levels, deployments and the sharing of the foreign exchange burden." This idea had originated in suggestions from Bator and other sympathetic voices in the Departments of State and Defense. Bator, whose role as White House staff officer exposed him to the sharply divided perspectives within the U.S. government on how to deal with the offset issue, was searching for a way to present the complex tradeoffs to the president. The Defense Department, in alliance with Treasury, insisted on full offset, ostensibly for balance of payments reasons. McNamara was quite willing to withdraw forces from Germany if the offset wasn't met, in large reason because he believed a much smaller U.S. force, combined with air mobility, could accomplish the function of deterrence. The State Department strongly opposed a tough approach to Germany and a strict link between offset and force levels, knowing how strongly the Germans reacted to any American withdrawals. (The United States had withdrawn 15,000 men in April for service in Vietnam, and this had produced a minor furor in Germany.) A deep cut in conventional strength might also make it difficult for Erhard to give up a "hardware" solution on the nuclear question, and perhaps play into the hands of the French, who argued that the United States would eventually leave Europe and abandon the Continent's defense. In early August the American embassy in Bonn had warned Washington that if it hoped to influence the German budgetary process, it needed to act "before the late-August cabinet discussions at which the Defense Ministry share of the overall budget total will be fixed." Bator presented the issues to LBJ, making a strong case for waiting and considering a new approach. He thought that the creation of some type of "mixed commission" of the United States, Britain, and Germany might serve to "protect our balance of payments" and hammer out a consensus "on an allied defense posture in Europe which will provide deterrence and the insurance of a reasonable conventional option."[112] He also hoped that, by placing the offset question in a much larger context, the president would be able to avoid the pressure to take "risks with the stability of German and alliance politics" in order to "make marginal gains in our balance of payments." Such risks might be necessary on the issue of nuclear sharing, Bator argued, but not on offset. Johnson agreed, showing a willingness to "gamble on waiting" in order to work out an agreed American position and to consider whether a trilateral process involving the British and Germans was the right approach to the issue.

In late August Johnson and his advisers gathered at his Texas ranch to work out the American position. During a long and heated meeting, McNamara, strongly backed by Fowler, made the case for holding the Germans to their deal and insisting on full offset. If Germany couldn't keep its part of the bargain, the United States would be free to make some needed cuts in its military presence in Germany. Fowler emphasized the continuing danger American deployments posed to the balance of payments. George Ball, representing the State Department in something of a lame duck status—his departure the next month had already been announced—made the case for taking a "softer" position toward the Germans, resisting any troop withdrawals and arguing for not making political and strategic decisions on narrowly economic grounds. The State Department also strongly urged creation of a trilateral process, joining with Bator in proposing that John McCloy, the former U.S. high commissioner in Germany, be asked to serve as American negotiator. After hearing the arguments, the president decided to approve the trilateral approach and immediately invited Wilson and Erhard to participate in the process. In his letter to Erhard, LBJ also gave McNamara satisfaction on one point: the United States would hold Germany to the existing offset agreement, even mentioning the need for it to be included in the German budget.[113] But Bator and his allies in the State Department felt they had achieved their objective in Johnson's decision to indicate to the chancellor that there would be much greater flexibility in future offset arrangements, including alternatives to strict military purchases, and that these could be discussed in their forthcoming meeting in September. They also hoped that a trilateral process, placed in the hands of a distinguished member of the East Coast foreign policy establishment, would ultimately reaffirm the U.S. commitment to NATO and Germany, even if the United States needed to make some cutbacks in its force levels.

The British jumped at the trilateral proposal, hoping finally to get American help with the Germans. (Previously the U.S. stance on the questions had been, "We wish you luck with your offset with the Germans," regarding it as not a matter for U.S. intervention.)[114] Wilson told LBJ that his "major concern" was to safeguard sterling, that he would have to move fast, since he needed to announce specific savings to Parliament by the middle of October, and that he "wanted to reach an agreed Anglo-American position so the Germans could not play one country against the other."[115] Johnson rejected Wilson's appeal for bilateral talks, pointing out how important it was "to avoid actions that might make the Germans feel they were not full partners on the team."[116] But Erhard proved far more resistant to playing on the team than Johnson expected. He replied that the trilateral idea would have to "be thoroughly prepared and its possible effect on the Alliance carefully examined," and that the idea could be discussed at their September meeting.[117] His resistance to the proposal was shared by Erhard's foreign minister as well. George Ball, during his farewell tour of Europe in early September, noted that Schröder disclosed an "appalling lack of understanding" of the problems that would result from a British withdrawal, and that the German foreign minister evidently did not understand the need to begin the trilateral talks as quickly as possible. Despite trying through a number of different diplomatic channels, from Ambassador McGhee to Erhard's banker nephew, American officials were unable to convince the chancellor that some planning and discussion of the offset issue, especially the current offset, was essential before he, Erhard, arrived in Washington. They were also unable to convince him that the Americans had made an important concession on future offset payments, a concession that Erhard could use in dealing with his political rivals. Bator told Georg von Lilienfeld, the German ambassador's deputy, that preliminary discussions would be very helpful in making the meeting a success, pointing to the example of Wilson's visit in July and the extensive discussions and planning that had taken place before the trip and made the trip a substantive success as well as public relations success. Nevertheless, the Germans rejected this approach, a decision that came directly from Chancellor Erhard.[118]

To a certain extent Erhard's reaction is not hard to fathom. He had what he believed to be an exceptionally good personal relationship with Lyndon Johnson and "assumed that the friendship was a kind of capital which could be spent to solve his political problem."[119] He was certain that if he could tell Johnson directly about his political problems, the president, who had never failed to ask him what he needed and what LBJ could do for him, would provide him with a resounding political "victory" that would silence his opponents and carry him through the temporary economic problems. However, there was more to Erhard's position than simple trust in Lyndon Johnson. In mid-August, Martin Hillenbrand, McGhee's deputy in Bonn, had reported on the "unhealthy" state of U.S.-German relations. With their "capacity for self-pity," Hillenbrand argued, the Germans saw their current international position as that of the Pruegelknabe, or "whipping boy." Despite their good behavior in the Kennedy Round and NATO crisis, he said they were being "singled out and criticized for anticipated, though not yet actual, failure to meet an offset which we obtain from no other country; they believe their security to be threatened by alleged plans for large-scale American troop withdrawals . . . [while] at the same time their primary national objective of reunification remains as much of a will-o'-the-wisp as ever, and they see little enthusiasm anywhere to do anything about it." Hillenbrand reported that Erhard himself, "harassed as he is on a number of fronts and struggling to maintain control over a fluid political situation, is feeling abused and nursing a certain sense of grievance over 'disappointing U.S. conduct.'" A few weeks after this analysis, the White House received a report of an off-the-record press conference in which Erhard, in discussing offset payments, "evinced a degree of firmness bordering on the belligerent." The chancellor had told the German reporters that McNamara's "demands" were "completely arbitrary" and must be "categorically rejected." When asked if he would display this attitude in Washington, "the chancellor had replied emphatically, 'You can bet on that,'" repeating the point on several occasions during the press conference.[120]

Ludwig Erhard, increasingly desperate, "scared stiff" at the prospect of his trip to the United States, and aware that "many of his party colleagues [were] sharpening their knives to take advantage of the first opportunity to finish him off," was playing a complicated game in September 1966.[121] He even considered having a diplomatic illness that could allow him to cancel the trip.[122] On the one hand, Erhard decided, as McGhee described it, to "throw himself on the President's mercy on the basis of his and Germany's past performances as a good ally."[123] On the other, the chancellor was also preparing to appear as the defiant spokesman for German interests in the face of the Americans, a posture that he may have hoped would save him if Johnson was not forthcoming. Whatever his thinking, Erhard clearly miscalculated, misreading both the political situation in the United States and how his friend Lyndon Johnson interpreted the politics of the alliance.

With Erhard's political position in Germany now so precarious, the Johnson administration reconsidered its own position. As the news from Germany continued to be grim, Bator told LBJ that "for us it is important—even more than Erhard's survival—that we not appear the culprit if he falls."[124] Although Johnson's advisers still disagreed on some issues, they agreed that the president should hold Erhard to the original payments schedule, conceding that he could meet some of that with the purchase of long-term bonds. McNamara and Fowler were willing to allow six to twelve months for the Germans to place orders for weapons, but they insisted that all the orders for weapons—the full $1.4 billion—be placed by the end of this "stretch-out" period. Ball and Bator argued that the United States should agree to reduce the amount for weapons orders by the amount of the bond purchases. McNamara was far more willing to contemplate troop withdrawals, arguing that they would not significantly reduce "military effectiveness."[125] To meet an estimated yearly gap of $500 million between what the Germans would pay and what the costs were, McNamara advocated reducing American spending in Europe by $200 million and considering the withdrawal of a significant number of American combat personnel, which he acknowledged might have a "traumatic psychological impact in Germany, in NATO, and in the United States."[126]

With press coverage on both sides of the Atlantic making it clear that Erhard "badly need[ed] a success at the White House,"[127] Johnson and Erhard met alone in the Oval Office, accompanied only by their interpreters. Erhard raised the two "big issues" he wanted to discuss, the offset problem and U.S. troops in Germany. In discussing the latter, Erhard told LBJ that "nobody was expecting a 'hardware' solution any longer," but that Germans wanted to know "how they would be protected in the event of the conclusion of a non-proliferation treaty." What they wanted was a "common solution under NATO." In effect, Erhard finally abandoned the German position on the MLF/ANF that had stalled the NPT negotiations, conceding that the Nuclear Planning Group would give the Germans their "voice" in such matters, and Johnson was quick to use this concession. Erhard went on to tell the president that the Germans realized how much they owed to the United States, and how deeply appreciative they were of American sacrifices for freedom in Vietnam. America's firm stand there had helped to secure Berlin and was a "beacon of hope" to the Germans. Erhard then shifted from declarations of loyalty to an implied threat, noting that a "different German government that might succeed his Government" might "not show the same loyalty and determination to cultivate close ties to the United States," and that although a new German government wouldn't leave NATO, this might lead to a "moral loosening" of the alliance.[128] Having established this context, Erhard then made his pitch: "Out of the current budget it would not be possible to fulfill all financial obligations under the current offset agreement to the full amount," and Germany needed more time. Erhard described the problems of the German economy and the budget cutting he had done, suggested other means to fulfill offset, and asked that the problem be handled in a "businesslike way."

Although Erhard emphasized repeatedly that he would honor the offset agreement and was only looking for more time, his refusal to allow lower-level discussions that could have worked out a concrete proposal suggests that the chancellor wanted something more dramatic from Johnson, even the forgiveness of some substantial amount of the offset. LBJ decided not to bargain and put Erhard back on the defensive. Johnson told the chancellor that his own problems were more severe, especially the balance of payments, and that "if the Germans could not keep their commitments it would put them in a very serious and disconcerting position." He allowed that the offset might be fulfilled by other means, such as nonmilitary purchases, but he also raised the specter of "certain reductions" in the U.S. troop level. Erhard backpedaled and immediately began to suggest other alternatives, but Johnson homed in on "a German commitment not being truly honored." He then suggested to Erhard that they let their experts see what proposals they could arrange, that compromises might be possible, and that he "did not want to be too inflexible, [since] otherwise he might win the argument but lose the sale." At this point Erhard slipped into his "whipping boy" role, telling Johnson how "bitter" it was for him "to hear the President say he could not trust the German word." The Germans would pay every "last penny" and make every effort to pay as much by July 1, 1967, as they could. Knowing that the meeting was almost over, Erhard shifted moods again, asking that the President visit Germany, a visit he asserted would get "a tremendous spontaneous reception." Johnson simply told him he would think about it.[129] Erhard emerged from the meeting "utterly dejected," perhaps deservedly so. He had gambled on a stunning success from the meeting, a success that Johnson would not give him.

Johnson's genuine affection for Erhard did not interfere with a cold and realistic judgment about Erhard's political strength and prospects. The amount the Germans wanted forgiven, or even the additional time they requested to fulfill the agreement, were all less important than Johnson's perception that Erhard could not deliver, that whatever bargain he struck would not be fulfilled. Erhard had not tried to work out proposals before the trip, he had been unable to secure the agreement of the Bundesbank to buy U.S. Treasury bonds, and he had refused to see the possibilities in the trilateral arrangement that Johnson had offered him. All these facts persuaded the president, despite his appreciation of Erhard, not to make a substantive deal

Johnson and Chancellor Erhard tour the Kennedy Space Center, September 1966. Erhard's expression may reflect his own sense that his mission to Washington had been a failure. (LBJ Library; photo by Yoichi Okamoto)

with the man the Germans called the Gummilöwe, or "rubber lion." Johnson even leaned toward more troop withdrawals, telling a sympathetic McNamara that evening: "Looks like to me, we ought to take advantage of this opportunity to make him tell us that he cannot afford to have our troops there."[130]

However, Erhard could not agree to any troop withdrawals. The two leaders remained stalemated and tried to put the best face on their talks. Their joint communiqué stressed that the Federal Republic "would make every effort fully to meet the current offset agree-

ment insofar as financial arrangements affecting the balance of payments are involved."[131] Johnson even took Erhard to Cape Kennedy
for the launch of a Gemini manned space mission, although this gesture may have only underlined the economic gap between the two
nations.[132] Erhard still tried to avoid facing the facts. When he returned to Germany, he told McGhee that he had told the president
he could not fully meet the existing offset agreement and that he had
not changed his position after their discussions. McGhee told Washington that Erhard was still fighting for his political life, and that
"if we push too hard, we might break the present government."[133]
Actually there was little that the United States could do to save
Erhard, and the Washington meeting was simply one more disappointment. Although a German newspaper close to the opposition
Social Democrats spoke of "a thinly veiled fiasco on all counts," and
such perennial critics as Franz Josef Strauss attacked Erhard's "naive
one-sided reliance" on the United States,[134] others were less critical
and even took the theme that "Erhard had emerged bloody but un-
bowed" and that there had been "neither victor nor vanquished"
in the Washington talks.[135] Indeed, although a number of German
politicians, most notably Helmut Schmidt, insisted that the United
States had "brought Erhard down," it seems abundantly clear that the
chancellor's fate was sealed much earlier in the summer.[136] In the
weeks preceding the trip, his top aide, Ludgar Westrick, had resigned,
and his defense minister had only barely survived a vote of no confidence. During Erhard's absence, CDU leaders held a number of
meetings about finding a successor. One recent analysis notes that "in
Germany the prevailing opinion was that Erhard's fate was sealed
anyway and the visit to Washington was just the last straw."[137] Erhard
was not able to overcome his own party's doubts about his leadership.
When in late October he was compelled to propose a tax increase to
cover his budget shortfall, the Free Democratic Party (FDP) left the
government, and Erhard resigned at the end of October. His resigna-

tion was widely seen as marking the end of an era in U.S.-German relations, with considerable uncertainty about what might follow.

The Editorial Writers Speech:
Johnson's European Vision

Although it was more a coincidence of timing than a planned gesture, President Johnson's most significant speech on Europe took place while the Erhard government was in its death throes. The idea for the speech had originated in the White House and had come out of the Acheson task force assigned to find ways to "increase the cohesion of NATO and the North Atlantic Community."[138] The group's report had suggested that by September, "when most of the decisions had been taken to respond to the disruptive actions of France, the President should make a major address expressing the continuing U.S. interest and participation in NATO."[139] But the speech was also a response to the president's long-standing concern with bridge building to Eastern Europe and the Soviet Union, an idea he had spoken of in May 1964, but that had been largely lost to public awareness because of Vietnam and countless other policy initiatives. In July 1966, in National Security Action Memorandum (NSAM) 352, Johnson "instructed that—in consultation with our Allies—we actively develop areas of peaceful cooperation with the nations of Eastern Europe and the Soviet Union." The major purpose Johnson cited for moving toward better relations was "to help create an environment in which peaceful settlement of the division of Germany and of Europe will become possible."[140] In August Bator sent to Johnson a detailed outline of the speech, describing it as "a major *framework-setting* speech on what we are about vis-à-vis Western Europe, Eastern Europe and the Soviets, and arms control." Bator suggested as a setting either a gathering of newspaper editors or a major university, but strongly recommended that Johnson give the speech after Labor Day, since "Europe generally closes up shop in August."[141] The Bator outline emphasized a point that Johnson had made earlier but that was still especially difficult for the Germans to swallow: Bridge building and reconciliation with the East would create an environment that "permits a peaceful European settlement." German reunification would come not at the beginning of this process but much later, as the hostility between East and West diminished. This formulation, although it had been U.S. policy for quite some time, had not been as openly and strongly put. And as the speech developed, largely under the guidance of Bator but with Johnson's directions in mind, it also emphasized respect for "the integrity of a nation's boundary lines" and consciously avoided traditional Cold War references to four-power responsibility in Germany, the need for free elections in Eastern Europe, or even the nonrecognition of East Germany.

President Johnson chose to give the address on October 7, to the National Conference of Editorial Writers in New York. Although there were political considerations involved in the timing of the speech—the administration was laying out its achievements only a month before midterm elections and also trumping Robert Kennedy, who was planning a European speech—the primary reason for the speech, as Bator briefed reporters, was to "re-assert in broad and general terms . . . what the President's policy toward Europe is."[142] Entitling the speech, "Making Europe Whole: An Unfinished Task," Johnson keyed it around two anniversaries, the end of the Berlin airlift and the ratification of the Partial Test Ban Treaty, to point up his insistence on deterrence and detente as the keys to his European policy. This was the "healthy balance" he pursued, and he used the speech to push three themes: the modernization of NATO, the integration of Western Europe, and the development of East-West relations. Johnson told the editorial writers, "We want the Soviet Union and the nations of Eastern Europe to know that we and our allies shall go step by step with them as far as they are willing to advance."

He listed a number of steps he would take to hasten "peaceful engagement" with the East, including liberalizing trade and travel restrictions and encouraging cultural and scientific exchanges. The president argued that these moves would have important consequences in the long run for Germany: "We must improve the East-West environment in order to achieve the unification of Germany in the context of a larger, peaceful, and prosperous Europe."[143] "Our object," Johnson emphasized, "is to end the bitter legacy of World War II."

In what was considered the most "newsworthy" aspect of the speech, Johnson also affirmed that the United States respected "the integrity of a nation's boundary lines" and encouraged the resolution of territorial and border disputes, a none-too-subtle reference to Germany's refusal to recognize the Oder-Neisse Line and the loss of its eastern territories. The Bonn embassy had sought a last-minute change that would have softened the reference, but the State Department insisted it remain to provide "gentle support to those people in Germany who want slowly to back away from a self-defeating position."[144] This approach drew immediate attention from the Erhard government, and State Secretary Karl Carstens prepared a long report for the Erhard cabinet on the present uncertainties of Germany's policy toward reunification. Carstens painted a bleak picture of Germany's situation, stressing that Bonn's policy on reunification now had no serious backing from the United States and actually compromised German security by provoking Soviet hostility. He noted that Johnson's speech made it clear that the Americans regarded the Oder-Neisse boundary as the permanent German-Polish frontier. He added that although the Vietnam War had hindered progress between the United States and the Soviet Union on detente, clear indications existed that the Soviets might be reassessing their position. These developments did not augur well for the Federal Republic, which was increasingly isolated from its allies. Erhard had no response at the cabinet meeting except to ask the members on their honor not to discuss the report. However, there was little honor left in the Erhard cabinet, and the report was leaked to the press, with the prominent magazine *Der Spiegel* stating that German foreign policy was at a "dead end."[145] The speech was clearly read in Germany as favoring new ideas for dealing with the East, and it indirectly contributed support to moderate Social Democratic Party (SPD) politicians in Germany, like Willy Brandt, and their ideas of *Ostpolitik*.[146]

Johnson's speech also coincided with a clear shift in Soviet policy and perceptions. As late as July 1966, the Soviet leader Alexei Kosygin, who divided responsibilities with party leader Leonid Brezhnev, told British prime minister Harold Wilson that Johnson was "virtually a mad man," akin to Mussolini, who "bombed innocent people in Ethiopia." Wilson's reporting of this attitude was no doubt partly intended to show himself as a mediator. The British leader noted that he had built up a position of trust with the Soviet leader and told LBJ that Kosygin "casts you as the bloodthirsty villain of the piece," and that all the world's problems "were increasingly seen through the prism of events in Vietnam." But if Kosygin seemed to indicate to Wilson that Vietnam was a stumbling block to detente, he also made it clear that Moscow's primary concerns were connected with its own troublesome former ally, China. The outbreak of the Cultural Revolution that spring, with the disorder and chaos it unleashed, terrified the Soviets. They feared that, in the atmosphere of radicalization set off in Beijing, "any relaxation of the Soviet attitude [toward Vietnam] might precipitate active Chinese intervention in the conflict to the point where Peking would 'virtually take over' North Vietnam and the conduct of the war." Wilson believed that Soviet concerns about China were "the root cause" of Moscow's reluctance to pressure Hanoi to negotiate with the Americans.[147]

Whatever reservations the Soviets had about dealing with Lyndon Johnson faded as the Cultural Revolution intensified. Johnson himself came to believe that "the Russians are obsessed with China," and that this obsession might afford opportunities for the United States.[148] (Political cartoons at the time pictured the United States and Soviet Union in the same foxhole, taking cover from artillery shells marked "Red China" and "Belligerence.")[149] In the Soviet Union, Andrei Gromyko told the Politburo, "We should not avoid agreements with the United States on questions of our interest if such agreements do not contradict our position of principle in regard to Vietnam. Needless to say, we should avoid a situation where we have to fight on two fronts, that is against China and the United States."[150] The "second front" that the Soviets envisioned was in Europe and particularly Germany, where they continued to fear any possibility that the Federal Republic might acquire nuclear arms. Kosygin, for example, despite his attempts to court the French, reacted angrily when de Gaulle told him that France would never sign a nonproliferation treaty, and reminded the French leader that "le grand problème, c'est l'Allemagne."[151] Despite the chill Vietnam put on relations, in January 1966 Kosygin resumed correspondence with Johnson via the secret "pen pal" channel that had not been used since February 1965. His message seemed to have been motivated by the Johnson-Erhard summit of December 1965 and the continuing possibility of a "hardware solution" like the MLF.[152] A more dramatic shift in the Soviet view became clear by the early autumn of 1966, when the two superpowers reached agreement on a treaty to ban nuclear weapons in outer space. When Gromyko sat down with Johnson in early October, an agreement on a nonproliferation treaty was very close. Aware of Erhard's concession that a hardware solution was now unnecessary, Johnson assured Gromyko that the president of the United States would never give up his veto over the "power of decision to fire nuclear weapons to anyone else." All he asked was that the Soviets not insist he accept wording that would damage NATO, since he was not asking the "Soviet Union to tear up the Warsaw pact and to have no allies." In classic Johnsonian prose, he said he and

Gromyko should "get our pencils out and work on an agreement."[153] Rusk amplified the point later that same day, when he told the Soviet leader that "if the Soviets should be worried about the possibility that some day a United States nuclear weapon might be fired by a German soldier on order of a German government, and without U.S. consent, he could assure Gromyko that this would and could never happen." Gromyko conceded that the Soviets would not insist that the treaty ban consultation with allies, and although he still had concerns about the U.S. approach, he acknowledged that "our positions are similar." Discussions over the precise wording of the first two articles of the NPT continued, but a basic understanding had been reached. The difficult point for the United States would come with convincing the NATO allies, especially Germany, that their concerns had been protected.

Johnson's European speech and its aftermath have been obscured in history by the Vietnam War.[154] Yet at the time, it was heralded immediately in the American press as "a bold new initiative on the part of the U.S. to achieve East-West reconciliation."[155] Senator Fulbright, by now alienated from LBJ over Vietnam, called the speech "a statesmanlike approach to our relationships with the Europe of today—not Europe as it has been in the past," and Harold Wilson telegraphed Johnson to praise his "great and imaginative speech" and to tell the president that he believed the Soviets, "despite Vietnam, . . . want to push ahead with relations in Europe and with you and that this desire has recently grown."[156] The speech was also recognized as a response to the French challenge, as expressing "a doctrine congenial in Europe, different from de Gaulle's, without quarrelling."[157] With headlines now proclaiming that the United States and Soviet Union had reached an agreement on banning nuclear weapons in outer space, and with reports that there had been significant progress on a nonproliferation treaty, commentators speculated that LBJ might "manage to achieve a full-fledged detente with Russia."[158] However, Johnson himself contributed to shifting attention away from the speech and its significance for East-West relations by deciding at this point to make a seventeen-day trip to Asia and a summit in Manilla, during which he would emphasize America's role as a Pacific power and pay a visit to the troops in Vietnam. Vietnam—although it did not prevent change and development in America's policy toward Europe—still cast a large shadow over those changes.

4

The Year of Achievements

In late 1966 the Johnson administration's European policy was in serious trouble. For the first time since the Korean War, America was engaged in a war in Asia while trying to maintain a significant armed presence on the European continent. However, while the Korean conflict had actually accelerated the American buildup in Europe and made NATO a real military alliance, Vietnam now threatened to unravel that commitment. Europe's lack of support for the war in Southeast Asia, coupled with its unwillingness to assume a greater share of the burden for its own defense, threatened to erode support for NATO in the United States. Johnson himself told the National Security Council in December, "We are fast approaching a day of reckoning," and that "we can't get the American people to support our NATO policy when they see the actions taken by the French, British, and Germans."[1]

The Germans posed the most immediate problem. The Erhard government, America's closest ally in Europe, had collapsed. Many Germans blamed the collapse on the United States, pointing to its excessive offset demands as well as its interest in a nonproliferation treaty they believed was directed against West Germany. This view, combined with the negative impact of media coverage of the Vietnam

War, resulted in a precipitous drop in public support for the United States in Germany. Those Germans who perceived "the basic interests of their country as in agreement with the U.S." plunged from well over 70 percent in June 1965 to just 16 percent at the end of 1966.[2] For his part, French president Charles de Gaulle continued his worldwide travels and his campaign against American foreign policy, especially the war in Vietnam, and denounced the United States in a speech in Phnom Penh, Cambodia, in September 1966. Contrasting France's "courageous" withdrawal from Algeria with the increasing U.S. escalation of the war in Vietnam, de Gaulle called American policy "more and more threatening for the peace of the world."[3] As one British diplomat put it, the speech, "though couched in language of conspicuous elegance, contains his most brutal and one-sided criticisms yet of American policies in Vietnam."[4] De Gaulle's antiAmerican rhetoric was matched by French policies of opposition on important economic issues. Both the Kennedy Round and the negotiations to reform the international monetary system were stalled, largely because of French resistance. The Treasury Department concluded that France was "practicing economic warfare" against the United States "within the framework of a national policy which calls for the weakening of U.S. strength and influence in Western Europe as a necessary condition of establishing French hegemony over that area."[5] With the authority to negotiate the trade agreement expiring June 30, 1967, and with the American balance of payments deficit continuing to be aggravated by Vietnam, the possibility of a crisis in the international economic system loomed. In Britain, the struggle to maintain the pound sterling's value led to a search for cutbacks in Britain's worldwide commitments, with increasing attention toward forces in Europe and those east of the Suez Canal. Complicating all of these issues was the ongoing war in Vietnam, which seemed no closer to resolution with 400,000 Americans in Vietnam than it had with 200,000 a year earlier. The intensification of antiwar protests at home and abroad further underlined the political costs for Johnson of waging a limited war for containment in Southeast Asia.

Johnson knew he was in trouble.[6] With the electorate worried about Vietnam, racial conflict rampant in America's cities, and inflationary pressures in the economy, the results of the midterm elections of 1966 delivered a bitter—if not wholly unexpected—blow. The Republicans gained forty-seven seats in the House, three in the Senate, and eight governorships. Johnson's own approval rating had slipped below 50 percent, with only 43 percent of the electorate approving of his conduct of the war and only 32 percent having a favorable view of the Great Society.[7] The *New York Times* noted that the elections had weakened, "perhaps critically," Johnson's influence with Congress and "did not add luster to his reputation as a party leader and candidate for re-election."[8] *Time* magazine noted that Johnson would now have even less room to maneuver legislatively than John Kennedy had after 1962, adding that "Kennedy's last days were plagued by a curmudgeonly, uncooperative Congress."[9] However, before pronouncing an obituary on Johnson's effectiveness, the *New York Times,* which was increasingly critical of the president, conceded that "Mr. Johnson, who served six years as the majority leader of a Democratic-controlled Senate during a Republican Administration, is no stranger to bipartisanship," and that the increasing friction between president and Congress "need not mean a legislative impasse."[10] Johnson might well emerge as even more effective, the paper conceded, especially if he abandoned his search for consensus and made a more partisan appeal for support.

This picture of a president in trouble, facing increasing opposition and intractable problems, is only one part of the story. Despite all of the difficulties he faced at home and abroad, Johnson had now put his stamp on American foreign policy. As British ambassador Patrick Dean recognized in early 1967, "[LBJ's] primary interest in foreign affairs is the improvement in relations with the Soviet Union," and

Johnson had "discreetly reoriented United States policy by admitting the need to work for an improvement in the general atmosphere of East-West relations as a prerequisite to the settlement of the German problem." Although it was "absurd" to suggest that the United States had turned its back on Europe, Dean told his London superiors that the United States was beginning to see itself "less as leader of the Atlantic Community and more as the Atlantic-Pacific Power whose best interest lies in encouraging, but not being too closely enmeshed in, the development of collective regional endeavors in all areas of the non-Communist world." He concluded that there would be "less sentiment and more hard-headedness in the American attitude to Europe" over the coming year. Indeed, over the course of 1967, the Johnson administration, through shrewd negotiation and careful weighing of the politics of its allies, crafted a series of agreements that solved several outstanding problems within the NATO alliance and fostered the development of a more liberal and open international trade and monetary system. At the same time, and despite both the Vietnam War and the outbreak of war in the Middle East, Johnson continued his push toward detente, meeting with the Soviet premier Alexei Kosygin at Glassboro in June 1967 and making significant progress in the drive toward a nonproliferation treaty and the beginning of serious arms control negotiations between the superpowers. It was a series of impressive achievements, largely obscured at the time —and since then—by the drama and tragedy of the Vietnam War.

The Trilateral Negotiations

Ironically enough, the Trilateral negotiations began before the collapse of the Erhard government, as the dispirited chancellor had finally agreed to them during his September talks with Johnson. Although the political turmoil in Bonn prevented the Germans from recognizing it as such, the selection of John J. McCloy as the chief

American negotiator was Johnson's clear signal that he would protect German interests in the negotiations. McCloy's long background in German affairs, along with his paternal regard for both NATO and the Federal Republic, made him an unlikely candidate to preside over the dissolution of the NATO alliance.[11] McCloy had already expressed his view that it was "tactically wrong . . . to link the number of American troops stationed in Germany with German payments."[12] He thought such a link exacerbated German insecurity over the American commitment, and that this had caused the deterioration in relations. Despite the pretext of undertaking a "review of our NATO policy," McCloy never wavered from his long-standing conviction that "NATO is vital to the security of the United States" and that the United States "should not withdraw any significant forces from the Central Region in Europe under current conditions."[13]

When McCloy arrived in Bonn, he decided to hold a meeting with the other members of NATO who were not participating in the trilateral exercise. He faced immediate hostility, with these countries calling the tripartite operation a "self-appointed group" that was "without prior consultation, to do what all members of NATO had an interest in, and what NATO was created to do and was actively undertaking in its current force planning exercise."[14] McCloy, assisted by his former aide Robert Bowie, who had come back to the State Department in the position of counselor, defended the exercise as essential to meet a crisis "which ran [the] real risk of producing [an] extremely dangerous attrition of NATO defense posture and required extraordinary and rapid action to cope with it."[15] A British diplomat described Bowie's "powerful intervention" in the argument, insisting that the NATO countries recognize the gravity of the problem in the United States, citing the Mansfield Resolution, and arguing that, in this case, the administration had made "a sacrifice of procedural propriety for the sake of reality."[16] At this point the diplomat rather sarcastically noted that McCloy made "a declaration of faith in the origi-

John McCloy, Henry Fowler, and Francis Bator at a meeting on the trilateral question, March 1967. Johnson used McCloy's reputation with the Germans to bring about an agreement on restructuring the NATO alliance. (LBJ Library; photo by Yoichi Okamoto)

nal purposes of the Atlantic alliance which my Canadian colleague subsequently described as a 'requiem for NATO.'"[17]

The British disdain for McCloy was based on more than his tendency toward sentimental paeans to NATO. London disapproved of his appointment, as well as of the announcement that the talks would begin in Bonn, noting that "McCloy is particularly liable to take the German point of view and this risk would be enhanced if the talks were in Bonn."[18] Over the next weeks the British attempted to get McCloy replaced, trying to use their connections to the Defense Department and McNamara to encourage a joint stand against the former high commissioner.[19] This gambit proved fruitless, even when decisions about the British role were the first major challenge faced by the negotiations. With the collapse of Erhard's government at the end of October, it became clear that there would be no trilateral agreement before Wilson's budgetary deadline to announce defense cutbacks. The prime minister defiantly told Eugene Rostow, the undersecretary of state, that the British government's position was that, at the end of twelve months, "we must either have the money to cover all the foreign exchange costs of our troops, or withdraw the troops." When Rostow brought up the Mansfield Resolution, the British prime minister dismissed it, and referring to his tiny pre-March 1966 parliamentary majority, said "that he had never claimed in aid with the president this kind of Parliamentary or electoral difficulty."[20] (Wilson's memory was very selective—he knew that his fragile majority had given him considerable leverage from the beginning of his time in office, beginning with the first sterling rescue package in 1964.) Nevertheless, faced with Johnson's powerful plea to avoid troop cutbacks that would lead the trilateral negotiations to "lose credibility and political usefulness in all three countries," Wilson relented. He accepted an offer from LBJ for the United States to place some "$35 million in orders" in Britain, to put off any decisions on troop withdrawals until after the trilateral exercise was completed.[21]

Wilson did not have an easy time selling his concession to his cabinet. Though Johnson had fretted about reaction on the Hill, especially from the "new Congress,"[22] Wilson's more left-wing cabinet ministers criticized the acceptance of "a subvention which imposed restrictions" on British foreign policy.[23] Wilson may have been inclined to delay the cutbacks because of his cabinet's other decision to make a second and determined effort to secure membership in the Common Market. British domestic politics had an important impact on that decision, as Wilson was undermining his Conservative political opposition, now headed by the strongly pro-Europe Edward Heath.[24] Wilson's turn toward Europe, although not the product of any great personal enthusiasm for European integration, would soon influence his assessment of the British position east of Suez and the devaluation question.[25] Although the United States applauded the "courageous" British decision to try once again to join the EEC, and LBJ asked if "there is anything we might do to smooth the path," administration officials recognized that de Gaulle remained the roadblock for that direction.[26]

Indeed, Charles de Gaulle's influence in Europe seemed at a high point in late 1966 and early 1967. The new German government, a Grand Coalition of the Christian Democrats with the Social Democrats, headed by CDU leader Kurt Kiesinger, immediately signaled its deference to Paris. Franz Josef Strauss, who had vilified Erhard's pro-American stance and whose bombastic and combative style raised concerns about a resurgence of German nationalism, received the important post of finance minister. With his doubts about the solidity of the American commitment, Strauss could create significant problems for the negotiations. Kiesinger, who had taken a low profile in the Atlanticist-Gaullist conflict, immediately offered an olive branch to de Gaulle. In the new government's first declaration of policy to the Bundestag, Kiesinger and Willy Brandt called for a "new beginning" and a renewed attempt to give meaning to the Franco-German Treaty of 1963. Symbolic politics were high on the agenda of both Kiesinger and Brandt, the new Social Democratic foreign minister. Both made their trips to Paris to meet with de Gaulle and assure him of their desire to strengthen relations with France. Watching Brandt on television after his visit to Paris angered McCloy, who told Johnson that Brandt's attitude "was too effusive and too obviously directed toward a make-up with France and a tactful detachment from the United States." McCloy told Brandt that he was "fearful of the result of all this Lili Marlene love affair," and reminded him that only a few days before his embrace of de Gaulle, Soviet premier Kosygin had been in Paris delivering "vicious attacks" on the United States and West Germany that had received no rebuttal from the French. The German behavior was sure to feed into the Mansfield sentiment of "a plague on both your houses" and to make it more difficult for the United States to stay in Europe. Germany, McCloy reminded Brandt, had to play two roles: "embracement of France and adherence to collective policies hostile to De Gaulle."[27]

Along with the Gaullist turn in German policy came another problem, more significant than most historians have recognized. The question of Germany's trustworthiness, an argument that underlay concerns ranging from the MLF to the economic integration of the European Community, resurfaced in powerful form in late 1966. The modest success of the National Democratic Party (NPD) in two state elections in Hesse and Bavaria, coupled with Kiesinger's Nazi background, heightened concerns throughout Europe that West Germany's Nazi past had not been overcome. The election results might have been dismissed as insignificant except for their connection with Germany's economic difficulties, a connection that raised disturbing historical associations. As Kurt Birrenbach observed among his American interlocutors, including McCloy, Bowie, and Eugene Rostow, the elections brought forth memories "of the unfortunate attitude of our Western neighbors at the end of the 1920s, which helped lead to the catastrophe of January 30, 1933."[28] Congressional opponents of the Mansfield Resolution, like the influential Republican senator Jacob Javits, used the specter of "neo-Nazism" in arguing that West Germany was in "a terrible state of flux and ambivalence" and that a unilateral American withdrawal might cause the West Germans to ask "whether they had better make a deal with the East or be left high and dry."[29] On the other side of the Iron Curtain, the Soviets expressed a similar concern about neo-Nazis, although this sentiment was now filtered through their increasing preoccupation with the Chinese threat. Premier Kosygin told Wilson during a February 1967 trip to London that there was a real danger in "underestimating Nazism in Germany," and that the increase in neo-Nazi support "gave comfort to the Chinese, who were only too happy to see Russia threatened from other quarters."[30]

The electoral success of the NPD also amplified the news that the new German chancellor had a compromised past. The first American reports described Kiesinger as "a Nazi party member from 1933 to May 8, 1945," who "served as a liaison officer between the Foreign Office and Josef Goebbels' Propaganda Ministry, and later as an SA officer and political commissar with the Wehrmacht."[31] The latter part of these allegations, about membership in the SA, proved to be incorrect, although Kiesinger himself admitted to joining the party in May 1933, claiming that he had hoped to moderate its excesses. Kiesinger presented himself as "representative of the majority of Germans," a *Mitläufer*, or follower, who had supported the party initially but had nothing to do with its horrendous crimes. However, as the debate within Germany intensified, Kiesinger did have one of his trusted subordinates ask the American ambassador how President Johnson stood toward his candidacy. The answer that came back, "President Johnson sends his regards to Kiesinger," was correctly interpreted as showing an American willingness to accept the German choice.[32]

Although the formation of the Grand Coalition was widely perceived as a defeat for American interests, Johnson and his aides also recognized the great potential benefits of this government. For one, with its broad base of support—technically the coalition commanded 447 out of 463 seats in the Bundestag—it might now be possible to make lasting agreements with a German government capable of carrying out its end of the bargain.[33] It was also clear that the new German government had a different perspective on the long-standing nuclear sharing issue. The presence of Willy Brandt, the former mayor of Berlin and highly esteemed Germans in the United States, played an important role in American thinking. Although representing the

Social Democratic Party, which had originally opposed NATO and the American alliance, Brandt's strong anticommunist record in Berlin gave him considerable prestige in American circles. His record as one who had opposed Hitler from abroad, while damaging his support among some Germans, gave him a moral credibility that helped offset Kiesinger's Nazi past. Brandt also enjoyed good personal relations with Lyndon Johnson, with whom he felt he had a relationship of "trust," despite Brandt's own misgivings about the Vietnam War.[34]

At his first NATO meeting, in December 1966, Brandt told Secretary of State Rusk that his government was ready to "forget" about any special "European clause" in the proposed NPT. Rusk reported to LBJ that "Brandt made a major impression . . . in demonstrating that the new German government will not be bound by the rigid theology of the Adenauer period and is prepared to probe the possibilities of better relations with Eastern Europe, including the east Germans."[35] The Grand Coalition, as one German journalist put it, wanted to leave "the trenches of the cold war," and accepted the United States moves toward detente.[36] Rusk and Johnson welcomed this development, and Rusk echoed the president in saying that "we should give them a chance to find out whether another approach might produce more results."[37] Johnson continued to send warm signals to Brandt of his approval of this early *Ostpolitik*. In July 1967 Johnson met with two German journalists close to Brandt and told them that the German government did not need his approval for new initiatives toward the East. In Johnson's view, as the "undisputed leader in the process of bridge-building . . . German bridge-building towards the east was highly useful."[38]

What both Johnson and Rusk overlooked in their enthusiasm for the new German initiatives was that Brandt went much further in his thinking on this issue than his coalition government—Kiesinger and his party feared that detente between the United States and the Soviet Union might "cement" the status quo of Germany's division, which they could not accept.[39] Still, it was clear that whatever problems its Gaullist wing might pose, the new German government was trying to fall in line with the direction of President Johnson's European speech of October 7. Kiesinger and Brandt were determined to make a serious attempt to improve West Germany's relations with Eastern Europe and the Soviet Union. In one of its first actions in power, the Kiesinger-Brandt government recognized the communist government of Romania. And in a shift that Americans had long quietly encouraged, the Grand Coalition changed the tone and terminology of dealings with East Germany, exchanging letters with the East German premier, Willi Stoph, and proposing easier arrangements for travel, Berlin passes, cultural exchanges, and other contacts with the "other part of Germany."[40]

However, the "new beginning" of the Grand Coalition also meant postponing the trilateral discussions. Though the talks had originally been expected to last six to eight weeks, the fall of the Erhard government and the new government's reluctance to resume discussions before it had settled other issues, delayed the talks into early 1967. Although continuing the negotiations was never in question, the Kiesinger government symbolically demonstrated greater independence by waiting until the end of January to approve their resumption. The new German representative, Ambassador Georg Duckwitz, would first travel separately to Washington and London, where, as Foreign Minister Brandt informed Ambassador McGhee, he would express strongly to the Americans and the British "the seriousness faced by the Germans in their budget."[41] The great advantage that Duckwitz possessed was that the Bundesbank, Germany's independent central bank, was now prepared to help the politically solid Grand Coalition government in ways it had refused to help the floundering Erhard government. Duckwitz also quickly recognized during his talks in Washington and London that one of the keys to resolving the negotiations with the Americans was an acceptable deal for the British. The U.S. fear that sharp British reductions would create great domestic pressure for America to follow suit had finally registered with the Germans, and Duckwitz now urged his superiors to find some formula that would help the British avoid troop cutbacks.[42]

The delays in resuming the trilateral talks also led to increasing problems between Washington and Bonn, with Washington worried about the direction of German policy and Kiesinger's approach to the United States. The Bonn's courtship with Paris, along with Kiesinger's strong criticism of the "atomic complicity" between Washington and Moscow over the nonproliferation treaty,[43] led LBJ to have his own "doubts" about whether the "German policy of friendship toward us" was really "unchanged."[44] Kiesinger's additional attacks on the United States for its lack of consultation with the Germans enraged LBJ, who said, "If I had a dollar for every time I consulted the Germans, I'd be a millionaire." LBJ already suspected that Kiesinger was "shopping around, seeing where he can make deals with de Gaulle and the others." Johnson now told McCloy to tell Kiesinger that "you have done business with me since World War II, and that you know that the way he's trying to do business with me in the newspapers is not going to work."[45]

In the midst of these irritations Johnson faced an important choice regarding the trilateral negotiations, a choice that his assistant Bator warned would "cast a very long shadow on our relations with Germany, with consequences for domestic politics." Johnson was faced with sharp divisions within the American government. McCloy, representing the stalwart East Coast foreign policy establishment but also supported by the Joint Chiefs of Staff, maintained an unwillingness to support any reduction in U.S. forces in Germany. If pressed, McCloy did allow that he might be able to live with a one-division reduction, but only if this could be negotiated with the rest of the allies and the Germans.[46] The State Department favored only a one-division reduction, couching this in terms of the "rotation of one

division and three air wings" back to the United States. McNamara
and the Defense Department, with the implicit support of Treasury,
remained firmly in support of a two-division reduction, a cutback
that would certainly lead McCloy to withdraw as the American negotiator. At the first meeting to consider these respective choices, Johnson refused to discuss the numbers that his advisers gave him. Rather,
he instructed them to develop a set of principles for the negotiations,
principles that would serve to make any decision of the trilateral discussions a joint allied decision rather than a unilateral American
move. These principles were sufficiently flexible to allow for any
Johnson decision, and at the same time they covered up the differences within the American position. Johnson also brought the Congress into the process, although carefully managing his meetings with
senators and congressmen to create the impression of congressional
support for maintaining the American position in Europe.

Three principles came out of the deliberations and were incorpo-
rated into LBJ's draft directive to McCloy. The first and most important was forcefully stated: "Force levels should be determined through
agreement among the Allies on the basis of security considerations,
broadly construed." The president was, as he made clear in the letter
to McCloy, "determined not to jeopardize the security of the Alliance" for financial reasons. The other two principles that Johnson
listed were that Germany itself should determine the level of procure-
ment (offset spending) it should make in the United States and Britain to bring its forces up to an appropriate strength, and that the
allies should deal with the remaining balance of payments consequences (deficits) by cooperation "in the management of monetary
reserves or by other agreed means."[47] On March 1, 1967, McCloy
met the president at the White House. When presented with this
draft, McCloy told LBJ that he was somewhat perplexed, noting that
there was "nothing on troop cuts," and that the instructions seemed
to put "primary focus on the UK/BAOR situation and on money."

He worried that they created the impression of "indecision," and asked if he could take a "line" in the negotiations that would stress that the president had "not reached final decision on troops," and that he wanted "to sit down with the UK and FRG in a cooperative way to see if we can avoid any cuts and unraveling."[48]

As talented and experienced a negotiator as he was, McCloy had recognized only a part of Johnson's strategy. Over the next hour, LBJ, mixing folksy metaphors—"I want to marry and live with the woman, but it is damned important to know how she feels"—with political analysis and kvetching about various political personalities, laid out his understanding of the situation, careful not to reveal to McCloy his own bottom line or what cuts he was prepared to make. Rather, Johnson pushed McCloy to find out what the Germans wanted and were prepared to pay, telling him that the Germans "are the key; they have a new Government; if they can come up with something to help the British, then maybe we can hold the line." Johnson explained to McCloy that the "congressional position is three to one for substantial cuts," noting that it wasn't just "doves" like Mansfield who wanted to cut but also conservative Democrats like Richard Russell and even his Republican predecessor Eisenhower, "who really thinks we ought to cut many more than just two divisions." Johnson wanted the Germans to be "realistic" about the situation he faced, telling them that he was not "ready to sign on any dotted line without knowing what they will do." In classic Johnson fashion, he related the problem to his own personal experience, telling McCloy that "I know my Germans . . . I lived in Fredericksburg [Texas], grew up in Fredericksburg; they are a great people; but by God they are as stingy as Hell." Johnson made it clear to McCloy that he couldn't confront the congressional opposition without knowing how the Germans and British were going to behave, that he needed something from them before he could "tackle" Congress. Painting what was consciously an overpessimistic picture "of the dark and dangerous ground" between now and 1969, Johnson warned McCloy, "My judgment is that we'll have to cut two divisions." McCloy responded with his own dire prediction, telling Johnson, "You are on the verge of the collapse of the Alliance. We are going back to the old world of dog-eat-dog—each nation for itself . . . in a much more dangerous world—the nuclear age." Almost immediately Johnson stepped back from this prediction of the apocalypse and reassured McCloy, saying, "I'll try to hold this Alliance together longer than anybody else will, longer than the British will, and longer than the Germans. But they have got to put something in the family pot." McCloy wondered, "Suppose the Germans come up with the money? Can you then hold the line?" Cautious as always, Johnson simply replied, "Perhaps, but you have to go over there and find out what they will do."[49]

Johnson's approach to his establishment negotiator accomplished two things: it kept his own decisionmaking options open, and it energized McCloy, who returned to the talks determined to take a tough line with the Germans. The British, whose intelligence in Washington was usually excellent, misread the result of the meeting, believing that "McCloy's views prevailed" because the administration was reluctant to see him resign.[50] London was still determined to insist on a full offset of its costs, as Wilson warned Rostow, for it was regarded as a "major issue of principle in the country and the Government could not go back on it." He also told the president's aide that "apart from anything else, it would be impossible for the Government to hold to its East of Suez commitments" unless it was offset for its costs in Europe.[51] McCloy had more success in dealing with Kiesinger. During the course of a long meeting with Kiesinger, McCloy made the chancellor aware of the president's "concern" and "resentment" about some of the chancellor's public statements, and he told him, "The President hoped that the Chancellor would understand his problems, just as he tried to understand Prime Minister Wilson's and the Chancellor's problems." Kiesinger backed away from this criticism and told McCloy that he when he had mentioned the word "complicity" in describing the origins of the NPT, he had done so "smilingly." The chancellor said that his own experts believed that the British would drastically cut their forces no matter what the Germans offered, and that some had the same impression of the U.S. position because of McNamara's and Mansfield's statements. Kiesinger was pleased to hear that this was not necessarily the case. Kiesinger clearly wanted Johnson to understand that German finances were in a "miserable mess," but that he would "try to find a way" at the next cabinet meeting. Kiesinger then returned to the "complicity" quote, taking pains with McCloy to correct any "misimpressions" that might have resulted. Indeed, Kiesinger went on at great length, trying to reassure McCloy, and by implication Johnson, that he had "a real friendship for the U.S. . . . and would do his best to cooperate."[52]

Knowing now of Kiesinger's desire to cooperate, McCloy returned to Washington for another meeting with the president. The main problem, he reported, remained the gap between British demands and the German offer, a shortfall that now amounted to about $40 million. Johnson pushed his advisers to come up with creative ways to fill the gap, insisting only that the United States not fill the entire amount. Johnson also outlined the makings of a deal in which America would cut one division, the United Kingdom would cut one brigade, and the Germans and British would split the $40 million deficit. Johnson and his aides then decided, as Bator put it, "that it is useful as well as proper for the more powerful to make the first move."[53] At the suggestion of Ambassador Duckwitz, they drafted a letter from Johnson for Kiesinger to use at his important cabinet meeting. Johnson pushed Kiesinger to do as much as possible to help the British, a gesture that would be "a real contribution to Alliance solidarity." He made it clear that he thought "a limited rotational plan" could satisfy "NATO's security requirements." He promised

Kiesinger to "hold the line against any steps which would significantly weaken NATO," but he pushed the Germans for help on the international monetary negotiations. LBJ also added a strong paragraph, against the advice of a number of his advisers, stressing the importance he attached to the Nonproliferation Treaty.[54] Kiesinger would have no illusions about nonproliferation's importance to Johnson, even as the president was reaffirming his commitment to NATO.

Johnson's letter made a "deep impression" on Kiesinger, who used it repeatedly during his cabinet meeting to support his arguments. The Germans decided to increase their offset purchases in Britain, although Finance Minister Strauss raised "unshirted Hell about this surrender to the Anglo-Saxons."[55] The British also made a concession, agreeing to credit toward the gap in their expenses money the United States was already planning to spend in Britain on relocating forces from France. They now recognized, as Michael Palliser told Wilson, "We are most unlikely to do better than this," especially when Johnson was forcing McNamara to make up part of the remaining gap with $20 million in new procurements within Britain.[56] There was now, as Bator reported to LBJ, the makings of a "workable three way bargain," a bargain that would demonstrate that "when the chips are down NATO pulls up its socks to come up with a sensible and responsible package."[57] Bator further emphasized to the president the particular value of the pledge from the Bundesbank, the so-called Blessing Brief, not to convert any of its dollars to gold, a pledge that, according to Bator, was the equivalent of putting the Germans on a dollar standard and giving the United States much greater flexibility in dealing with its balance of payments deficits.[58]

Although the outlines of an accord existed, a major stumbling block remained over the specifics of the American plan to "rotate" a division and its air wings out of Germany. Kiesinger told LBJ that he had particular concern about the continuing presence of "massive Soviet forces" in East Germany whose strength in recent years had been increased. In principle, the Germans believed in tying the withdrawal of allied forces in Germany to Soviet reductions.[59] However, after studying the U.S. plan, which kept one brigade in Germany at all times and rotated the other two back to the United States, the Germans were satisfied in most respects except one—the air element. The Germans believed that the American plan to redeploy 144 aircraft back to the United States—fully half of the U.S. planes on German soil—was too great a reduction. They dug in their heels on this point, and McCloy urged Washington to show some flexibility. However, McNamara strongly resisted backing down on this issue, and it appeared that the president would have to break the deadlock.[60]

In the midst of what should have been a straightforward compromise, other issues arose to complicate the bargain. On April 14 the United States presented a new version of the Nonproliferation Treaty to NATO members, with plans to gain their approval for submitting it to the Soviets at the end of the month. The German reaction became even more strident and angry, directed against both the notion of a *diktat* by the United States and Soviet Union and the possibility that the treaty would allow inspections by Soviet and Eastern European officials of West German nuclear facilities.[61] There was also a widely reported rumor that the American company General Electric was advertising its own relative freedom from controls compared with its German rivals in the nuclear industry.[62] Many Germans were coming to see nonproliferation as an infringement on their own economic and scientific development, a "Morgenthau Plan squared," as former chancellor Konrad Adenauer put it.[63] The United States, from its position, recognized that German views on the trilateral talks were indirectly influenced by this concern, as the Germans feared being left defenseless in the face of Soviet power and abandoning a position that might help to bring about German reunification. Johnson also recognized that he would need German help on other issues, particularly the Kennedy Round and the negotiations over international money, where the Germans could serve to isolate the French and pressure them toward reaching an agreement. As Bator advised him, "We are reaching a crucial moment on a lot of fronts and the Germans are in a key position."[64]

LBJ's Trip to Europe

Konrad Adenauer, legendary founding father of the Federal Republic, chancellor for fourteen years, and then critic of his successor's policies, died on April 19, 1967, at his home outside Cologne. Although ninety-one at the time of his death, Adenauer had maintained an active role in German politics, using his last speech, in February of that year, to call for the creation of a United Europe armed with its own nuclear weapons.[65] Johnson, who had been criticized for not attending Winston Churchill's funeral in January 1965, quickly decided to attend Adenauer's funeral himself, thus making his first visit to Europe as president.[66] Johnson had turned down previous invitations to come to Europe, including repeated offers from Erhard, as he sought to avoid an inevitable comparison with Kennedy's triumphal visit of June 1963. The trip to Adenauer's funeral was improvised, and some, including the U.S. ambassador to Germany, George McGhee, later maintained that Johnson's visit "accomplished little of significance apart from paying tribute to the creator of postwar Germany."[67] This conclusion, however, is wrong. Attending the funeral of Adenauer offered LBJ an opportunity to avoid a direct comparison with Kennedy—no one expected cheering throngs at a state funeral—while at the same time taking personal command of European diplomacy at a crucial time.

Johnson was careful to observe the traditional formalities of the state funeral. Although traveling with a large entourage—one that inevitably invited criticism for its heavy-handedness in carrying out the "president's wishes"—Johnson made a special personal visit to the

Adenauer family at their hillside home in Bad Honnef to convey his respects.[68] Though LBJ met privately with both Wilson and de Gaulle, who also attended the funeral—Johnson even sparred with de Gaulle about a possible visit to France, telling the French leader rather disingenuously that "this is an election year and that he [did] not think that he [would] do much traveling"—the main focus of his attention was Kiesinger. (He had also brought Kiesinger's daughter, who was married to an American, along with the presidential entourage.) Johnson remained leery of the German chancellor, still smarting over his public criticisms of American policy. Cautioned by Bator that "you are three times his size—and . . . he knows it," Johnson used a variety of techniques in his approach to Kiesinger. During their first meeting, Johnson referred once again to his own partial German ancestry and his youth in a German community in Texas. He assured the chancellor that the United States "would never disregard the interests of the Chancellor and the German nation." Kiesinger then launched into a long lecture about the "quality" of the consultation between the United States and Germany, suggesting that it had been deficient and that the way to strengthen the alliance was "through complete and candid exchange of views in an atmosphere of trust." This criticism triggered Johnson's temper, although his response was more sarcastic than explosive. Picking up on the chancellor's reference to "quality," Johnson referred repeatedly to the high "quality" of the men in his administration who consulted with their German counterparts. Johnson made it clear that the public criticisms of Kiesinger, those that were "spread all over the *New York Times* and other papers," were feeding the congressional critics of his policy, who wanted much greater cuts in U.S. forces in Europe. He specifically mentioned the chancellor's "complicity" charge, assuring him that "he had always had good and friendly feelings towards the German nation and the German people." Although Kiesinger responded by assuring the president that he was convinced of the "out-

LBJ and Chancellor Kurt Kiesinger (right) in Bonn, April 1967. Johnson's wary look captures his irritation with Kiesinger's "lecturing" about the proper consultation with allies. (LBJ Library; photo by Yoichi Okamoto)

standing quality" of the men advising the president and that he had his own problems with the Bundestag, the short meeting ended with Johnson warning Kiesinger that despite his thirty years in Washington dealing with Congress, "he sometimes did not have much control over its decision."[69]

The two men agreed to delay the major substance of their talks until their next meeting. After the first meeting, some German officials feared that Kiesinger had treated Johnson "as if he were complaining of the conduct of a minor NATO ally or EEC partner," and they worried that he had gone too far in pushing the president.[70] For his part, Johnson thought the German leader somewhat "pompous" and in a "very nervous and emotional state."[71] Learning through one of the chancellor's aides that Kiesinger was largely willing to go along with U.S. policy if "there is a place for German unity," Johnson was determined to use his second meeting with Kiesinger to push for German cooperation on the whole range of issues involved in his European policy. Again Johnson allowed Kiesinger to assume the initiative and reassure the president that the Germans "did not only want to continue those good relations [with the United States] but indeed to *try to make them better and closer*" (emphasis in the original). The chancellor talked generally about the changes in German public opinion, changes he attributed to the fact "that the cold war had abated to a certain extent and that people had not yet become adjusted to the new period properly." Kiesinger now focused on the German question, noting that as recently as the last period of the Eisenhower administration there "were some people who were saying that the U.S. had sold out to the Soviet Union and was no longer supporting the cause of German reunification." Kiesinger admitted that "a certain relationship between the Soviet Union and the United States was necessary in view of the power and the heavy responsibilities of these two countries." Johnson interrupted to affirm U.S. support for German reunification and the alliance, and to assure the chancellor that he had "strong feelings" about the Soviets, "just as much as Adenauer did," but that "he just did not talk so much about them." Kiesinger then continued, assuring Johnson that neo-Nazi right-wing parties were not real threats in contemporary Germany, and that Germans perceived Erhard as "naive" in his dealings with the Americans and this had led to his fall from power. Kiesinger added his suggestion that there should be a shorter time limit on the Nonproliferation Treaty. Finally, he mentioned in vague terms that he might help on the international money and troop reduction issues.

After Kiesinger's long exposition, Johnson shifted into high gear, accepting the chancellor's view of German opinion but depicting the

Johnson with German president Helmut Lübke (center) and French president Charles de Gaulle at Chancellor Konrad Adenauer's funeral, April 25, 1967. In one of the rare photos of Johnson and de Gaulle together, it is symbolic that a German stands between them. (LBJ Library; photo by Yoichi Okamoto)

problems he faced with Congress in vivid detail: "People were saying to themselves: Why should we continue to spend over a million dollars? Why should we keep on maintaining our troops there? Why should we not let them handle their own defense? They are grown up now. They have rebuilt their countries. They can take care of themselves." Johnson again affirmed that he was opposed to such sentiments, that "he wanted to be friends with Germany" and to speak up for reunification. He then turned to specifics. Washington had already changed the NPT text twenty-five times to meet German objections. There were no secret deals "behind the barn," as the news media reported. The United States did not regard Erhard as a "softie" but rather as a man "who was wise to see the danger of an isolationist trend which was growing in the U.S." and was willing to make concessions to head it off. When Kiesinger tried to interject about proposed American withdrawals of "172 planes," Johnson caught him with the numbers and pointed out that the withdrawal was actually of 144 planes, out of 662 in Europe as a whole. Kiesinger quickly backed off from any more specific suggestions, telling LBJ that "they should not try to decide too many difficult problems at once." Johnson now hammered away on a range of issues, pushing for German support for the Kennedy Round, the international monetary negotiations, the NPT, and the conclusion of the trilateral talks. He dramatically took and shook Kiesinger's hand and renewed a pledge he had made to Erhard, that "the U.S. would stand by his side against any aggression by the Soviet Union." Then Johnson used the occasion to observe that the Germans looked well fed and that they could provide more aid to "the people of Asia" and "support his food program" in that region.

Johnson had turned the tables on Kiesinger. Americans at the meeting perceived that "the Chancellor was feeling slightly uneasy about the emphatic, determined and simply-worded delivery of the President's thoughts." Kiesinger, whose training as a diplomat combined with a personal style that was both graceful and eloquent, normally had the advantage in such conversations, but he was "unable to control the direction of the conversation" with the president. Johnson, for his part, "appeared completely at ease throughout the conversation." And indeed LBJ had accomplished what he wanted to, forcing the German chancellor to realize that Johnson, too, faced significant problems at home and that it was important for Kiesinger to cooperate with him in minimizing the friction in the relationship. The way was now clear for a final compromise on the trilateral negotiations.

Only days after he returned to Washington, Johnson faced the question of aircraft withdrawals. The Germans proposed that the

United States redeploy only 72 planes instead of 144. McCloy recommended the compromise figure of 96. McNamara would only agree if the Germans allowed the withdrawal of an additional 10,000 men. Johnson overruled McNamara once again, agreeing with Bator that the decision was "a favor to Kiesinger" and that McCloy should make it clear that Washington hoped this would "make it easier for Kiesinger to cooperate on other fronts where he has domestic difficulties," including nuclear nonproliferation, international money, and the Kennedy Round.[72]

At the conclusion of their meeting on April 28, 1967, McCloy signed the Trilateral Agreements along with his British and German counterparts. The three had agreed to a variety of new arrangements to sustain the Western presence in Germany, and to recognize that, as McCloy later put it, "the financial burden of our troops abroad and the balance of payments complications that presented" were indeed "common problems" to the alliance.[73] "NATO was still in business," Johnson wrote later in his memoirs, proving "once again that if there is a will to do so allies can work out their most difficult problems, in spite of divisive domestic political pressures."[74] But the Trilateral Agreements were only a first step in the complicated and complex web of arrangements Johnson sought in restructuring the alliance and "growing out of the Cold War."

The Kennedy Round, Act II

Like a running back with blockers and a clear path to the end zone, Johnson made it clear to Kiesinger that he planned a full agenda for Europe that spring, and that the Kennedy Round was one of his most important goals. The vice president, Hubert Humphrey, also lobbied every European leader during his trip early in April. Even Senator Robert Kennedy, although having now broken with LBJ over Vietnam, still used some of his time during a trip to Europe to press

Kiesinger to help win approval of the Kennedy Round, something that would be seen as a tribute to his late brother.[75] Dean Rusk warned Europeans of "incalculable consequences for the American attitude toward the whole Atlantic relationship" if the Kennedy Round failed.[76]

But time was running out, as Johnson's congressional authorization to negotiate the trade compact ended June 30, 1967. The length of time allowed for the negotiation can be attributed in part to a significant historical development. The Kennedy Round was the first major international negotiation in which the European Economic Community attempted to act as a single entity, a milestone in the history of the EEC, but one that generated enormous delays. Within the confines of the EEC, President Charles de Gaulle's France fought so resolutely to protect the Common Agricultural Policy that no serious talks could begin until the EEC made its first agricultural offer in August 1966.[77] Even then it was clear that the Europeans would proceed on a policy that meant, for most agricultural products, "very high support prices and tightly protected markets."[78] Part of the U.S. strategy in dealing with the EEC was to propose generous offers, with the hope that this would generate "the most effective pressure possible on the EEC to improve its offers."[79] However, these U.S. offers received mixed reviews at home. After Johnson's political vulnerability became clear in the midterm elections, Senate minority leader Everett Dirksen publicly attacked the U.S. position in the talks. In a speech to the Trade Relations Council, Dirksen proclaimed, "The United States appears intent upon concluding an agreement which will not repair the damage to our farmers, while inflicting new damage upon our manufacturing industries," and he said that it looked as if the United States was offering to give the Europeans "our shirt in exchange for a handkerchief."[80] The death of U.S. Trade Representative Christian Herter in late December removed the political cover that the prominent liberal Republican and former secretary of state had provided. There was no obvious replacement with Herter's Republican status, and as Herter's deputy, William Roth, had been doing most of the work during Herter's illness, Johnson appointed Roth the new U.S. trade representative in Geneva, even though he lacked the ties to Congress that Johnson would have wanted. As the time passed into spring 1967 and approached the end of the president's TEA authority, Roth worried, "Time is [so] damn short that it will be a miracle if we can put the pieces together."[81]

To put the pieces together, Johnson approved Bator's suggestion of "a very small command group" operating from the White House and positioned to "backstop" Roth and his negotiators in Geneva. The advantages of this approach from Johnson's point of view were fewer press leaks as well as the greater capacity of such a small group to spell out clearly "the critical choices" for presidential decision. Given the group's covert setup, with its separate communications link humorously named Limdiss-Potatoes (limited distribution—potatoes), Bator apologized to LBJ "for making this sound like a battle plan. However," he pointed out, "not only five years of work, but your entire trade policy is at stake."[82] Johnson appreciated his aide's attempt to maintain secrecy and defend presidential prerogatives. Although he would leave most of the technical details of the negotiations to Bator, Roth, and their advisers, Johnson was deeply interested in a successful outcome, and keenly sensitive to the issues in domestic politics and his relations with Congress that the trade agreement represented.[83]

Two major areas of dispute remained in the Kennedy Round trade negotiations, both with strong congressional overtones. The first involved a dispute over the American selling price (ASP), a system of tariffs on four classes of imports—benzenoid chemicals, rubber-soled footwear, canned hams, and wool knit gloves.[84] As the official history of the Kennedy Round explained, the tariffs on these products were based on the wholesale price of a comparable item produced *in the United States*—in contrast to the usual practice of basing tariffs on the wholesale price in the *country of origin*.[85] (In effect, this was a form of legal American protectionism achieved by the chemical industry.) The Europeans initially wanted the ASP abolished without any reciprocating concession. When it was clear that the United States would not consider this proposal, the EEC demanded that the elimination of the ASP be included within the Kennedy Round agreement as a part of the package. The problem this option presented was that only Congress could eliminate the ASP, and Congress would not want to have itself seen as "pressured" by the EEC to make this decision by having it linked to the overall Kennedy Round agreement. The American negotiators knew that the ASP was a problem—Johnson had approved Roth's recommendation to eliminate it in February—but they wanted to keep it separate from the Kennedy Round package and obtain concessions for its elimination.[86]

The other issue that complicated the final talks of the Kennedy Round was agriculture, particularly the U.S. demand for guaranteed access to the European feed grain market. Roth advised Johnson to drop this demand in return for getting the EEC to drop its own insistence on a minimum price for grain imports, something that kept efficient U.S. producers from competing. This would complicate the president's relations with the farm groups, but Johnson was willing to take that risk. The president also intervened when the issue of canned hams threatened to break down the negotiations. Long upset about the treatment that agriculture had received in the Kennedy Round, Secretary of Agriculture Orville Freeman wanted the United States to withdraw its offer to cut its tariff on canned hams by 50 percent and to "bind" the duty at that reduced level. (To bind a tariff meant to agree not to raise the tariff without compensating foreign suppliers.) Freeman was concerned about the U.S. meat industry, which had been affected by rising imports. Roth and Bator argued that withdrawing the offer would, to use the word that had been frequently used during the trilateral negotiations, "unravel" the agreement and lead the EEC to withdraw its modest agricultural offers. Freeman's opposition split the Washington command group and called for a presidential compromise. Flying back to Washington on Air Force One on May 8, the president decided to accept a compromise Bator proposed, to withdraw the offer to cut the tariff but to keep the offer to bind the present fairly low tariff on canned hams.[87]

Despite the president's decision, Roth reported a "wake-like atmosphere" in Geneva with the continuing failure of the United States and the EEC to reach an agreement by the self-imposed deadline of the evening of May 9. Bator sought to encourage the Geneva team, and he warned them that it was the administration's "firm view" that "we must avoid breaking off negotiations," especially since there were some signs of movement in the EEC position. Roth reassured Bator the next day that "happily I had not pulled the plug" on the talks and that the new date for concluding the negotiations was May 14.[88] For their part, the British remained skeptical about the EEC's flexibility. Their negotiator, Sir Richard Powell, told London that after two days of intense discussions, "The EEC pursued their accustomed tactic of pressing for concessions, pocketing without payment anything they could pick up and then pressing for more: in the process using methods for which bazaar haggling would be too dignified a term."[89]

In the midst of this haggling, Johnson sat down with his advisers for a final consideration of the U.S. position in the talks. Bator told him that the United States would come out of the agreement in "rough terms" "about even" with the EEC, though Japan and the United Kingdom would "get more" than the United States would. Acknowledging that his calculations were "pretty arbitrary," Bator still believed they were "conservative" in their estimate of the benefits. Nevertheless he recognized that the fact that the U.S. export surplus might be reduced meant the Johnson administration did face "a public relations problem" in presenting the agreement. Bator told the president that the EEC had finally accepted that the ASP problem would be solved through a "two-package approach," with the United States in the first package agreeing to cut its tariffs by 50 percent on chemicals, with a corresponding reduction of 20 percent by the EEC. In the second package, which would stand on its own and require congressional action, the ASP would be eliminated, the United States would cut most chemical tariffs further, and the EEC would reduce its chemical tarriffs another 30 percent. Bator recognized that Congress might balk at this arrangement but said that it "was a good bargain for us." Agriculture might also pose a problem, as the results with the EEC were modest, amounting to about $100 million or "an average tariff cut of about 12%." Anticipating Secretary Freeman's objections, Bator suggested that LBJ stress the agricultural benefits coming from other nations that were more substantial. In Bator's view, Johnson would have to make the judgment of whether these results were enough "to avoid a major political war with the farm community." The president's deputy closed his memo by urging LBJ to initial the bargain, asserting that the real issue was not the level of tarriffs but "holding to a reasonable set of trade rules without which international trade would become jungle warfare, commodity by commodity, and country by country." The failure of the Kennedy Round would risk a "spiraling protectionism," as well as having the political effect of encouraging "strong forces now at work to make the EEC into an isolationist, anti-U.S. bloc."[90]

Bator was preaching to the converted. Although Johnson was always a tough bargainer and could sound like a protectionist and a nationalist when describing how other countries would "screw us to death," his basic belief in the benefits of free trade was unshakable. Even Johnson's knowledge of the deep discontent within the farm belt, a discontent that would likely hurt the Democrats in 1968, did not deter him from his support for the Kennedy Round.[91] Johnson orchestrated a meeting with his cabinet and other advisers, producing unanimous support for the Kennedy Round. In typical fashion, he reserved his decision until after the results of the final bargaining session were known.[92]

That session included some difficult discussions with the British, whom Roth believed were "completely unhelpful." U.S. officials thought the British were "stonewalling" on a number of issues, including the overall balance of concessions between London and Washington, and various aspects of the agreements on import prices for grains, tarriffs on plastics, and steel duties. Roth again feared that the British position would lead to a "general unraveling with the risk that the entire house of cards will crumble." The Bator command group's response was to go to London "on every channel and hit them with all we have, short of Presidential intervention with Harold Wilson."[93] Bator telephoned his friend Michael Palliser, Prime Minister Wilson's private secretary, and stressed that this was "political business of the highest sort" and that the president "considers the successful outcome of the negotiations a matter of the greatest concern." Palliser considered Bator's message "highly alarmist," but the British soon contended that there was a "misunderstanding" of their position.[94] Powell, the British negotiator, also thought that the Washington reaction was "much exaggerated," but the British agreed to make a number of concessions. After several marathon sessions in the last days, with "the risk up to the last that the Community might not agree to some minor agricultural concessions," the negotiators reached a final agreement early in the morning on May 16.[95] Johnson telegraphed Roth to thank him for "a first-rate job."[96]

Although Roth later thought "we could have done better here or there," the Kennedy Round was a substantial achievement for U.S. economic diplomacy. As one recent study noted, in terms of the original objectives of a 50-percent tariff cut, the reductions averaged 36 to 39 percent, with about two-thirds above 50 percent. The Kennedy Round "contributed to the substantial rise in the value of world exports in the early 1970s as the tariff cuts were phased in."[97] At the time, America's most important NATO partners were pleased with the Kennedy Round. Despite their own economic problems, the British believed that the agreement was "a highly satisfactory outcome,"[98] as did the Germans, who deemed it the best result that could have been expected.[99] The Germans had agreed to maintain their support for the CAP, in return for which the French yielded in their resistance to allowing the Kennedy Round to come to an agreement.[100] The U.S. debate proved a more difficult one, and Johnson had to deal with an increasingly skeptical Congress. He warned the legislators that the movement toward liberal trade "is a steep climb up a slippery slope." It was possible to slip back and to fall into "an economic cold war where nobody trusts anybody and everybody stagnates." The president also connected the outcome of the Kennedy Round with his larger political goals. Noting that this was "a time of stress and re-direction for the Atlantic community," Johnson told Congress that "we can emerge stronger and more mature. Or we could dissolve into rival islands." As with the Trilateral Agreements, Johnson was determined that the alliance would not unravel on his watch, and that its redirection toward detente and the peaceful management of disputes would not be ruined by protectionist and nationalist forces. This determination reflected Johnson's core beliefs, but his was not an easy case to make in the political atmosphere of the times.

In the midst of an increasing atmosphere of protectionism and concern about America's economy, the Kennedy Round proved to be the last major international trade agreement for more than a decade. The Eighty-ninth Congress never approved the elimination of the ASP, though it did resist other protectionist measures that were proposed.[101] Historical assessments of the results of the Kennedy Round vary widely. Most economists remain highly supportive of the movement to liberalize trade, and they extol agreements like the Kennedy Round for having contributed to the general increase in living standards throughout the world in the last half-century. Ernest Preeg, one of the negotiators of the agreement, argued that for nonagricultural trade alone, the Kennedy Round meant an increase in industrialized world trade on the order of $2 billion to $3 billion annually.[102]

Yet there are strong critics of the bargains that American leaders made. Alfred Eckes, one of the most prominent, concludes that the United States achieved "few of its initial goals," emphasizing the failure to "open agricultural markets or increase opportunities for exports from developing countries."[103] He stresses that during the implementation period for the treaty, from 1968 to 1972, "the U.S. trade surplus vanished and a sizable deficit emerged." From a different perspective, Thomas Zeiler argues that, in the Kennedy Round, "the United States got many trade advantages, but . . . the EEC won *its* aim of lowering industrial tariffs while maintaining agricultural barriers." Indeed, Zeiler sees the Kennedy Round as a "significant indication of the end of U.S. hegemony," with the EEC "now a formidable and effective challenger to U.S. power."[104] (However, as Thomas Ilgen has noted, "With so many issues and with countries ranking the importance of such issues very differently, it is not surprising to discover that outcomes were dominated by no single state . . . in short, the United States orchestrated the launching of a trade liberalizing scheme over which it had less and less control.")[105]

The critics fail, however, to judge the outcome of the Kennedy Round in the larger context of successful alliance politics. No trade agreement generates only winners—some Americans were adversely affected by the lower tariffs, although the recession of 1969 and the subsequent economic turmoil of the 1970s exaggerated the impact of freer trade on U.S. industry. Even Eckes admits that there were other factors that caused a deterioration of the U.S. trade performance after the signing of the Kennedy Round, including inflation, lagging productivity gains, an overvalued dollar, and increasing energy costs, and he concedes that the Kennedy Round was "perhaps not the most important."[106] Critics also tend to overestimate the leverage the United

States had, especially on the agriculture issue.[107] Agriculture was at the heart of France's European policy, and pressing harder on this issue would probably have led to the collapse of the talks and increased strains within the alliance. There was much greater shrewdness and vision in the Johnson administration's refusal to threaten the EEC's unity by pressing too hard on agriculture. The development of a more united Europe, which, as Zeiler notes, was indeed an achievement of the Kennedy Round, played a critical role in the long-term strategy of the United States to triumph peacefully in the Cold War. An integrated Europe proved a source of strength—and, at times, competition—for the United States, but it effectively brought Germany thoroughly into the Western alliance and proved an extraordinarily appealing magnet for the trapped citizens of the Soviet empire in Eastern Europe.[108] To the extent that the American economy suffered from the Kennedy Round—and the evidence for this is debatable—the larger political objectives that were achieved, strengthening the alliance and the cohesion of the West, far outweigh the short-term economic dislocations. There was some hyperbole in Johnson's claim that the Kennedy Round was "the most successful multilateral agreement on tariff reduction ever negotiated,"[109] but history has borne out the great difficulties of achieving such agreements, as well as the significance of this success.

"International Money": Special Drawing Rights and the Reform of Bretton Woods

A few days after the Kennedy Round negotiations ended, Francis Bator spoke with his British friend Michael Palliser, assuring him that the pressures that were brought to bear on the British toward the end of the Kennedy Round were "by no means artificially generated" but reflected the high priority the measure had for President Johnson. Preparing for Harold Wilson's scheduled visit to Washington at the end of May 1967, Bator told Palliser that the administration's next priority was to get agreement on the plan for creating new international monetary reserves. Bator told Palliser that the United States was well aware that Britain could "not get out in front" on this issue, as the fragility of sterling weakened the British voice on such matters. America saw the Germans as "the key," and once again the problem would be France.[110]

The French had a better chance to block this U.S. initiative than they had the Kennedy Round, in part because of the change in fortune of the U.S. balance of payments. In the almost two years since the United States had proposed the reform of the international monetary system, its balance of payments had deteriorated significantly. Whereas for a time in 1965 it had appeared that the United States would be experiencing balance of payments surpluses, the demands of Vietnam, supplemented by the beginnings of the Great Society, now produced significant deficits. The $1.42 billion deficit for 1966 represented an increase of only $123 million over the deficit for 1965, but the deterioration aroused immediate concern.[111] Increasing deficits raised the risk of an attack on the value of the dollar, although the German agreement not to exchange dollars for gold, stated in the Blessing Brief, strengthened the U.S. position. For the most part the president was reluctant to adopt the tough policies favored by "balance of payments hawks" in his Treasury Department. At one point he bluntly told the chairman of the Federal Reserve Board, William Martin, "I will not deflate the American economy, screw up my foreign policy by gutting aid or pulling troops out, or go protectionist just so we can continue to pay out gold to the French at $35 an ounce."[112] Johnson's heretical thoughts on this subject were nurtured by Bator, who had been telling him for some time that "a run on gold which would force us to declare a moratorium on sales is not the end of the world." Bator said he believed that "the present rules of the international money game place an excessive burden on the U.S." and that, properly handled, "we could within a few months negotiate new rules which would make far more sense all around."[113]

Bator's heresy on the dollar-gold link may have been music to the president's ears, but for political reasons Johnson wanted to avoid the type of financial crisis Bator sketched, even if such a crisis afforded the United States opportunities for action. The president's priority was not "solving" the balance of payments problem, and then facing the undesirable consequences of such a solution. However, to avoid the domestic pressure to act on this issue, Johnson needed a success in monetary reform. During his visit to Germany he told Kiesinger how important the United States believed a successful outcome of the liquidity talks was, and that he hoped Germany would cooperate. But this was an issue that posed significant problems for the Germans. The same day that Johnson and Kiesinger were having their first bilateral meeting, the German economics minister, Karl Schiller, met with Johnson's national security adviser, Walt Rostow, and assured him that "I know where we have to end up in this monetary matter. Please tell your people not to be too rigid."[114] In truth, the Germans remained very skeptical of the U.S. plans, seeing the desire to create liquidity as a means of financing America's payments deficit. They noted suspiciously that "the amount of new liquidity required annually was stated by the U.S. side as being roughly comparable to that currently injected by the U.S." through its payments deficit. At a meeting of EEC finance ministers in Munich in April 1967, the Germans joined with the French in favoring "a vaguely defined drawing rights approach" against "the more effective reserve unit approach" supported by the Dutch and Italians.[115] There were authoritative leaks from Bonn that "the Germans went along with the French because of their resentment at the American pressure."[116] Even Erhard, with all his sympathy for the American stance against France, did not support Washington on this issue. McGhee warned that the German cabinet would break with the French on this issue only as a last resort and only if the French "persisted in positions which threatened solutions that the Germans, in the light of their own interests, considered reasonable and desirable."[117]

To lobby the Germans on this issue, Johnson turned again to John J. McCloy, asking him to return to West Germany to try to persuade its bankers and financial leaders to endorse the American position. Washington was particularly concerned that the German position had moved closer to that of France—namely, to supporting a drawing rights scheme that was more like credit than the creation of an actual new asset. The Germans also seemed willing to accept a joint EEC position, even though the French "never agree to EEC solidarity in areas that, like international monetary sphere, are not covered by the Treaty of Rome, unless it suits their interest."[118] The undersecretary of the treasury, Frederick Deming, insisted to McCloy that he needed to refute General de Gaulle's claim that the "United States' interest in reserve creation results from a desire to continue financing our balance of payments deficit. This is *not the case.*" Rather, the United States believed that new reserves were essential for "the continued development of the world's monetary and trading system without lapsing into cumulative restrictions on capital movements and on trade itself." Deming assured McCloy that the United States did not expect that reserves would grow more than 2 or 3 percent per year, a figure that was "quite conservative" and that he hoped would appeal to the German bankers.[119]

McCloy's trip coincided with the Six-Day War in the Middle East, which diverted the attention of U.S. policymakers from European matters and even the war in Vietnam. McCloy probably spent as much time reassuring the Germans about America's response to the Middle East crisis as he did discussing the monetary question. Nevertheless, he did meet with modest success. Hermann Abs, the president of Deutsche Bundesbank and an extraordinarily influential figure in German politics, expressed his support for the U.S. position.

Abs told McCloy that Otto Emminger, the German representative in the Group of Ten and also a director of the Bundesbank, was a close friend of Kiesinger's and would be important to persuading the chancellor to act. When McCloy went to see Emminger, he found that he, too, was antagonistic to the French position but convinced that "to get France isolated, it was necessary to give the others (EEC) the impression that they have used all possibilities to bring France along."[120] The best thing Washington could do to help this process would be, in Emminger's view, to get out more "propaganda" on its position and to convince Europeans that the whole exercise wasn't designed just to finance the American deficit. When he saw Kiesinger two days later, the chancellor expressed the same concern that there would be enough "discipline" to prevent the misuse of any new reserves. In general, the Germans also conveyed to McCloy that the Middle East crisis had helped to underline the need for the type of "contingency planning" represented by the liquidity negotiations.[121]

As helpful as the Germans sounded, their position had limits. During a meeting of American and German financial officials in Washington in June 1967, Economics Minister Schiller made it clear that they would not budge on their insistence on an effective EEC veto of any new reserves created, by requiring that the reserves receive an 85 percent approval vote to be activated. Treasury Secretary Fowler grew angry, telling Schiller that the "world looked at the EEC as 'hard-nosed central bankers preoccupied with gold.'" Schiller responded that the Grand Coalition government was different from the Erhard regime, and it would not automatically follow the United States, and that they wanted to "revive the Franco-German treaty." After all, Schiller remarked, America should be pleased with all this Franco-German cooperation: "The EEC had been a U.S. 'baby,' with George Ball one of the fathers." Fowler cooly replied that it had been designed "as an outward-looking baby." The treasury secretary went on to say that at the time of Bretton Woods, Western Europe was a "wrecked battle ground." American "blood and treasure had helped revitalize it." Fowler then added: "Was it asking too much of Western European nations now to play by the rules of the game?" Schiller could reply only, "We will reach a solution."[122]

Toward the end of this long meeting, both Fowler and Bator emphasized "the increasing 'linkage' between the liquidity negotiations, the balance of payments problem, and United States military expenditures abroad, including western Germany." The German officials did not like this implied pressure, and reacted strongly. But Fowler made it clear that "modern military and political alliances must have a financial wall," a formulation that brought home to the Germans the fact that the United States saw this monetary reform as far more than a technical issue, and considered its success connected to its presence in Europe and its leadership of the Western alliance. Fowler also indicated that the United States would be willing to call the new asset "drawing rights" instead of units, so long as it served the function of reserves. But he wanted a solution prepared before the annual meeting of the International Monetary Fund in Rio de Janeiro in September.[123]

The Germans, understandably, felt battered by all sides on this issue. In a series of Franco-German meetings in July, the French pressured their German counterparts to resist the American proposal. De Gaulle repeatedly emphasized to Kiesinger and Brandt that the issue was "très importante" and that Europe needed to be protected from American inflation. The French leader appealed for "solidarity" in the negotiations, implicitly promising that German support would yield greater French cooperation in other matters. Kiesinger tried to put off the French leader by repeating that he wasn't an expert on the issue, but he also appeased de Gaulle by insisting that the Americans would have to compromise.[124]

The United States did compromise on minor issues, but the American position prevailed on the most important matters. At the end of

August 1967, after a series of meetings of the Group of Ten at Lancaster House in London, the solution was announced as special drawing rights in the fund, and the special drawing rights (SDR) were then endorsed at the IMF meeting in Rio. The London negotiations were exceedingly complex, but a major impasse was breached when the Canadian finance minister Mitchell Sharp agreed to present a compromise position formulated by the American delegation as his own, a procedure that effectively isolated the French.[125] (Schiller had refused to put forward the U.S. plan, though he supported it once the Canadians had.) On the main stumbling block with the French, whether the SDR would be more like an asset ("paper gold") than a credit, the U.S. viewpoint prevailed, but with a minor compromise. The rules governing the creation of the SDR were more restrictive than the Americans wanted, and since the net use of SDR involved the payment of interest, the SDR did have some characteristics of credit. "In effect," as Thomas Ilgen has argued, "the United States succeeded in creating a new reserve unit, while the French managed to assure only limited control over its use."[126] When the U.S. delegation returned to Washington, President Johnson praised their accomplishment as the "greatest forward step in international financial cooperation since the creation of the IMF."[127]

The SDR exercise did not prove as significant as Johnson's praise implied. Subsequent events—in particular Richard Nixon's decision in 1971 to sever the dollar-gold link and move to a world of flexible exchange rates—changed the entire nature of the debate about the international monetary system. This has led some to argue, as noted historian Harold James has, that "the SDR appeared as the last and most controversial of the gadgets devised to deal with the weakness of the U.S. payments position, rather than the beginning of a new approach to managing the international order."[128] But in this case appearances are deceiving. Within the context of the time—and especially the French challenge to the U.S. position—the SDR solution was a skillful exercise in alliance politics, demonstrating within the forum of international finance the choices and consequences that the industrialized nations faced, and requiring them to adjust their differences. It sharply underlined what Barry Eichengreen describes as the continuous "cooperation among governments and central banks" that characterized the Western alliance system during the Cold War.[129] Special drawing rights may not have proved as lasting an innovation as its creators hoped, but the process undertaken would serve as an important precedent during the periods of economic uncertainty and turmoil in the 1970s and 1980s.

Progress on Nonproliferation and Arms Control

In the midst of the crises he faced in the spring of 1967—especially the rising tensions in the Middle East and the Vietnam War—Johnson wrote to Soviet premier Kosygin, arguing that there were two areas in which they could cooperate: arms control and nuclear nonproliferation. Johnson maintained that it would be easier to convince other nations to sign on to the nonproliferation treaty if the two superpowers could show their willingness to bring the nuclear arms race under control.[130] A little more than a month later, the two leaders would be sitting across the table from each other at a small college in Glassboro, New Jersey. The Six-Day War had highlighted another region where U.S. and Soviet interests clashed, and it had further underscored the need for direct talks.

As Kosygin was scheduled to speak at the United Nations to bolster his defeated Arab allies, Johnson invited him to come to Washington as well. Eventually the two leaders agreed to meet in Glassboro, New Jersey, located almost exactly between New York and Washington, and their talks took place at Glassboro State College. The negotiations were frustrating to Johnson, as Kosygin was clearly not in a position to discuss the serious issues of arms control that

Johnson and Soviet premier Aleksei Kosygin at the Glassboro summit in June 1967. Although the concrete results were few, the summit meeting symbolized Johnson's attempt to move the superpowers toward detente. (LBJ Library; photo by Yoichi Okamoto)

Johnson wanted to debate. As LBJ later wrote, "Each time I mentioned missiles, Kosygin talked about Arabs and Israelis."[131]

The talks did not lead to any breakthroughs, though they may have contributed to ending an impasse in the nonproliferation talks. The United States and the Soviet Union had clashed repeatedly about Article III of the proposed treaty, which provided for safeguards and inspections. Deferring to its allies, especially the Germans and the Italians, the United States wanted to allow the Europeans to continue using the safeguards of their own regional organization, Euratom, while setting up a transition period of some three years for the International Atomic Energy Agency (IAEA) and Euratom to work out a system for IAEA to verify Euratom's safeguards. For the Europeans, the desire to uphold Euratom had a variety of motives: support for European integration, resistance to any Soviet or Eastern bloc inspection of nuclear facilities, and fear of industrial espionage through the IAEA. For its part, the Soviet Union flatly rejected any provision allowing Euratom to provide inspections under the treaty, seeing it as a way for West Germany to escape true international control.[132] At Glassboro, Johnson suggested to Kosygin that together the United States and the Soviet Union table a nonproliferation treaty, minus only the controversial Article III. Kosygin did not answer Johnson directly, but the Soviets agreed to study the question. Over the next two months the United States continued to push the issue. Finally, on August 10, 1967, the Soviets quietly informed the American delegation in Geneva that they were prepared to "table the NPT jointly with us with a blank Article III." As Rostow told the president, "Now the game will move to the non-nuclear powers; and some months of negotiations lie ahead. But it is something of an event."[133] The draft texts elicited numerous suggestions for possible changes, but the prospects for the NPT were now significantly improved. Indeed, *U.S. News and World Report,* a conservative voice within the American media, posed the question, "What's really going on between the U.S. and Russia?" and concluded it was "peace." The magazine went on to say that after examining the various steps LBJ had taken toward the Soviet Union, and his management of the Middle East crisis and talks at Glassboro, "Johnson had emerged as the apostle of peace in spite of the war he was waging half a world away."[134]

In August 1967 Johnson conferred again with Chancellor Kiesinger. The intervening months since their meeting in April had seen significant achievements, but once more they were facing a challenge. In early July the German government had announced that it would need to make cuts in its defense budget. In the complicated game of coalition politics, the defense minister, now Gerhard Schröder, warned that these cuts would lead to a reduction in German armed personnel of some 60,000. Kiesinger was angry about Schröder's figures, telling his defense minister that they would be "a shock to our domestic and foreign policy."[135] Kiesinger also realized what the impact would be in the United States, where Lyndon Johnson would see in the German cutbacks lethal ammunition for the Mansfield forces. This issue would even overshadow continuing concern about the impact of the NPT on Germany.

In preparing for Kiesinger's visit, Bator asked the president to commit to a "strategy session," since "this will be a critical meeting—not quite in the league with Glassboro, but close enough to call for very careful preparation." Johnson's NSC deputy urged the president to "lay out for Kiesinger—and draw him into a dialogue about—the basic components of our European policy."[136] Johnson did just that, taking Kiesinger for a walk in the White House Rose Garden and spending considerable time explaining his own political situation, the world situation he faced, and his own concerns about the alliance. He told the chancellor about the Russian decision to table the NPT without Article III, but placed this within a larger picture of his own efforts to ease tensions with the Soviets. Once again, he stressed the congressional reaction to the cutbacks, telling Kiesinger that Congress reacted strongly when word came that the Germans would cut 60,000 men. This elicited a quick denial by Kiesinger, who stressed that the reduction would be much less and would not exceed 15,000. Johnson then talked of consultation, saying how important it was that "the men at the top had complete trust and confidence in one another . . . It should be the same kind of process as between two brothers running a business jointly . . . Did the Chancellor agree to that?"[137]

Kiesinger certainly did, and their discussions went exceedingly well. Hubert Humphrey once told an interviewer that Johnson at his persuasive best was like a "cowboy making love,"[138] and in his talks with Kiesinger the president made a conquest. Ambassador McGhee,

Johnson and Chancellor Kurt Kiesinger in Washington, August 1967. Johnson's second meeting with the chancellor went so well that the American ambassador in Bonn reported afterward on an "absence of controversial issues." (LBJ Library; photo by Yoichi Okamoto)

who had spent the last months repeatedly asking American leaders to stop pressing the Germans, reported that the atmosphere in Bonn after the Kiesinger visit was one of a "pervading calm—an absence of controversial issues." All of the major issues of the past year—offset, the NPT, the Kennedy Round, U.S. investment in Germany, international liquidity—had faded in importance. McGhee even added that with the completion of the "highly successful meeting [between Johnson and Kiesinger], a new period in German-American relations—one long in the making—began."[139]

In a more peaceful era, any administration that had put together such a string of successes in its foreign policy would have been hailed for its diplomatic genius. But September 1967 was not a normal time. With American cities like Detroit in flames, and the war in

Vietnam dragging on, Lyndon Johnson could not take much comfort from these important successes. Although he had moved the Atlantic alliance in the direction of detente, begun the process of thawing the Cold War, and negotiated important changes in the world's trade and monetary system, Johnson could not escape the long shadow of the war in Southeast Asia.

5

The Long 1968

As he entered his fifth year as president, facing Vietnam, racial conflict, and widespread public discontent over his personality and policies, Lyndon Johnson still towered over the landscape of American
and world politics. Calling its choice "inescapable," *Time* magazine
named him its Man of the Year, commenting that he "was the topic
of TV talk shows and cocktail party conversations, the obsession of
pundits and politicians at home and abroad, of businessmen and
scholars, cartoonists and ordinary citizens throughout 1967."[1] Johnson's public approval rating had stood at its all-time low of 31 percent
in October 1967, with 46 percent of Americans expressing frustration with the progress of the Vietnam War.[2] A march on the Pentagon
in October 1967 had highlighted domestic unrest over the war, while
at the same time numerous antiwar demonstrations took place in
Western Europe, with more than 3,000 demonstrators attacking the
American embassy in London and thousands demonstrating in Co-
penhagen, Amsterdam, Oslo, and West Berlin.[3] Senator Eugene Mc-
Carthy, now leading the "dump Johnson" movement within the
Democratic Party, decided to run for president.[4] Johnson found it almost impossible to leave the White House without attracting hostile
protesters. During his appearance at Cardinal Spellman's funeral in
New York in December, demonstrators across from St. Patrick's Ca-

thedral held signs that read "Napalm: Johnson's Baby Powder," and chanted the by now familiar refrain, "Hey, hey, LBJ, how many kids did you kill today?"[5] Nevertheless, despite the polarized atmosphere within the country and the growing opposition to Johnson's policies among the people and in Congress, *Time* concluded that "once the Republicans nominate a candidate and Old Campaigner Johnson can start shelling the foe, the President will again be the favorite."[6]

As with many predictions about the remarkable year 1968, this one was confounded by Johnson himself, when he decided to withdraw from the presidential race on March 31, 1968. Yet although 1968 is largely portrayed by historians and contemporaries as "the year everything went wrong," the "nightmare year," and a "year of unmitigated disaster" for the Johnson administration, Johnson's last year as president contained significant achievements.[7] Despite the prevailing disorder of the year—the riots, the demonstrations, and the assassinations of Martin Luther King, Jr., and Robert Kennedy—Lyndon Johnson, although politically weakened by his decision to step aside, nevertheless remained able to direct American foreign policy toward important and long-lasting goals. His administration used the "gold crisis" of March 1968 to demonetarize gold and begin the dismantling of the Bretton Woods international monetary system. Johnson obtained a tax increase that helped yield a surplus in both the federal budget in 1969 and the U.S. balance of payments by the end of 1968. And although Johnson would leave office in January 1969 with his failure to end the Vietnam War foremost in his mind, his search for "areas of agreement with the Soviet Union" went far toward changing the nature of the superpower confrontation and significantly reducing the danger of nuclear conflict.[8]

The Challenge to the Dollar

In August 1967, more than eighteen months after Gardner Ackley, chair of the Council of Economic Advisers, had advised Johnson about the need for a tax increase to deal with the danger of inflation, and eight months after LBJ had proposed a 6 percent surcharge, the administration finally sent a special message to Congress calling for a 10 percent surcharge on corporate and individual income taxes. Johnson warned that without a tax increase, the federal budget deficit could exceed $28 billion and pose a "clear and present danger to America's security and economic health."[9] Outside of the decision to escalate the war in Vietnam, no decision of Johnson's presidency has come under more attack than his refusal to push for a tax increase earlier in his administration. Historian Irving Bernstein proclaims that "the Great Inflation . . . can be pinpointed to President Johnson's decision to commit American forces to Vietnam in July 1965. It would continue for 17 distressing years."[10] Critics also have linked this decision with Johnson's "credibility gap," arguing that he deliberately avoided such a request for a tax hike in the same manner that he deceived Americans about the scale and extent of the Vietnam War.[11] The economist Lester Thurow also identified the Johnson fiscal and monetary decisions as the cause of "the great inflation of the late twentieth century."[12] Another recent account concludes that Johnson's "strong desire for both guns and butter was a trap from which neither he nor the country could escape, a trap for which the president was mostly responsible."[13]

Although the connection between Vietnam and the inflation of the 1970s has become the conventional wisdom, there are skeptics. David Hackett Fischer has convincingly shown that the inflationary surge that so many scholars associate "mistakenly" with Vietnam began in Western Europe some four to five years before the 1965 decision to escalate. Johnson's policies, in Fischer's view, had an "impact because they reinforced an existing trend and increased its momentum." The real roots of "the price-revolution of the twentieth century," Fischer argues, were in "demographic trends and economic structures."[14] Johnson's reluctance to ask for a tax increase was a decision connected with his larger goals. LBJ was reluctant in late 1965 to force Congress to enact a tax increase by a call for national mobilization, a call that would make it extremely difficult to keep the war limited and avoid a larger confrontation with China or Russia. (That he still hoped that Hanoi might choose to settle the conflict also played a role in his calculations about the need for a tax increase.) At the same time, the Federal Reserve's actions in late 1965 helped produce a "credit crunch" that sent the American economy into a brief "mini-recession" in 1966. It then became harder for Johnson to make the case for a tax increase.[15] Arthur Okun, who succeeded Ackley as the chairman of the Council of Economic Advisers, believed that from September 1966 till mid-1967 it even looked as if the Federal Reserve's tighter monetary policies might actually bring the economy under control, and "that all the dangers were on the other side of possibly falling into a recession."[16] Johnson also argued that there was little support for a tax increase in Congress, the business community, organized labor, or even his own cabinet.[17] As late as January 1968 the Gallup Poll showed 79 percent of Americans opposed to an increase in taxes.[18]

Johnson's delay in pushing for a tax increase was also connected to his concern for the Great Society programs he had sponsored. Johnson knew that any request for a tax increase would bring calls for cuts in domestic spending on programs that were still in their infancy. As was so often the case on political questions, Johnson proved to be right. As soon as the administration proposed its tax hike, Representative Wilbur Mills, the powerful chairman of the Ways and Means Committee, opened hearings on the bill. Mills, whose personal relations with Johnson were already strained, was a conservative Democrat and an opponent of many Great Society programs. Viewing Johnson as a free-spending liberal, Mills was determined to use his position to block any tax increase without significant spending reductions.[19] Despite supportive testimony from the Federal Reserve and many economists, in October the Mills-led Ways and Means Committee put aside the tax bill until "the President and Congress reach an understanding on a means of implementing more effective expenditure reductions and controls."[20]

With his own economic policies stalled, Johnson had less flexibility as another crisis with the British pound developed in November 1967. As late as September 1967, both Wilson and Chancellor of the Exchequer James Callaghan had assured American officials that the British government was still opposed to devaluation.[21] However, the international situation, as well as the long-term problems of the British economy, continued to work against such resolve. Earlier in the year, the Middle East war and the closing of the Suez Canal had damaged the British balance of payments.[22] The hoped-for resurgence in British exports did not take place, in large part because of the slowdown in the German economy. Another dock workers strike in October, along with the failure of the Bank of England's interest rate increases to stem the outflow of reserves, contributed to the crisis situation. As Treasury Secretary Henry Fowler told LBJ, the British were now *"scraping the bottom of the barrel,"* seeking a $3 billion support package and indicating as never before so clearly *"that, without help, they will be forced to take the plunge"* and devalue.[23]

Faced with this blow to his government's standing, Harold Wilson wanted to travel to Washington to meet with Johnson himself, believing that the president could be convinced to help sterling because of his own electoral prospects in 1968.[24] To avoid any market reaction to such a sudden trans-Atlantic summit, Wilson proposed using the need to consult about the Vietnam War as a pretext for the meeting.[25] Ambassador David Bruce, undoubtedly toning down LBJ's reaction, told the prime minister that the president's attitude toward such a trip was "very, very negative," and that such a visit would "wreck the existing personal relationship between the Prime Minister and the President to which the latter attached great value."[26] British ambassador Dean echoed this sentiment, stressing Johnson's difficulties with

Congress. He told Wilson that "Congress is in a filthy mood, and the president is in a corner himself."[27] Persuaded that such a visit would be counterproductive, Wilson still sought to convince Johnson to help with the pound, playing on Johnson's sense of recent history. "As a loyal disciple of Roosevelt," Wilson wrote, "the President would be aware from his memories of the economic cut-throat world of the 30s where this might lead. As LBJ he will know what the political and defense implications mean in the 60s."[28] Wilson did not leave it to LBJ to spell out such possibilities, stressing again the possibility of British cutbacks east of Suez and in Europe, as well as the possible impact of a sterling devaluation on the value of the dollar. He hoped, as he sent his representatives to Washington, to make "their flesh creep" with his warnings about the horrible consequences of devaluation.[29]

Beset with their own list of global problems, Americans were hard to scare in late 1967. Nevertheless, the administration did not give up on the pound, and Johnson insisted that the British be given every opportunity to defend sterling. Accepting the view of both Fowler and Rostow that the "risks are just too great" to let sterling go and relieve its "long agony," Johnson pushed his advisers to construct a support package with the reluctant Europeans.[30] Less concerned than earlier about possible British withdrawals, Johnson and his advisers worried primarily about the prospect of an attack on the dollar after British devaluation. "Go at them," the president told Frederik Deming, the undersecretary of the treasury, when Deming expressed his pessimism about gaining European cooperation.[31] Yet Johnson also hedged his bets, trying to ensure that if devaluation did occur, it would be kept to 15 percent and thus not induce a wave of competitive devaluations.[32]

In the end the Europeans—mainly the Germans—proved particularly reluctant to save sterling again, and the British could not escape devaluation, lowering the value of the pound from $2.80 to $2.40. This was a more modest devaluation than many of Wilson's advisers wanted, especially those less tied to the "special relationship" and more interested in entering Europe. The French also criticized Wilson for not going far enough and for missing "a great chance for demonstrating independence from America."[33] American officials, in contrast, were pleased by the new rate for the pound. They understood that the British were trying to avoid causing significant problems for the international monetary system.[34] For his part, Wilson assured Johnson that "the way we are handling our problem now is . . . designed to leave the dollar as little exposed as possible."[35] Wilson also tried to reassure the president that the British decision would not affect any defense commitments in Europe or east of Suez, although he was far less unequivocal than in the past.

In his memoirs, Johnson commented that the news of the British devaluation was "like hearing that an old friend who has been ill has to undergo a serious operation. However much you expect it, the news is still a heavy blow."[36] Treasury Secretary Fowler remarked to the press that now the dollar was "in the front line," and Johnson reaffirmed that the United States would stand by its commitment to buy and sell gold at $35 an ounce.[37] He also used the British crisis to his advantage in a meeting with congressional leaders, emphasizing that the devaluation "now brought the requirements for fiscal action and the tax increase into even sharper and more critical focus."[38] Using an expression that would receive considerable public attention, Johnson told the leadership, "We will rue the day if we fail to face up to these critical responsibilities."[39] Treasury Secretary Fowler reiterated Johnson's point about the necessity of acting quickly on an "expenditure reduction and tax increase package," adding that "markets don't wait."[40]

The gold market bore out the wisdom of Fowler's comment. In the week after devaluation, the gold pool—an organization formed in 1961 by the United States and eight other countries to buy and sell gold as necessary to maintain the price at $35 an ounce—suffered losses of $641 million, with the U.S. share at 59 percent.[41] French policy complicated this development. France had withdrawn from the pool earlier in the year but chose to reveal its move in the leading newspaper *Le Monde* on Monday, November 20. Throughout the week the French press continued to report that Britain faced serious difficulties in stabilizing the value of the pound and that an increase in the price of gold was imminent.[42] Despite this active French involvement in the speculative attack on the dollar, the United States held the rest of the Europeans behind its policies. At a meeting in Frankfurt at the end of the week, Undersecretary Deming, representing the administration, secured a multilateral commitment to the price of $35 an ounce, and the gold market began to stabilize.[43] But the Europeans also indicated to him that the "calming of the international monetary system" depended on the United States adjusting its own payments position and taking domestic actions such as a tax increase.[44]

As the United States struggled to deal with this financial crisis, it was clear that it faced a formidable obstacle in the increasingly strident and hostile President de Gaulle. Throughout 1967 de Gaulle had been outspoken in his attacks on American "hegemony" and the need for Europe to stand against "the preponderance of America."[45] On November 27, 1967, de Gaulle followed the French announcement on withdrawing from the gold pool with one of his most famous press conferences. Over the course of a few hours, de Gaulle attacked America's ally Israel and the Jews themselves as "an elite people, sure of themselves and dominating"; predicted that Quebec would separate from Canada; rejected British membership in the Common Market because of American influence on London's policies; and denounced, yet again, the Bretton Woods system and urged a reliance on gold for international transactions.[46] Only a few days later, the French chief of the defense staff, General Charles Ailleret, published an article that announced a new French strategic doctrine.

Bearing de Gaulle's imprint, the policy Ailleret proclaimed was one in which France would now be prepared to defend itself "*mondial et tous azimuts*—world wide and from all points on the compass."[47] (A British analyst termed this "national independence run completely wild.")[48] In the space of just a week, de Gaulle signaled his complete independence from the United States and NATO, as well as his willingness to undermine the basis of American power and commit France to frustrating U.S. global objectives.[49] Johnson wrote in his memoirs that when the French announced their withdrawal from the gold pool, "I was tempted to abandon my policy of polite restraint toward de Gaulle."[50] At the time, Johnson did not conceal his anger in private discussions, and in a December 1967 telephone call to Senate leader Mike Mansfield, he complained of the desire of the French and the Soviets "*and all of our enemies*" (my emphasis) to acquire U.S. gold and bring the dollar down, "busted like the pound was busted."[51]

While remaining publicly restrained, the administration worked out a program to prevent Paris from bringing the dollar down. In late December, while Johnson went on a whirlwind global trip that took him to Australia for Prime Minister Harold Holt's funeral, South Vietnam for a speech to the troops at Cam Rahn Bay, and Italy for a meeting with the pope, his advisers hammered out the details of a balance of payments program. Fowler had warned Johnson that the news would be grim about the balance of payments deficit; he had initially predicted it would be $2.6 billion but now, after the British devaluation, he was thinking it would be in "the $3 to 4 billion range."[52]

To avert a speculative campaign against the dollar after the figures were announced in February, Johnson wanted a strong program that would act as a preemptive strike against the markets. Although he gave his advisers considerable freedom to devise a plan, LBJ insisted that they not recommend unilateral protectionist measures that

would cripple the free trade system. Johnson had held off protectionist measures earlier in the year, and he refused to do anything that
might damage the achievements of the Kennedy Round. Johnson also
insisted that the program be limited to what he as president could enact administratively. For this reason he delayed proposing the lifting
of the gold cover, the legal requirement that the United States have
sufficient gold reserves to cover 25 percent of the paper money in cir-
culation. This requirement, which could be lifted only by congressional legislation, tied up some $10 billion of the nation's gold sup-
ply.[53] Johnson feared that if he proposed lifting the gold cover in his
balance of payments program, Congress might refuse to go along—
just as it had with the tax increase—and its refusal would cripple the
effect of the balance of payments program on the international markets.[54] As the final balance of payments program was assembled on
December 29, LBJ decided to send a high-level mission to Europe
and Japan to explain his decisions. This mission would also discuss
with the allies the possibility of cooperative action, and, most important, it would convey to them a sense of the domestic political pressures Johnson faced, and how they could help each other in dealing
with such pressures. For Johnson, the balance of payments question
was essentially a political one, and he reiterated the belief that had led
him to so vigorously support the creation of a form of international
money in the special drawing rights: "The world supply of gold is insufficient to make the present system workable—particularly as the
use of the dollar as a reserve currency is essential to create the required
international liquidity to sustain world trade and growth."[55]

With his characteristic preference for drama and surprise, Johnson
announced the balance of payments program on New Year's Day
1968. "Sounding like [John] Kennedy at his most conservative," as
historian Diane Kunz has written, Johnson reaffirmed the importance
of the balance of payments to the American dollar and the international monetary system.[56] He also used the occasion to push Congress

once again for his tax increase, while at the same time asking Americans to avoid nonessential travel outside the Western Hemisphere. (Liberals were dismayed by this gesture—a political cartoon pictured a sword-wielding LBJ about to sacrifice a helpless American tourist on the altar to a biblical golden calf inscribed "gold policy.")[57] The most dramatic step that LBJ implemented was a program to restrain direct business investment abroad and require businesses to repatriate foreign earnings to the United States. The president also ordered the Federal Reserve to restrict foreign lending by banks, hoping to save some $500 million in this manner.[58] Finally, the administration asked the Congress to approve a program to help American exporters and encourage tourism within the United States.

Johnson achieved a significant psychological impact on the markets with the program, an impact that exceeded the actual content of the proposals. Although the program provided another occasion for domestic criticism—Chicago economist Milton Friedman lamented, "How low we have fallen!" and criticized the restrictions on overseas private investment[59]—it seemed to be working. A week after the announcement, his advisers reported that there was "widespread optimism that speculation in gold should be substantially halted."[60] However, more than the specifics of his proposals, Johnson's method of dealing with the allies makes this episode revealing. Many of his advisers, including Fowler, had strongly advocated imposing a border tax that would have amounted to a permanent export rebate and import surcharge of about 2.5 percent. The danger was, of course, that such a tax would spur retaliation by other countries and end up restricting trade. Though assured by Fowler that such a tax was allowed under the rules of the General Agreement on Tariffs and Trade, Johnson sent his delegations to the allies, including France, with the message that while he was considering such a move, he had not yet made a final decision. Nicholas Katzenbach, the undersecretary of state, told Harold Wilson that LBJ believed the main purpose of the border tax proposals was to "contain the protectionist sentiment in Congress and to stimulate import interests to develop their own pressures on Congress." Katzenbach also stressed that the president faced an "influential current of opinion" that "complained about the drain of U.S. Armed Forces abroad." The central point that the American representatives conveyed was that Johnson was trying to deal with a substantial domestic political problem in a way that would not lead to significant U.S. troop withdrawals or to the undermining of the free trade system. But that to do so, "It was essential for him to have something concrete to deal with protectionist pressures."[61]

Johnson ultimately decided against a border tax, a proposal that Undersecretary of State Eugene Rostow had feared would be taken as a "profound change in the direction of our trade policy."[62] But he had made his point to the Europeans and the Japanese, that he faced significant challenges to his authority in the coming election year of 1968. In his State of the Union address on January 17, 1968, he also called for Congress to pass legislation lifting the gold cover. Katzenbach assured LBJ that "without exception, the people we talked to are aware of the tremendous burdens the President carries, and all (except France) spoke with admiration that forceful and positive action had been taken."[63]

However, those burdens increased exponentially toward the end of January 1968. On January 21 the North Vietnamese began a siege of the U.S. Marine base at Khe Sahn. Two days later the North Koreans seized the U.S.S. *Pueblo* spy ship in international waters and took its crew captive.[64] And at the end of the month the North Vietnamese and Viet Cong launched the Tet offensive, carrying their battle into South Vietnam's cities and American living rooms. As the British ambassador advised Harold Wilson before his February trip to Washington, "The fact is that the administration is at full stretch and almost wholly preoccupied with matters of immediate import to the U.S."[65]

Wilson's meeting with Johnson, the last the president would have with a major European leader, could easily have been overshadowed as well by the British cabinet's decision in mid-January that, as part of the new austerity budget, Britain would accelerate its planned withdrawal from the Persian Gulf and Far East by five years. The former Rhodes scholar Dean Rusk, not known as a man of passions, reacted strongly to the decision, telling British foreign secretary George Brown that the withdrawal would "have profound and detrimental implications for the U.S. and the U.K." and that "it was a catastrophic loss to human society."[66] However, Johnson had his own problems on his mind when he met with Wilson. After an outburst against his domestic opponents and an expression of frustration with the Russians for having done so little to help in Vietnam, Johnson simply read from a briefing paper that compared current financial problems, especially sterling's situation, with the 1931 financial crisis that had deepened the Great Depression. Johnson warned Wilson that his advisers feared a run on the pound might provoke a monetary crisis. For his part, Wilson exuded confidence that there had already been a marked improvement in Britain's export performance. Johnson's preoccupation with Vietnam showed in his unwillingness to press the prime minister any further, and the meeting ended with Wilson's suggestion that a "feminine hand"—namely Barbara Ward, a British author and economist whom LBJ often quoted—had written the excessively pessimistic briefing paper.[67] (She had.) Johnson's laughter at the suggestion capped what the British believed to be a successful trip, which "could not have gone better and has done everything possible to smooth the path" for the implementation of the British withdrawal plans.[68]

A month later Wilson had reason to come back to the Barbara Ward document that LBJ had shown him. In a message to the president on March 15, the British prime minister took some satisfaction in noting that Ward envisaged a "remorseless development of events which could land us back in 1931. At that time you thought it might come from the weakness of sterling, in fact it has come through the scramble for gold."[69] Wilson was enjoying the irony of watching the Americans now fight to preserve the value of the dollar.

The "Gold Crisis" of March 1968 has received increasing attention in recent years, even being designated the "most serious economic crisis since the Great Depression shook the Western world."[70] Some argue that it demonstrated that "the economy was verging on disaster."[71] That it was, as *Time* magazine designated it, "the largest gold rush in history," is undeniable.[72] But the crisis itself has been misunderstood and its effects exaggerated, in part because of its coincidence with the decision to deescalate the war in Vietnam and Johnson's withdrawal from the presidential race. Indeed the crisis actually afforded the administration the opportunity to move away from the tyranny of the gold-dollar link and begin to forge new and more flexible arrangements for the development of the international monetary system.

Despite the favorable impact of the president's balance of payments program, speculative pressures intensified in February and early March. Some of these resulted from the increasingly unclear Vietnam situation, with the aftermath of Tet leading to doubts about the American commitment. In addition, the National Advisory Commission on Civil Disorders issued its report about the summer riots of the previous four years and described the United States as moving toward "two societies, one black, one white—separate and unequal."[73] The commission called for a massive new program of federal expenditures to deal with this racial divide in American society.[74] More directly linked to the gold crisis was the continuing stalemate over the tax increase legislation, which raised doubts about America's ability to curb its deficits. The beginning of the congressional debate about lifting the gold cover contributed to the speculative fever, with the influential New York senator Jacob Javits recommending that the United States cease supporting the dollar rate by simply refusing to

Francis Bator meeting with LBJ, November 1968. Bator played a crucial role in John-son's European policy, and was called back to duty in Washington during the Gold Crisis of March 1968. (LBJ Library; photo by Yoichi Okamoto)

buy or sell gold. France may also have played a role. The French press remained a source of speculation about a change in the price of gold, which could only rebound favorably for General de Gaulle's objectives. Wilson referred to this when he suggested to LBJ that "there have been signs of a hidden hand in operation against the dollar and the pound—and not all that hidden either."[75]

During the first week of March 1968 the gold pool countries had to put some $300 million worth of gold into the market to stabilize the price. That weekend, at a meeting of central banks in Basel, bankers reaffirmed "their determination to continue their support to the pool, based on the fixed price of $35 per ounce of gold."[76] But their statement served only as an additional trigger to speculators, and during the first four days of the week of March 11, the gold pool lost $769 million. Sterling was also under attack, with the Bank of England having run down its reserves to preserve the $2.40 rate. As Walt

Rostow told LBJ, "We can't go on as is, hoping that something will turn up." He urged the president to close the London gold market and call an emergency meeting of the gold pool countries in Washington for the weekend. Noting Fowler's impression that "the attitude on the Hill" was "one of almost anarchistic willingness to pull down the temple around their ears on the grounds that our budgetary expenditures are out of control," Rostow said that finding a solution to the crisis went "to the heart of our nation's capacity to carry its external commitments; maintain the world trade and monetary system; and avoid a serious domestic breakdown in our economy."[77]

Some of Rostow's fears were legitimate—if expressed in a characteristically exaggerated and almost apocalyptic form. But Johnson was already trying to reconcile these larger objectives with a solution to the crisis. As Dallek's biography makes clear, by this point Johnson had already decided to move in the direction of negotiations, deescalation, and a "slow withdrawal strategy" in Vietnam, and was structuring the decisionmaking process to yield that outcome. (His famous meeting with the so-called Wise Men—Acheson, Ball, Bundy, and so on—many of whom were worried about the gold situation—was not a decisive turning point in Johnson's thinking.)[78] LBJ decided as well, as he told Harold Wilson, that while the West needed a "more sensible way of handling international money," any "change in the official price of gold would be unacceptable to me."[79] The Washington meeting followed the blueprint drawn up by Johnson and his advisers, and "the Johnson Administration [was] able to control the discussions and their outcome."[80] The Americans put forward a suggestion made by the governor of the Italian central bank, Guido Carli, who in November 1967 had proposed a two-tiered gold market in which the United States would supply only central banks with gold at $35 an ounce, while on the private market gold would be allowed to float freely, determined by supply and demand.[81] Governments had to agree not to buy gold for official purposes and then sell it on the private market and to work together to provide additional support for the British currency. The creation of an intergovernmental gold market would protect the American gold supply from the forces of the private market. The United States also pushed for the activation of special drawing rights at the scheduled Stockholm meeting of the Group of Ten at the end of the month. The SDR would be a useful tool to offset the need for gold as an international reserve.[82] In the end, the administration won a considerable victory, although it was largely obscured by the other domestic political news of the day: Robert Kennedy's entry into the presidential race.[83]

General de Gaulle denounced the results of the Washington meeting and sent Finance Minister Michel Debré to attempt to block the adoption of the special drawing rights proposal at the Group of Ten meeting in Stockholm at the end of March. At the conference, Treasury Secretary Fowler again assured those in attendance that the United States would address its deficit problems, "and that we would bring our own financial house in order and, specifically, that we would pass the tax bill."[84] Despite Debré's attempt to rally other members of the Common Market to him with the argument that the Americans "were dumping unwanted dollars on the world," the U.S. position prevailed.[85] The Germans, who were crucial to any attempt to block the American initiative, refused to join with the French, with Chancellor Kiesinger bluntly telling de Gaulle that his anti-American outbursts were gradually costing him the trust of the German people.[86] Debré returned from Stockholm and told de Gaulle that the French had been "abandoned" by their European partners and that their "submission" to the American "ukase" (edict) was "total and humiliating."[87]

The United States did make a number of small compromises, especially in regard to the veto the EEC could exercise on special drawing rights. These were made, as Rostow told LBJ, to "help Germany, Italy, Belgium, and the Netherlands take the political heat at home of dividing with the French on this fundamental issue. They had to be able to show that they were not knuckling under to the U.S. but were acting to protect world prosperity on an issue where France was unreasonable."[88] This isolation of France, as the British observed, was of "considerable political significance." Debré himself was "willing to make concessions, as long as he could portray it at home as a victory for the French."[89] The finance ministers gave the French some cosmetic changes in the wording of the approval of special drawing rights, but the French still refused to endorse the package deal.[90] Stockholm, however, proved to be the "last fling of the French attempt to destroy confidence in the dollar."[91] The explosion of unrest in France in May 1968 devastated the country's newfound fiscal strength, leading to a "massive foreign exchange hemorrhage" that would find the French approaching the IMF for an emergency loan in June 1968.[92] In what was a classic case of irony in international politics, the pressure on the French was alleviated only by a rescue package "of Federal Reserve credits and a withholding of snide commentary" by American leaders.[93] In late November when the French franc again faced possible devaluation, the Johnson administration, "rather than chortling at the twist of fate," tried to support de Gaulle and France and to prevent the "disruptive effects on the international system."[94] After the French president chose not to devalue, Johnson sent de Gaulle a message "expressing our hope that his course would succeed and assuring him that the United States was ready to cooperate in any way possible."[95] De Gaulle wanted to publicize Johnson's message to his own people, revealing a change of heart in the general after so many years of assertive independence and defiance of the American hegemon.

By April 1968 the United States succeeded at least temporarily in its long-term objective of changing Bretton Woods, but as Rostow noted, "the tax bill [had] now become as much of a world issue as the controversy over the price of gold."[96] Such a connection between an ostensibly domestic American issue and the international order hardly came as a surprise to Lyndon Johnson. The president exploited the fears created by the gold crisis, especially with senators like John J. Williams, a Republican from Delaware and an outspoken fiscal conservative who now became convinced "of the need for a deflationary tax." As one analyst of the politics behind the tax-increase legislation wrote, the gold crisis was "the most significant dynamic element impelling movement toward the tax."[97] Johnson continued to fight the attempt by Congressman Wilbur Mills to link the tax increase with cuts in domestic spending, but he eventually agreed to a $6 billion spending reduction. When he signed the bill on June 28, the president termed the domestic spending reductions "unwise," and he delayed making any reductions until he saw what action Congress would take. As Joseph Califano has noted, "Johnson did indeed have the last laugh." Congress could not even cut the $4 billion that LBJ was willing to cut, and Johnson refused to make any other reductions. "Fiscal 1969 ended with a $3.2 billion surplus—and the Great Society programs survived."[98] Not only did Johnson succeed in creating a federal budget surplus, but also his balance of payments program and the additional taxes helped to bring the deficit in the balance of payments under control. The U.S. balance of payments registered a surplus of $1.67 billion in 1968 and a $2.81 billion surplus in 1969.[99] In remarking on these overlooked legacies, which the Nixon administration would inherit, LBJ's old friend John Connally stated, "The most remarkable thing about [Johnson's] last year in office is not how embattled he was but how much he achieved under the circumstances."[100]

The Drive for Arms Control

Coping with the economic problems exacerbated by Vietnam was only one facet of Johnson's last troubled year in the presidency. Johnson also made a concerted effort to build on the Glassboro summit and improve relations with the Soviet Union. Despite the Vietnam War, the administration pushed forward its efforts toward the "bridge building" it had proclaimed in the president's October 7, 1966, speech, and it gradually laid the basis for the arms control negotiations and detente that would come to fruition under Johnson's successor.

Curbing the spiraling costs of the arms race became a central priority for Johnson in his last two years as president. After the October 1966 breakthrough on the Nonproliferation Treaty, Johnson sent the experienced diplomat, Llewellyn Thompson, back to Moscow to pursue an arms control agreement with the Russians. Johnson told Premier Kosygin that he faced "great pressures from members of Congress and public opinion" to deploy a defensive missile system, an antiballistic missile, or ABM, in response to the Soviet deployment of such a system. Rather than face the "colossal costs" involved in such an escalation of the arms race, Johnson sought negotiations—negotiations that could produce a "mutually acceptable and stable balance of forces, verifiable to the maximum extent possible by our national means." This was a matter not only of "the greatest importance but of considerable urgency."[101]

Johnson renewed his appeal to Kosygin at Glassboro, but the Soviet premier rejected the equation of defensive systems like the ABM with an escalation of the arms race. Kosygin even seemed appalled that McNamara made the argument it would be "cheaper" for the United States to overcome a Soviet ABM with more offensive weapons. This was an indirect reference to the MIRVs (multiple independently targeted reentry vehicles), which were under development and on the verge of deployment by the United States. Kosygin even came close to losing his temper, proclaiming at one point that "defense is moral, aggression is immoral."[102] Retreating into Marxist orthodoxy, Kosygin misunderstood McNamara's point and called it a "commercial approach to a moral problem which was by its very nature immoral."[103] Kosygin also contended that he "failed to see true possibilities" for arms control negotiations "while the Vietnam war continues and while the Middle East situation remains unsettled."[104] Although these regional issues may have affected Soviet consideration, the truth was that Kosygin had come to Glassboro with no mandate from the other Kremlin leaders, especially the increasingly dominant party leader, Leonid Brezhnev, to give Johnson any definite answers.[105] The delay also allowed the Russians to continue their own buildup of forces, which, as Rostow told LBJ, was "not alarming; but I suspect it will be exploited as a political issue in 1968." U.S. intelligence indicated that the increase in the number of Soviet intercontinental ballistic missiles (ICBMs) meant that the "Soviets almost certainly believe that their strategic position relative to that of the U.S. has improved markedly" and that therefore they "may take a harder line with the U.S. in various crises than they have in the past." But from Johnson's point of view, the Soviet buildup had the unintended advantage of making possible—as well as desirable—a stabilization of the arms race that could serve as the basis for an ongoing detente and relaxation of tensions between the superpowers.

In mid-September 1967 the administration announced its decision to proceed with the development of a limited ABM system, giving as a justification both the prospect of a Chinese threat in the 1970s and Moscow's continuing work on its own missile defense system. Nevertheless, Defense Secretary McNamara's speech announcing the policy made it clear that the administration still preferred to negotiate a ban on such defenses. If such talks failed, McNamara lamented, both the United States and the Soviet Union would be forced to continue "our foolish and feckless course" of ABM development.[106] Rusk reassured both Gromyko and Dobrynin that the United States still wanted talks on strategic arms, but the Soviets continued to delay. In January 1968 Johnson repeated "his sense of urgency" to Kosygin about making "progress towards limiting the strategic nuclear arms race" as well as curbing arms deliveries to the Middle East. Although his annual budget would request $1.2 billion to start production on an ABM system, Johnson tried to reassure Kosygin that the United States "in no way seeks military advantage; on the contrary, [it] seeks a solution through a limitation on arms based on a full appreciation by each side of the national interests and security of the other."[107] But Kosygin's only response was to say that the Soviets were "studying the problem" and "would give their views later."[108]

Johnson used the occasion of his March 31 speech, in which he announced a limit on the bombing of North Vietnam and his withdrawal from the presidential race, to repeat to Dobrynin that "the U.S. and U.S.S.R. had shown in many matters that we could work together for constructive results; for example, in the Non-Proliferation Treaty."[109] And indeed the United States and the Soviet Union had worked to make the NPT a reality: by May 1968, Secretary Rusk was expressing his appreciation to Deputy Foreign Minister Kuznetsov for the "close cooperation" that had taken place in the handling of the Nonproliferation Treaty. Rusk also urged that the two governments stand firmly against any changes in the treaty.

For the United States, this meant taking a tough stance toward the Federal Republic of Germany, where there remained significant opposition to the NPT within the Grand Coalition. Rostow met with the CDU chairman, Rainer Barzel, in February, assuring him that the United States had "defended vigorously the German national interests" in the NPT discussions with the Soviets, especially over such issues as the role of the European atomic agency, Euratom, in inspecting facilities, and the question of the duration of the treaty.[110] Chancellor Kiesinger made it clear to Ambassador McGhee that he was flexible about the NPT and that despite rumors about his dealings with Eastern European countries and accusations that he was following a "Gaullist policy," he wished to "steer the course" of close consultation, which he discussed with Johnson during their August 1967 meetings.[111] Johnson administration officials walked a delicate line between reassuring the Germans and keeping the Soviets on board for the signing of the treaty. Rusk even tried to advise the Soviets on German domestic politics, telling them that there was an "internal problem" in the FRG, and urging them not to make an issue of the negative statements made by a German observer at the UN discussions on the treaty. He added that "the members of NATO were strongly interested in assurances of FRG adherence to NPT," making it clear that the United States understood the importance to the Soviets of German compliance with the treaty.[112]

Johnson himself celebrated the successful passage of the treaty with a commencement address at Glassboro State College on June 4, 1968. In the speech, which was largely overshadowed in the American news by the murder of Senator Robert Kennedy late that evening, Johnson talked about the "year of achievement—and frustration" in U.S.-Soviet relations, remarking—with Vietnam and the Middle East in mind—that "making peace is a tough, difficult, slow business—often much tougher and often much slower than making war." He stressed his own belief that "the old antagonisms which we call the 'cold war' must fade—and I believe they will fade under stable, enlightened leadership," and he called again for negotiations with the Russians to "avoid a costly anti-ballistic missile race."[113] When the signing of the NPT was set for July 1, Johnson renewed his appeal to Kosygin, who finally agreed in late June to a joint announcement on the occasion of the NPT signing that talks "on limitation and reduction of offensive strategic nuclear weapons delivery systems as well as systems of defense against ballistic missiles" would begin in the "nearest future." The president also hoped to begin the negotiations himself by leading the American team in a trip to Moscow. Over the next six weeks, work within the administration proceeded rapidly, resulting in a type of "freeze proposal" on ICBMs and limits on new defensive systems.[114] A breakthrough seemed at hand. The United States and the Soviet Union planned to make a joint announcement of the beginning of the Strategic Arms Limitations Talks (SALT), including plans for a presidential visit to Moscow in October, on August 21, 1968. Despite the ongoing war in Vietnam, Johnson was poised to take the decisive step he had hoped for in lessening nuclear danger.

Bridge Building, Czechoslovakia, and the Frustrations of Detente

By almost any measure, the subdued coverage in the American media of the signing of the nonproliferation agreement, compared with the much greater attention given to the Partial Test Ban Treaty of 1963, is striking. A British diplomat told Prime Minister Wilson, "It is a tribute to the improved East/West relationship in spite of Vietnam, that on the whole people no longer feel the same fear of the Soviet nuclear threat. This is of course unfair, since the NPT is an infinitely more important measure of disarmament."[115] By the summer of 1968, the atmosphere of East-West relations did seem to be changing in profound ways. Along with the movement toward arms control, the Johnson administration's efforts to build bridges to Eastern Europe seemed to be achieving results. The "Prague Spring" seemed to show that detente in Europe was leading to a liberalization of the strict Soviet rule over its empire and a degree of convergence that promised the possibility of a Europe "whole and free."

Confirmed by National Security Action Memorandum 352 of July 1966 and reinforced by Johnson's October 7 speech that same year, the administration's efforts to build bridges to the Eastern bloc encompassed a variety of initiatives. Some involved economic issues, such as reducing export controls on East-West trade, extending export-import bank credit guarantees covering Eastern Europe, easing Polish debt burdens, and financing American exports for a Soviet-

Italian Fiat auto plant. Others were more rhetorical and atmospheric, such as avoiding harsh Cold War rhetoric and deliberately downplaying symbolic occasions such as the fifth anniversary of the building of the Berlin Wall or the tenth anniversary of the outbreak of the Hungarian revolution. Still others had practical significance for increasing contacts between the blocs, such as negotiating a civil air agreement with the Soviet Union, liberalizing U.S. travel laws dealing with visits to communist countries, and exchanging cloud photographs from weather satellites. But the Eastern bloc's political and material support for North Vietnam put limits on the degree to which the administration could get bridge-building measures through Congress.

One of the most significant but largely overlooked initiatives of the Johnson administration began as part of the Acheson committee's report of June 1966. Along with its recommendations for NATO reforms and East-West bridge building, the Acheson committee advocated the creation of "An East-West foundation or University" whose purpose would be "to provide Western instruction in subjects of acute practical importance to Eastern Europeans, e.g., agriculture, business administration, and modern management techniques." The proposal stalled when Secretary Rusk worried that it might compromise the U.S. policy of nonrecognition of East Germany, and Johnson did not announce it in his October 7 speech. But Bator kept the proposal alive in a memo to the president of November 30, 1966, in which he proposed the appointment of McGeorge Bundy to explore the idea and explained that "those of us who have worked on the idea have in mind an institution based on the proposition that *all* advanced economies—capitalist, socialist, communist—share the problem of efficiently managing large programs and enterprises: factories and cities, subway systems and air traffic, hospitals and water pollution. There is great demand—in Russia and Yugoslavia as well as the U.K. and Germany—for the new techniques of management designed to cope with these problems."[116] Johnson approved Bator's request, and the appointment of Bundy and the proposal were both announced in December 1966. The subject arose briefly during the Glassboro talks, and Bundy continued to pursue it in talks with both the NATO allies and his Soviet counterpart, Jermen Gvishiani, the deputy chairman of the State Committee for Science and Technology and the son-in-law of Soviet premier Kosygin. However, the German question continued to bedevil the initiative, despite suggestions by Bundy to Gvishiani that the Soviets include the East Germans as a part of their delegation to the first meeting scheduled for June 1968 in Sussex, England. At the last minute the Soviets decided not to attend, using as an excuse new tensions over Berlin. The Sussex meeting proceeded anyway, with representation from West Germany, France, Italy, the United Kingdom, and the United States. It created a small planning group under the British representative, Solly Zuckerman, Wilson's chief scientific adviser. A few weeks later Gvishiani wrote to Bundy to express a continued interest in the project, with the hope that the issue of East German participation would not create difficulties. Over the next three years, the International Institute for Applied Systems Analysis (IIASA) would take shape. Finally established in 1972 in Austria, with the Soviets, the United States, and most of Europe as members, the IIASA even outlasted the Cold War and succeeded in "punching many small holes in the Iron Curtain," as its leadership later observed.[117] Another account noted, "It was hardly self-evident to IIASA's founders that Easterners and Westerners could work together productively on common problems . . . [and that they could] create something that would not crumble with the first political crisis between the U.S. and U.S.S.R."[118] To this extent, IIASA was an important Cold War bridge, preserving contacts throughout the 1970s and 1980s.[119]

By the end of 1967 this general movement toward detente in Europe was confirmed by the NATO countries in the Harmel report, which called for the alliance to coordinate its approach to the East based on the two principles of deterrence and detente. In effect, the Harmel report affirmed the approach to the East that Johnson had outlined in his October 7, 1966, speech. Earlier in the year Johnson had feared that the Harmel initiative might be blocked by the French and that the alliance would be unable to come to "a satisfactory solution for the future of NATO."[120] As the negotiations proceeded and a strong statement of alliance purpose was drafted, Rusk warned of French obstruction. He insisted that despite the "danger" of a final French withdrawal from the alliance, the NATO countries could not allow themselves to be "blackmailed."[121] The risk of such a French action was taken seriously by the other allies, especially given the radicalization of de Gaulle's policy in late 1967. However, the Harmel exercise proved to be a triumph of American diplomacy, assisted by the Belgians, the Canadians, and especially the Germans. At the final working group session in late November, the French decided that they preferred "the embarrassment of compromises to the risk of rejection," and they "entered energetically into the drafting" of NATO's statement of purpose.[122] The successful adoption of the Harmel report at the NATO meeting in December 1967 once again isolated the French and forced de Gaulle to acquiesce in what he hoped would prove a fruitless exercise in alliance diplomacy. The French tried to convince themselves that with the Harmel report they had agreed to little more than "in-depth exchanges on questions of common interest."[123] But this reinvigoration of NATO's mission, placing it in accord with Johnson's own policy preferences, was an important "turning-point for the Alliance and its long term validity," reinforcing the traditional military justification for NATO and now providing it with a "more forward looking *raison d'être.*"[124]

Following on the heels of the adoption of the Harmel report were the political changes in Czechoslovakia. On January 5, 1968, Alexander Dubček was elected first secretary of the Communist Party, replacing Antonin Novotny, who remained president. Dubček began quickly to implement reforms, including the lifting of censorship restrictions in March. Novotny's subsequent resignation meant that, as U.S. ambassador Jacob Beam observed, "For the first time in history, a Communist regime has purged [a] top leader by bringing popular pressure to bear on him." The liberalization and democratization encouraged by Dubček over the next weeks astonished Western observers and led to the hopeful designation of the Prague Spring. This "reawakening of political life" in Czechoslovakia was "obviously" in the American interest, but the question of how to respond to the developments was unclear. Undersecretary of State Eugene Rostow thought the United States should give the Soviets "a deterrent signal," since "it will be too late once they cross the border." But his position was a lonely one, strongly opposed by the overwhelming majority of State and Defense Department officials. Haunted by the memory of the U.S. response to the Hungarian revolution of 1956 and the belief that the Eisenhower administration, by talking loosely about the "rollback" of Soviet power in Eastern Europe, had encouraged the Hungarians to revolt and then abandoned them to the Russians, American officials were determined to follow what Defense Secretary Clark Clifford's aide George Elsey referred to as a policy of "nonaction" with regard to the Czech situation.[125] This view was shared by the Europeans, especially the Germans, who made it clear to Ambassador McGhee that they wanted no part of any policy that might even appear to interfere in Czechoslovakia, including "the output of Radio Free Europe, Radio Liberty, and RIAS."[126] The State Department agreed, and told McGhee that "it would seek to avoid any military provocation by U.S. forces within Germany and was restraining the content of broadcasts in an effort to avoid any pretext for Soviet military action in Czechoslovakia."[127] With the Czech government giving its own indications that it approved of the U.S. policy, the Johnson administration was determined to hold to this aloofness, es-

pecially as it sought arms control negotiations with the Soviets. However, when tensions mounted in late July 1968 with Soviet military
maneuvers near the Czech border, Dean Rusk did call Dobrynin to
complain about Soviet allegations that the United States was interfer-
ing in Czechoslovakia and warned him that any Soviet action would
have "a very negative effect on our relations."[128] British foreign secretary Stewart also wanted to give a "gentle warning" to the Soviets that
the "encouraging signs of an improvement in East/West relations
would all be drastically set back if the Russians walked into Czechoslovakia."[129] Washington did not object to the additional British
warning, although Charles Bohlen told the British ambassador that
he worried about any "appearance of ganging-up" that could be exploited by Soviet propaganda.[130] Such warnings from the West were
deliberately low key, and there was some doubt about whether they
would have any effect. As one British diplomat recorded, he did not
believe that "anything said to the Soviet Ambassador will deflect the
Soviet leaders from whatever action they consider to be necessary."[131]
This hands-off policy was even observed at the level of covert operations. As one recent study makes clear, there is "absolutely no evidence that either the State Department or the CIA took any measures
to use the Prague Spring as a means of destabilizing or subverting the
Soviet bloc, in spite of constant Soviet propaganda about the sinister
efforts of Western imperialism to do so."[132]

The Prague Spring, along with the general atmosphere of detente
encouraged by the Johnson administration, served to strengthen the
case of those within the Senate who wanted the United States to reduce its forces in Europe. Stuart Symington, the senior senator from
Missouri, led the charge in the spring and summer of 1968 with an
amendment to the military appropriation bill that would cut U.S.
forces in Europe to 50,000, a drastic reduction from the more than
300,000 men stationed there. Johnson was not averse to reductions,
but he wanted any further U.S. reductions to be balanced by Soviet

withdrawals. With strong U.S. support, NATO approved a resolution at its June 1968 meeting in Reykjavík that called for "balanced and mutual force reductions in Europe."[133] However, this did not reduce the domestic pressure for immediate and unilateral cuts. Pressed by Defense Secretary Clifford to come up with a plan for reductions, the Joint Chiefs of Staff contended that it could bring home 100,000, but that anything more would lead it to recommend a complete withdrawal from Europe. Clifford believed it was essential for the administration to cut forces, telling the president that he was "unrealistic" to resist these domestic political pressures. However, Johnson dug in his heels, taking what Clifford characterized as a "hard, hard, hard line" that there would be "no cutting of forces in Europe by even *one* man during his administration" (emphasis in the original). The administration sought to convince senators that passage of the Symington amendment would lead to the collapse of NATO, a German refusal to sign the Nonproliferation Treaty, and a likely German search for nuclear capability. If this chain of events unfolded, the Russians would never agree to cut nuclear weapons. However, such a scenario did not impress Symington or his allies, who found it ironic that now the administration was arguing that American forces were necessary to keep an eye on the Germans rather than deter the Russians.[134] Only Johnson's personal intervention helped block the measure that "in the summer of 1968 seemed likely to pass."[135] This debate also underscored the degree to which the Johnson administration was committed to the status quo in Europe, and to a U.S. presence there that preserved a non-nuclear Germany and allowed the process of detente with the Soviets to evolve in a context of stability and predictability.

That predictability was shattered by the Soviet invasion of Czechoslovakia on August 20, 1968. Moscow's unwillingness to allow any challenge to a ruling Communist Party, the so-called Brezhnev doctrine, underlined the limitations to the vision of building bridges to Eastern Europe. However, when Soviet ambassador Dobrynin came to the White House to deliver the news to Lyndon Johnson, he found a man so focused on announcing the beginning of strategic arms talks the next day that he completely failed to appreciate the import of Dobrynin's message. The tapes of the conversation make for bizarre reading, as Dobrynin conveys the message of Soviet intervention, with its pretext of an "invitation" by the Czech government against "a conspiracy of the external and internal forces of aggression against the existing social order," Rostow summarizes Dobrynin's message in his own words, and the president promises to study it and moves almost immediately to the question of the timing of the announcement of the arms control talks. Dobrynin himself recorded his relief that Johnson was so oblivious, noting that the president offered "me a whisky (I would have agreed to drink anything at that moment) and began to tell entertaining stories about Texas. He was good at it."[136]

In Johnson's defense, the Soviet intervention came as a "rude shock" to almost all of his top advisers, who had expected the Russians to "stabilize" the situation without using the blunt instrument of military force.[137] After Rusk's warning in July, both Rusk and Rostow had told the president that the "real crisis has subsided" in Czechoslovakia and that "the Soviets will not move militarily against them."[138] From the American perspective, the Czechs seemed to have learned from the mistakes of the Hungarians, as they had continually reassured Moscow that their internal changes did not signal any deviation from the Warsaw Pact. Rusk characterized the Soviet decision as contemptuous of the United States, and bluntly remarked that it was like "throwing a dead fish in the president's face."[139] U.S. officials had naively believed the Russians would not jeopardize the fruits of detente—namely SALT—by taking such an outright military action. Rusk told the cabinet that "the political costs the Soviets would have to pay was one reason we thought they would not move."[140] After listening to Rusk's exposition, President Johnson added sadly, "The Cold War is not over."[141]

Johnson's muted reaction, characterized in one account as "no more than perfunctory protests and token retaliatory moves," does illuminate the degree to which he was fixated on arms control negotiations with the Soviet Union as the final legacy of his administration.[142] Johnson believed, as Rusk put it in his memoirs, that the "United States and the Soviet Union share a massive common interest in the prevention of all-out nuclear war," adding that the two sides must "find some way to live together on this planet."[143] In Johnson's mind, there was nothing that the United States could do to help the Czechs, and the Soviets understood that as well. Johnson recognized that the division of Europe would not end without Soviet acquiescence and an overall lessening of tensions between the superpowers— Europe, to the Urals or not, was simply not the master of its own fate—and LBJ set his mind toward trying to continue the process of reducing tensions despite the invasion. Johnson even hoped that when the Czech situation calmed down he might be able to revive the idea of a trip to Moscow to begin the arms talks.[144] The British took the same view, arguing that "if it was right to work for detente before, it should be right again, and while making it clear to the Russians that we regard, and will continue to regard, their action in Czechoslovakia as disgraceful, and that we are keeping up our guard, we should gradually resume contacts and the interrupted dialogue."[145]

The French took a position that was consistent with General de Gaulle's own understanding of postwar history. The general denounced the invasion but invoked the idea that the Soviets were following the "politics of blocs," which had been "imposed on Europe by the Yalta Agreement." In speaking to Americans about the invasion, de Gaulle did not hesitate to heap blame on the Germans for showing too great "a zeal" for good relations with Czechoslovakia during the Prague Spring.[146] Although de Gaulle may have seen the invasion as confirming his own position about the Yalta system, the fate of Czechoslovakia was also a stinging rebuke to French diplomatic efforts to equate Eastern Europe's relationship with Moscow with that of Western Europe and the United States. De Gaulle's idea of a European concert of powers without the United States was dead. Along with the disorders of May 1968, the Czech invasion and its aftermath contributed to the slowly emerging Franco-U.S. *rapprochement* at the end of the Johnson administration.

Johnson's deep disappointment over the "postponement" of his Moscow trip did not prevent him from drawing a new line with the Soviets and using the Czech situation to strengthen the Western alliance. His administration now issued a clear warning to the Soviets not to continue with the Brezhnev doctrine by taking action against either Romania or Yugoslavia, both countries that had split from Moscow's orthodoxy on foreign policy. Neither country had enacted real internal liberalization or democratization, and both proved less threatening than Czechoslovakia to the Soviet model of communism. The administration's position of concern for both countries went further than previous American actions, coming close, especially for Yugoslavia, to a security guarantee. (Although Secretary of Defense Clifford told his aides that "if the USSR moves into Rumania, there's nothing we can do.")[147] To what extent the Soviets actually responded to such warnings or were actually deterred remains unclear, but the simple fact is that they did refrain from acting against either country.

The invasion of Czechoslovakia sent "shivers" through Western Europe, as the U.S. ambassador to NATO, Harlan Cleveland, put it. The West Germans seemed to appreciate the U.S. insistence on a stronger conventional defense, a message that Johnson put across in talks with various German emissaries, including the CDU spokesman Kurt Birrenbach. Although the Soviet action had taken the steam out of the Symington amendment and the move to withdraw troops,

Johnson told Birrenbach that "isolationist sentiment was latent" in the United States and that the "Europeans were sleeping while Rome burns." LBJ told the influential German politician how vital it was to use this crisis to strengthen NATO, and that it was time for "Europe to take matters in its own hands." The key, as always in LBJ's mind, was the Germans, and it was important for them to take action. Birrenbach needed relatively little persuasion on this point, and he returned to Bonn emphasizing the need for German initiative. In this case the government's response was more forthcoming, and Kiesinger agreed to increase the military budget and improve the readiness of German forces.[148]

In the final days of his administration, Johnson pursued both a settlement in Vietnam and an arms control summit with Moscow. Although LBJ knew the Russians might be in favor of a summit to soften the criticism they were getting for the Czech invasion, or as he characteristically put it, "to take some of the polecat off of them," his own desire to leave office as a peacemaker was equally strong.[149] Johnson and his advisers believed that after "many long and tedious months spent in an effort to work out concrete proposals," with the technology of weapons production advancing rapidly, and after such a long wait for the Soviets to act, any further delay, even if justified by a presidential transition, was unconscionable. When Soviet premier Kosygin met with former defense secretary Robert McNamara in Moscow in early November and pressed him about the need for serious arms control negotiations, Washington saw this as an indication that the Soviets still wanted to talk with Johnson, possibly because of their uncertainty about Nixon.[150] However, the administration's persistent efforts to interest the Soviets in a meeting ran the risk, as the Joint Chiefs of Staff protested, of dividing NATO and giving "tacit approval" to the Russian action in Czechoslovakia.[151] Johnson did seek president-elect Richard Nixon's approval for a last-minute summit, which Nixon wisely refused to give.

Johnson and German political leader Kurt Birrenbach, September 1968. Johnson made it clear to the West German leader that he expected Europe to do more for its own defense in the wake of the Soviet invasion of Czechoslovakia. (LBJ Library; photo by Yoichi Okamoto)

Johnson's efforts for a summit have come under harsh criticism, with historian George Herring characterizing the president as clinging "desperately, even pathetically" to his hopes for the last-minute redemption of a summit.[152] Yet it should be recalled that even some of Johnson's fiercest critics wanted him to act expeditiously. Senator Fulbright, joined by the *New York Times,* urged the president to call a special session of Congress to ratify the Nuclear Nonproliferation Treaty and urged Johnson to meet immediately with Kosygin to discuss arms control.[153] In John Prados's recent treatment of this issue, he concluded that "Johnson concerned himself with the substance, the need [for the negotiations,] not his own popularity." Johnson believed that unless the talks began promptly, the momentum to deploy MIRVs and to build expensive ABM systems could not be curbed.

And as Prados concludes, if Johnson had been able to negotiate the freeze on nuclear weaponry he sought in 1968, a real parity in nuclear weapons might have saved both superpowers billions of dollars and avoided many of the adverse domestic political consequences of the 1970s and 1980s. It is perhaps most surprising, in this post–Cold War world, to realize that even "after two SALT agreements, two strategic arms reduction treaties, plus a treaty eliminating intermediate range nuclear missiles, today there continue to be more nuclear warheads atop land-based rockets than there were in 1967."[154] Indeed, as Glenn Seaborg, the chairman of the Atomic Energy Commission under Johnson, later wrote, "Of all the tragedies that befell Lyndon Johnson, this must rank among the most grievous."[155]

Lyndon Johnson Reassessed

Lyndon Johnson did not go softly into the night. Although he was effectively a lame duck after his March 31 speech, Johnson never liked being compared to "a crippled waterfowl."[1] As is clear from his attempt to restart negotiations with the Russians, Johnson was determined to continue his pursuit of a stable and realistic relationship with the Soviet Union, despite the invasion of Czechoslovakia. Although he did not call Congress back into a special session as J. William Fulbright and others suggested, he lobbied individual senators to support the Nonproliferation Treaty. He even took the unusual step in January 1969 of delivering his last State of the Union address in person, something no president had done since John Adams.[2] In that speech, he defended the domestic achievements of his Great Society but acknowledged the "turbulence and doubt" within the country. He also repeated his faith in the resilience of the United States and his hopes for peace in Vietnam and the world. Pronouncing his own epitaph as he closed his speech, Johnson said, "I hope it may be said, a hundred years from now, that by working together we helped to make our country more just—more just for all its people—as well as to insure the blessings of liberty for our posterity. I believe it will be said that we tried."[3]

Not surprisingly antiwar protestors dogged Johnson's final hours as president, some demonstrating outside the Capitol building wearing buttons bearing the ambiguous but hostile message, "LBJ will go down in history."[4] And certainly that sentiment has proven correct, at least in the popular estimation of recent presidents. Best-selling author Robert Caro's biographical study, though still unfinished, paints Johnson in the harshest light, as a power-hungry opportunist "unencumbered by even the slightest excess weight of ideology, of philosophy, of principles, of beliefs." Caro writes that LBJ was a man of "utter ruthlessness and a seemingly bottomless capacity for deceit, deception, and betrayal."[5] George Reedy, Johnson's former press secretary, published a memoir describing his former boss as "a miserable person—a bully, sadist, lout, and egotist."[6] The general public seems to have absorbed much of this viewpoint. In considering presidents from Franklin Roosevelt to Ronald Reagan, Harris surveys in the early 1990s indicated that the public rated Johnson near or at the bottom in eleven categories. Only 1 percent chose Johnson as likely to be ranked best among those presidents, and Johnson was in last place, below Richard Nixon, as "the president setting the highest moral standards"; only 3 percent said Johnson was a president who could "get things done."[7] Defeat in Vietnam, coupled with growing antigovernment sentiment during the 1980s, contributed to this extraordinarily low estimation. For many Americans, Johnson is a convenient scapegoat for the failures of the idealistic promises of the 1960s.[8] Popular movies like Oliver Stone's *JFK* even picture him at the center of a conspiracy to kill John Kennedy in order to plunge the nation into war in Vietnam. Although Johnson's reputation may have risen slightly in recent years, there remains something quite personal in the intense hostility of the collective memory of Lyndon Johnson.[9] It reminds a sympathetic observer of the story told about an LBJ encounter with Dean Acheson. Complaining bitterly about the enormous public affection toward John Kennedy and the coolness toward him, Johnson wondered aloud why people didn't like him. "Mr. President," Acheson told him, "you're not a very likeable man."

Scholars, perhaps because of their more liberal political orientation, have been considerably more generous in their assessments of the Johnson presidency than the public has been. In the ritual polls of prominent historians, LBJ is almost invariably ranked in the above-average or even near-great categories. Arthur Schlesinger has noted that this ranking reflects the view that Johnson's "domestic and foreign record [is] so discordant."[10] Schlesinger's observation points to the fact that most attempts to reevaluate LBJ have rested on a consideration of his domestic achievements, especially such milestones in America's progress as the Civil Rights Act of 1964 and the Voting Rights Act of 1965. Even liberal critics such as Senator George McGovern and the economist John Kenneth Galbraith have found themselves reassessing Johnson. McGovern suggested in a *New York Times* article in 1999 that apart from Woodrow Wilson and the two Roosevelts, Lyndon Johnson was "the greatest President since Abraham Lincoln."[11] Galbraith placed Lyndon Johnson "next only to Franklin D. Roosevelt as a force for civilized and civilizing social policy essential for human well-being and for the peaceful coexistence between the economically favored (or financially fortunate) and the poor." Galbraith, although not regretting his own role in the antiwar movement, did lament the degree to which "we allowed the Vietnam War to become the totally defining effort of those years, and likewise of history. In the Johnson years it was Vietnam and nothing else. And so in history it remains."[12]

But it shouldn't. The Vietnam War should not be allowed to block a more dispassionate assessment of Johnson's foreign and domestic policies. This study argues that the Johnson administration's conduct of policy toward Europe deserves consideration as one of the most important achievements of his presidency. The first and most fundamental reason for this is that Lyndon Johnson built significantly on

John Kennedy's initiatives toward reducing the danger of a nuclear holocaust. This was—and rightly should have been—the overriding imperative of the Johnson presidency, one that shaped his diplomacy toward Europe. With its great wealth and potential, Europe still stood at the center of international diplomacy. As Dean Rusk once acknowledged, any fundamental disturbance to the positions of both superpowers in Europe, especially in Germany, would greatly increase the danger of nuclear war. Although Richard Nixon's presidency is normally associated with the flowering of detente with the Soviet Union, Johnson's achievements—most significantly the Nuclear Nonproliferation Treaty—stand out as creating the essential basis for easing relations. Soviet ambassador Anatoly Dobrynin writes in his memoirs that it is "an interesting contrast to the conventional wisdom" about Kennedy and Johnson that "in Johnson's time we had no serious conflicts in Soviet-American relations" like Berlin or Cuba.[13] Johnson was able to further the long-term process, begun by Kennedy after the Cuban missile crisis, of "thawing out" the Cold War. Through his bridge-building initiatives with Eastern European countries and the whole rhetorical tone of his presidency, Johnson sought to redefine the relationship between the United States and Soviet Union, as well as the relationship between Western and Eastern Europe. His October 7, 1966, speech now stands out as an unheralded yet significant milestone in the pursuit of detente. In Johnson's insistence that change within a clearly divided Europe would come with peaceful development and slow evolution, not stark confrontation or rollback schemes, the president even foreshadowed the peaceful revolutions of 1989.[14] Johnson's use of the "hotline" during the Six-Day War and his subsequent Glassboro summit with Kosygin began a series of U.S.-Soviet discussions of both the life-and-death arms control issues and the various regional conflicts dividing them. (The hotline had been established after the Cuban missile crisis, and LBJ's use demonstrated its value.) Indeed, Johnson's thawing of the Cold War was so pronounced and widely accepted that the world's media largely yawned when the NPT was signed, in contrast to the fanfare that surrounded the Limited Test Ban Treaty five years earlier.

As his approach to the nuclear-sharing question in NATO revealed, Johnson considered the subject of nuclear weapons with the greatest care.[15] As Thomas Schelling has written, Johnson's repeated emphasis that "there was no such thing as a conventional nuclear weapon" and that their use would require "a political decision of the highest order" contrasted sharply with the attempts in the Eisenhower-Dulles era to plan for the possible use of nuclear weapons in crisis situations. Johnson's approach, as Schelling notes, reinforced "the nuclear taboo," a taboo that has contributed to "the nearly universal revulsion against nuclear weapons."[16] Using the Nuclear Planning Group to provide West Germany with participation in decisionmaking and making nuclear nonproliferation a centerpiece of American diplomacy were fundamentally President Johnson's decisions, and those decisions continued to influence U.S. foreign policy long after the Cold War. The NPT itself was extended indefinitely in 1995, a tribute to its long-term significance to American foreign policy.[17]

Along with his encouragement of detente, Lyndon Johnson also emerges as an effective leader of the Atlantic alliance, a leader who worked within multilateral structures to make American diplomacy effective. This conclusion runs against the conventional historical wisdom that someone as "provincial" or "culture-bound" as Johnson could conduct a successful foreign policy, or that Johnson's Vietnam intervention demonstrates his own commitment to the unilateral exercise of American power. In fact, as Francis Bator has written, "It is not . . . all that surprising that someone like Johnson, who had comparatively little interest in and knowledge of the substance of foreign affairs but was a master of politics and of power and had been enormously successful as Senate Majority Leader, would be both shrewd and wise in coping with the cluster of overlapping, inter-connected problems we faced in Europe."[18] Indeed, Johnson's profound understanding of power—he once said, "I do understand power, whatever else may be said about me. I know where to look for it, and how to use it"—allowed him to recognize intuitively something that historians and political scientists now understand about the Cold War international order.[19] As John Ikenberry puts it, "The American postwar order was an open or penetrated hegemony, an extended system that blurred domestic and international politics as it created an elaborate transnational and transgovernmental system with the United States at its center."[20] Within the fragmented and relatively transparent U.S. government, it was often possible for allies to influence the process of American decisionmaking beyond the formal workings of multilateral institutions like NATO. This open or penetrated hegemony changed the nature of foreign policy. Within the institutions and decisionmaking forums of the West, both in security structures like NATO and in economic arrangements like the Group of Ten, foreign policy issues were increasingly "domesticated," with transnational and transgovernmental networks and coalitions playing an important role. As Ikenberry concludes, "The United States became the primary site for the pulling and hauling of trans-Atlantic and trans-Pacific politics."[21] The U.S. presidency could—if properly led and managed—stand at the center of such pulling and hauling within and outside of the American government, with the ability to organize coalitions that cut across national borders and to pursue objectives that might fail to win sufficient support within a purely domestic context. Properly understood, the international political environment in the West became increasingly similar to the American domestic political system, within which a skilled practitioner like Lyndon Johnson could flourish. In his earlier career Johnson had faced the challenge of moving from regional politics to the national stage. As head of the Western alliance, Johnson understood instinctively what political scientists like Ikenberry refer to as the "Janus-faced" nature of alliance politics, as Johnson was forced to "balance international and domestic concerns in a process of double-edged diplomacy."[22] Even Johnson's universalism, his conviction that people everywhere—despite their cultural or racial differences—had the same aspirations for peace, economic betterment for their families, and education for their children, no longer seems naive or provincial in a world where the language of universal human rights has achieved such strength and resonance.

Lyndon Johnson believed that other leaders were influenced by "the same grammar of power; whatever their countries' sizes or shapes, they shared a common concern with questions of rulership: which groups to rely on, which advisers to rely on, and how to conduct themselves amid the complex intrigues of politics."[23] It was this type of insight that allowed Johnson to deal successfully with Charles de Gaulle and steer NATO through its most severe internal crisis, the withdrawal of France from the integrated defense system.[24] This crisis clearly had the potential to unravel the alliance. Indeed, given the simultaneous reduction of tensions with the Soviet Union, there were many, including de Gaulle himself, who saw such a development as desirable. Johnson's public restraint toward the French leader infuriated some of the most cosmopolitan and experienced foreign policy men in Washington, including former secretary of state Dean Acheson and Undersecretary of State George Ball. In this case, however, Johnson proved far more perceptive than his advisers about the best way to handle the politics of de Gaulle's defiance, and about the overall limitations that de Gaulle would face. Recognizing that de Gaulle's public stance was rooted in French domestic politics and the need to overcome the national humiliations of recent history, Johnson's measured diplomacy avoided giving de Gaulle the ammunition he needed for his campaign against American hegemony. Johnson's approach served first to isolate the French from the rest of Europe and allow for the reconstitution of NATO as an even stronger and more cohesive organization, now dedicated to both deterrence *and* detente.[25] After the convulsions in Paris of May 1968 exposed the limits to de Gaulle's policy of *grandeur*, it was Lyndon Johnson who began the process of reconciliation with the French leader. Once again, although the Nixon administration is often credited with changing America's approach to de Gaulle's France, that process was well established before Lyndon Johnson left office.[26]

If Johnson's handling of de Gaulle can be considered a success, what of his dealings with the leaders of the Federal Republic of Germany and Great Britain? Critics often assail a Vietnam-obsessed Johnson for his "tough" handling of Ludwig Erhard, his role in the German leader's downfall, and the overall "deterioration" of U.S.-German relations during this period. Again the picture is far more complicated. Vietnam did have an impact on the relationship, but the more significant issues for West Germany were nuclear sharing, the Nonproliferation Treaty, and the impact of detente on the prospects for German reunification. Johnson successfully maneuvered the Germans into accepting the NPG "software solution" and eventually making a virtue out of their non-nuclear status. Even more important was Johnson's October 7, 1966 speech, which made it clear that the United States favored those elements in Germany seeking a new policy toward East Germany, Eastern Europe, and the Soviet Union. Although the American enthusiasm for Willy Brandt's *Ostpolitik* would diminish during the Nixon-Kissinger years, Johnson's own vision of German reunification as part of a larger process of "making Europe whole" was an important milestone in Cold War politics.[27] Bridge building and detente may have held within them the danger of the West's becoming too complacent and accepting of communist rule in East Germany and Eastern Europe, encouraging the West to look the other way when faced with communist violations of human rights.[28] But the degree to which those systems were peacefully undermined by their contact with and knowledge of the West—and the sharp contrasts their citizens could see—makes it difficult to argue persuasively for a more militant approach.

The confrontation with West Germany over the offset payments question, and its role in the collapse of the Erhard government, were byproducts of Johnson's diplomacy. It is ironic that, of all the European leaders with whom Johnson negotiated, Erhard was his personal favorite. However, contrary to some of the portraits of LBJ as being sentimental and prone to personalizing issues, the president could be coldly realistic in his dealings with foreign leaders. Erhard's political ineptitude at home made him an unreliable partner in Johnson's plans for the alliance. As difficult as his dealings with Kurt Kiesinger would prove to be, Johnson quickly realized that Kiesinger's Grand Coalition government could carry out its agreements. Although the direct American role in the downfall of Erhard was exaggerated by Erhard's political opponents, the event proved a blessing in disguise, as it helped to bring about the Trilateral Agreements as well as effective German political support for the Kennedy Round and the negotiations over international money. Johnson's overall insistence—in which McNamara played the bad cop to LBJ's good cop—that the West Germans could and should do more for their own defense also contributed to what one analyst has called "a little-noticed event [of the late 1960s] but one of seminal importance . . . the emergence of the German Bundeswehr (army and air force) as a first class fighting force."[29] Germany's more significant role in manning the front lines of the alliance's conventional defense would prove crucial to the health and stability of NATO over the next two decades, especially as America itself retreated in the wake of its Vietnam defeat. And although public sentiment in Germany became much more critical of the United States during the Johnson years—an almost inevitable development even without Vietnam, given the Germans' unvarnished and somewhat romantic enthusiasm for Kennedy—relations between the U.S. and West German governments were far more cooperative and harmonious in 1968 than during the early 1960s.[30]

With regard to Harold Wilson and the British, historians have almost uniformly emphasized the divisions created by Vietnam, with many taking the occasion to pronounce the death of the "special relationship." There is no question but that the two men had a very testy relationship over Vietnam. Johnson expressed little of the sentimentality toward Britain that both Kennedy and Eisenhower had for its wartime role in the Grand Alliance. He became increasingly annoyed with Wilson's frequent attempts at mediation of the Vietnam conflict, suspecting that Wilson's impulses came from domestic politics and his need to appease Labour's left wing.[31] A long-time advocate of detente with the Russians, Wilson considered Johnson too inclined toward using military force in Vietnam. Wilson may also have felt constrained by Britain's economic dependency from criticizing the U.S. position in Vietnam too harshly. When asked once why he didn't take a harder line against the Vietnam War, Wilson replied—in a manner Johnson would have understood—"Because we can't kick our creditors in the balls."[32] At Adenauer's funeral, Wilson told a bemused Kiesinger that "the President was a straight shooter—he shot, but he was always straight in the way he did it."[33] But these select comments do not paint the whole picture. There was an extraordinary degree of interaction, involvement, and influence between the U.S. and British governments during this period, with intense U.S. involvement in such matters as the British budget process and subsequent reciprocal British influence, especially on U.S. approaches to the alliance. Britain was not the fifty-first state, as many at the time feared, but its part in the American governing system went far beyond that of a separate sovereign state in international relations theory. To an extent much greater than many have thought possible, both Johnson and Wilson compartmentalized their relationship and learned to live with their differences over Vietnam and to work together effectively in matters where they shared a similar outlook. Wilson, indeed, seems to have "admired, respected, and genuinely warmed to the American President," and long after Wilson left office he described LBJ as a "very, very great man."[34] Johnson did not have the same warmth of feeling for Wilson, but he recognized how to work effectively with him. Though some of his flattery went over the top, Johnson's direct dealings with Wilson, especially as "politician to politician," seem to have made their mark with the prime minister. The president's ability to keep Wilson from making unilateral cuts in the British forces in Germany, cuts that would have strengthened Senator Mansfield's position that the United States should do likewise, is one example of Johnson's effectiveness. Through careful and timely negotiations and bargains, the Johnson administration helped Wilson and his Labour government with two objectives that the British prime minister favored but might not have been able to achieve on his own: keeping a British presence east of the Suez Canal and maintaining the value of the pound sterling. That the pound was eventually devalued in November 1967 and an accelerated British withdrawal east of the Suez was announced in January 1968 were disappointments to American policymakers. But the delay itself had enabled the United States to cope with both events more successfully than if they had taken place in October 1964, July 1965, or even July 1966.[35]

The British were also crucial allies in the Johnson administration's efforts to reform the international monetary system. Dynamic economic growth and prosperity were central objectives of Johnson's presidency, both at home and abroad. His free trade convictions are apparent in his effort to see the Kennedy Round talks successfully completed. Johnson's attentiveness to such economic matters is often overlooked. He rarely gave speeches on economic subjects—in a classic Johnson expression, he once told John Kenneth Galbraith, "Did y'ever think, Ken, that making a speech on ee-conomics is a lot like pissing down your leg? It seems hot to you, but it never does to anyone else."[36] Yet Johnson mastered the subject and was determined not to sacrifice his larger political goals to preserve an international financial system that venerated gold for $35 an ounce. Most historical accounts portray the move away from Bretton Woods and the problems Johnson faced with the balance of payments and the value of the dollar as examples of the "cancerous effect" of the war in Vietnam.[37] Clearly Vietnam aggravated these issues, but the underlying problems were structural. The Bretton Woods system, devised for the early postwar era of American predominance with its fixed exchange rates and rigid gold-dollar relationship, was increasingly less suitable in a world with multiple sources of economic strength and high rates of capital mobility.[38] With finance ministers and governments still fearing that flexible exchange rates would bring back the chaos of the Depression years, and with the French advocating a new "gold standard" that was likely to put the brakes on international economic growth, American leaders struggled to reform Bretton Woods within these perceived political limits. They did so through international consultation in a manner that allowed for significant compromise, especially with the emerging power of the European Economic Community.[39] Johnson's men outmaneuvered de Gaulle with the Special Drawing Rights Agreement in August 1967, but it took the gold crisis of March 1968 for the president to be able to take an important step toward demonetarizing gold with the two-tier system. Nixon would administer the final blow to the system with his economic program of August 1971, but once again the outlines of the change had preceded him.

All of Johnson's achievements in regard to Europe, the alliance, and the international economic system nevertheless remain in the shadow of the Vietnam War. What effect did the war in Southeast Asia have on the president's policy in Europe? This study runs against the conventional wisdom to argue that Vietnam actually had relatively little effect on the major outlines of U.S. policy toward Europe during those years. As traumatic as the war proved for American domestic politics and society, the diplomatic record does not support the idea that the war decisively undermined other aspects of U.S. foreign policy. Indeed, although the war hurt the image of the United States in Europe and undermined the popularity of America, governments and political leaders still cooperated with U.S. policies they perceived to be in their interest and opposed those they did not.[40] The Soviet Union did freeze its relationship with the United States after the initial escalation of the war in 1965, and a Johnson summit with Soviet leaders in 1965 was a casualty of the war. But even the communist superpower, with its need to offset China's appeal by showing solidarity with the struggling revolutionaries of Vietnam, came back to the negotiating table with the Americans when it saw that it might achieve a nonproliferation agreement that would serve its interests in Europe.

Perhaps Johnson would have achieved much more in European diplomacy without the Vietnam War overhanging his efforts. However, it is impossible to construct a foolproof counterfactual history in which the tragedy of Vietnam is magically eliminated, and historians can see the extent to which it distorted, changed, or undermined the other objectives of the United States. All that historians can do is assess what was achieved or not achieved despite the draining commitment to drawing a stable and definite "line in the sand" in Southeast Asia such as the one that existed with the Berlin Wall in Europe. Johnson gambled that fighting a limited war in Vietnam would enable him to continue his program of domestic reforms without the danger of a right-wing reaction or a "Who lost Vietnam?" debate within the United States.[41] He also gambled that fighting a limited war would allow him to move ahead with "thawing" the Cold War in Europe, demonstrating to the communist world that he was prepared to live in peace where the lines between the two sides were clear.[42] To Johnson, revolutionary violence, "wars of national liberation," were an unacceptable way to change those borders.[43] This study argues, in effect, that Johnson won one gamble and that his pursuit of limited war did allow him to move ahead with the Soviet Union because his domestic opponents could not paint him as an appeaser, the Democrat who had lost Vietnam.[44] Historians with access to Chinese documents also make it clear that Johnson's limited approach prevented a direct war with China, the eventuality that was so feared by Charles de Gaulle and that was one of the arguments he used with other Europeans to undermine their support for the U.S. position in NATO.[45] However, Johnson's limited war in Asia, fighting "in cold blood" as Dean Rusk put it, and his attempt to nurture detente in Europe also cost him the ability to appeal to American passions against the communists, for fear of igniting the anticommunist powderkeg.[46] In the end, Johnson lost his other gamble to preserve a viable noncommunist regime in South Vietnam, a defeat that damaged American foreign policy as well as America's domestic stability. However, it is important to recognize that much more was at stake than simply South Vietnam's viability, and American foreign policy of these years should not be simplified into the story of this defeat. Sometimes tragedy and achievement are interwoven strands in the historical narrative, impossible to separate without unraveling the entire story. It may be very difficult for Americans to accept, but Michael Lind's contention that Vietnam was a "necessary war" in the international and domestic context of the times may be much closer to the truth than the perception that the conflict was pointless or even immoral.[47]

This book's argument, however, does not stand or fall in terms of whether the Vietnam War was necessary. What I have sought to do is to present Johnson and his foreign policy achievements with more balance than previous accounts, and to answer Robert Dallek's challenge that we assess Johnson's choices in terms of their wisdom and benefit to America's and the world's well-being. Lyndon Johnson guided the United States with a policy that balanced the solidarity of the Western alliance with the need to stabilize the Cold War and reduce the nuclear danger. His administration began a process of treating Western and Eastern Europe as a whole, recognizing that the division of the continent could be overcome only through a patient and sustained effort to reduce tensions and build bridges between East and West. LBJ sought and furthered the process of expanding international trade and monetary cooperation with the goal of creating the prosperity and economic conditions that would decrease poverty and help ensure peace. Charles de Gaulle once said that "Roosevelt and Kennedy were masks over the real face of America. Johnson is the very portrait of America. He reveals the country to us as it is, rough and raw."[48] De Gaulle did not mean to flatter Americans with this comparison of their recent leaders, but in retrospect, he may have given the United States an unintentional compliment.

Tables

TABLE I
Balance of payments, 1958–1976

Year	Current account balance[a] ($US millions)				Capital account balance[a] ($US millions)			
	U.S.A	U.K.	W. Germany	France[d,e]	U.S.A.[b]	U.K.[c,d]	W. Germany[d]	France[d,e]
1958	784	964	1,387	-174	N/A	-1087	-490	190
1959	-1,282	426	950	712	N/A	-247	-1,465	-820
1960	2,824	-715	1,077	770	-6,442	802	427	-67
1961	3,822	17	712	1,135	-5,194	-887	-1,066	192
1962	3,387	342	-488	862	-6,192	-8	-67	409
1963	4,414	347	166	432	-6,778	-277	569	705
1964	6,823	-966	132	-102	-8,654	-868	-333	916
1965	5,431	-126	-1,554	761	-6,790	-888	535	126
1966	3,031	309	123	171	-2,929	-1,618	-151	286
1967	2,583	-705	2,503	205	-6,087	-1,213	-2,963	170
1968	611	-577	2,964	-1,059	1,033	-1,810	-1,531	-2,606
1969	399	1,222	2,032	-1,798	2,081	-420	-5,062	738
1970	2,331	1,970	872	-152	-12,587	1,314	4,142	1,899
1971	-1,433	2,869	848	526	-28,512	4,574	3,331	2,702
1972	-5,795	524	853	284	-5,386	-1,580	604	1,290
1973	7,140	-2,274	4,571	1,402	-13,324	414	4,863	-1,168
1974	1,962	-5,350	11,031	-4,230	-11,041	3,762	-10,497	2,292
1975	18,116	-3,062	3,787	2,564	-24,294	312	-5,064	-6,488
1976	4,295	-1,423	4,197	-5,312	-19,430	-5,065	-437	2,294

Sources: OECD *Main Economic Indicators, 1955–1971* (for all non-U.S. data from 1958–1963), *1960–1975* (for U.K. capital account data from 1960–1963), *1964–1983* (for all non-U.S. data from 1964–1976); *Economic Report of the President, 2001* (for all U.S. data), unless otherwise noted.

[a] Balances for United Kingdom, France, and Germany, when given in pounds, francs, or DM, are converted using year-end spot exchange rates for each year.

[b] Calculated as negative sum of net outflow of U.S. official reserve assets and net outflow of foreign official assets, minus the balance on the current account.

[c] Capital account data for the U.K. for the years 1958 and 1959 come from *IMF Balance of Payments Yearbook, 1957–1961,* Summary Statistics.

[d] For Germany: Prior to 1964, capital account data are calculated as net current plus capital transactions minus current balance. From 1964–1976, the capital account balance is given by net capital movements. For the U.K. (1960–1976) and France (1973–1976), capital account balances represent net capital movements.

[e] Data for France from 1958 and 1959 come from *IMF Balance of Payments Yearbook, 1957–1961,* Summary Statistics, and are for the franc area. French capital account data for 1960–1966 come from *OECD Economic Survey: France, 1970* and represent the balance on official settlements minus the balance on the current account with non-franc countries. French capital account data for 1967–1972 come from *OECD Economic Survey: France, 1975* and represent the balance on official settlements minus the balance on the current account with the rest of the world.

TABLE 2
eficit/surplus, investment abroad, 1958–1976

	urplus[a] (illions)	Budget surplus as % GDP[a]	Investment abroad ($US millions)
	-2.8	−0.6	N/A
1959	12.8	−2.6	N/A
1960	.3	0.1	4,099
1961	−3.3	−0.6	5,538
1962	−7.1	−1.3	4,174
1963	−4.8	−0.8	7,270
1964	−5.9	−0.9	9,560
1965	−1.4	−0.2	5,716
1966	−3.7	−0.5	7,321
1967	−8.6	−1.1	9,757
1968	−25.2	−2.9	10,977
1969	3.2	0.3	11,585
1970	−2.8	−0.3	8,470
1971	−23.0	−2.1	11,758
1972	−23.4	−2.0	13,787
1973	−14.9	−1.1	22,874
1974	−6.1	−0.4	34,745
1975	−53.2	−3.4	39,703
1976	−73.7	−4.2	51,269

Source: *Economic Report of the President, 2001,* Appendix B.
Investment figures represent net outflows of U.S.-owned assets abroad for selected years.
[a] A negative number represents a budget deficit.

TABLE 3
Inflation rates, 1958–1976

	Inflation (% change in consumer price index)			
Year	U.S.A.	U.K.	Germany	France
1958	2.8	2.9	2.1	15.4
1959	0.9	0.7	1.0	5.7
1960	1.5	1.0	1.5	4.2
1961	1.1	3.6	2.3	2.5
1962	1.1	4.0	2.9	5.2
1963	1.2	2.1	3.0	4.9
1964	1.3	3.3	2.3	3.3
1965	1.7	4.7	3.2	2.7
1966	3.0	3.9	3.6	2.6
1967	2.8	2.4	1.6	2.8
1968	4.2	4.7	1.6	4.5
1969	5.4	5.5	1.9	6.0
1970	5.9	6.3	3.4	5.8
1971	4.3	9.4	5.2	5.4
1972	3.3	7.1	5.5	6.1
1973	6.2	9.2	7.0	7.3
1974	11.0	15.9	7.0	13.7
1975	9.1	24.3	5.9	11.7
1976	5.7	16.5	4.3	9.6

Source: Data from International Financial Statistics.
Inflation$_t$ = (CPI$_t$ − CPI$_{t-1}$)/CPI$_{t-1}$

Abbreviations Used in Notes

AAPD	*Akten zur Auswärtigen Politik der Bundesrepublik Deutschland*
CDU	Christian Democratic Union
CF	Chronological File
DBPO	*Documents on British Policy Overseas*
DDF	*Documents diplomatique français*
FO	Foreign Office
FRUS	*Foreign Relations of the United States*
HSTL	Harry S. Truman Library
LBJL	Lyndon B. Johnson Library
MAE	Ministère des Affaires Étrangères, Paris
NARS	National Archives and Records Service
NL	Nachlass
NSAM	National Security Action Memorandum
NSF	National Security File
PRO	Public Record Office
TNN	Trilateral Negotiations and NATO
USIA	United States Information Agency
VHS	Virginia Historical Society
WHCF	White House Confidential File

Notes

PRELUDE

1. Michael H. Hunt, *Lyndon Johnson's War* (New York: Hill and Wang, 1996), pp. 3–4.
2. William J. Lederer and Eugene Burdick, *The Ugly American* (New York: Norton, 1958), pp. 11–32. "Lucky Lou" sounds very suspiciously like "Landslide Lyndon," one of Johnson's more famous nicknames. For a recent discussion of the book's influence, see Robert D. Dean, "Masculinity as Ideology: John F. Kennedy and the Domestic Politics of Foreign Policy," *Diplomatic History* 22, no. 1 (Winter 1998): 36–37. Dean recognizes the significance of the book in revealing the mentality of the time, but he fails to recognize its limits in explaining the entirety of Kennedy-Johnson foreign policy, a policy that not only fought the Cold War but attempted to reach a detente with the Soviet Union.
3. Robert L. Hardesty, *The Johnson Years: The Difference He Made* (Austin: Lyndon B. Johnson Library, 1993), p. 190. The toilet story was first published in David Halberstam's famous book *The Best and the Brightest* (New York: Random House, 1972), pp. 435–436. The former aide, Douglas Dillon, in a letter to the LBJ Library, angrily denies that LBJ treated him that way. LBJL, Douglas Dillon, Oral History, p. 1. Richard Goodwin describes his own interview with LBJ while the president was so disposed, in Richard Goodwin, *Remembering America: A Voice from the Sixties* (Boston: Little, Brown, 1988),

pp. 256–257. Alonzo L. Hamby, *Liberalism and Its Challenges: From F.D.R to Bush*, 2nd ed. (New York: Oxford University Press, 1992), p. 231.

4. Henry Kissinger, *White House Years* (Boston: Little, Brown, 1979), p. 18.

5. Bruce Kuklick, quoted in Stephen Winterstein, "Teaching the Vietnam War: A Conference Report," *Foreign Policy Research Institute Newsletter* 6, no. 4 (July 2000): p. 2.

6. H. R. McMaster, *Dereliction of Duty: Lyndon Johnson, Robert McNamara, the Joint Chiefs of Staff, and the Lies That Led to Vietnam* (New York: Harper Collins, 1997), pp. 50–51.

7. Fredrik Logevall, *Choosing War: The Lost Chance for Peace and the Escalation of War in Vietnam* (Berkeley: University of California Press, 1999), pp. 79–80, 339–340.

8. David Kaiser, *American Tragedy: Kennedy, Johnson, and the Origins of the Vietnam War* (Cambridge, Mass.: Belknap Press of Harvard University Press, 2000), p. 287. Walter Heller tells a similar story in comparing Johnson and Kennedy on economic questions, though he emphasizes Johnson's quickness and speed at grasping what he needed to know on an economic question. By contrast, Heller notes that it was more fun to work with Kennedy because of the depth to which he would penetrate economic questions, although Heller admits, "I'm not sure he needed to go so deeply into some of these things for him to make valid decisions on economics." Kenneth W. Thompson, ed., *The Johnson Presidency* (Lanham: University Press of America, 1986), p. 184.

9. One contemporary account that captures the burdens under which Johnson labored is Louis Heren, *No Hail, No Farewell* (New York: Harper and Row, 1970). A British journalist, Heren tracks the Johnson presidency from its tragic beginning through its unlamented end, recognizing many of the social and cultural assumptions and prejudices that affected the perception of Johnson. An insightful work of political journalism, Heren's book refers to the "curse of the South" that was on Johnson (p. 19). Another contemporary work, also by a British journalist, quotes A. J. Liebling's remark that "Southern politicians travel badly, like sweet corn. By the time they reach the cities of the north they have become overripe, offending delicate Northern palates. This is what has happened to Johnson." Michael Davie, *LBJ:*

A Foreign Observer's Viewpoint (New York: Duell, Sloan, and Pearce, 1966), p. 27.

10. Jan Jarboe Russell, "LBJ Sounds Off," *Slate* (www.slate.com), August 23, 1997.

11. George Christian, *The President Steps Down* (New York: Macmillan, 1970), p. 259. See also Richard Barnet, *The Alliance* (New York: Simon and Schuster, 1983), p. 295.

12. Herbert Block, *The Herblock Gallery* (New York: Simon and Schuster, 1968), p. 12. The cartoon appeared on June 30, 1965, in the *Washington Post*.

13. Thomas Stern, Oral History, Georgetown University Archives, Foreign Service Oral Histories, pp. 9–10. On that same trip to Germany, one of the presidential advance men reacted with disgust when he saw that the bedroom in which the president would sleep had built-in bookshelves: "You can't expect the president to wake up in the morning and look at books." Johnson's insistence on a powerful hot shower also led his assistants to insist on the installation of a special pump in the embassy, which eventually ruined the pipes of the old building. Martin J. Hillenbrand, *Fragments of Our Time: Memoirs of a Diplomat* (Athens: University of Georgia Press, 1998), pp. 241–242.

14. Waldo Heinrichs, "Lyndon B. Johnson: Change and Continuity," in *Lyndon Johnson Confronts the World*, ed. Warren I. Cohen and Nancy Bernkopf Tucker (New York: Cambridge University Press, 1994), p. 26.

15. Doris Kearns Goodwin, *Lyndon Johnson and the American Dream* (New York: Harper and Row, 1976), p. 202.

16. John Connally, *In History's Shadow: An American Odyssey* (New York: Hyperion, 1993), p. 63.

17. Horace Busby, a close associate of Johnson for many years, wrote a response to the attacks by some of Johnson's associates on the negative portrait of LBJ in Robert Caro's biography. Busby noted, "There were many Lyndon Johnsons. Some were admirable, brilliant, even, on occasion, awesome. Others were deplorable and detestable, small, abusive, unworthy of his high stations. To acknowledge this is not an act of disloyalty; it is only an act of honesty." *Washington Post*, March 29, 1983.

18. A notable recent work—still only in Italian—is Massimiliano

Guderzo, *Interesse nazionale e responsabilità globale: Gli Stati Uniti, l'Alleanza atlantica e l'integrazione europea negli anni di Johnson 1963–69* (Florence: Aida, 2000). Robert Dallek, in his otherwise exhaustive and balanced biography of Johnson, barely mentions European policy. Robert Dallek, *Flawed Giant: Lyndon Johnson and His Times, 1961–1973* (New York: Oxford University Press, 1998).

19. H. W. Brands, *The Wages of Globalism* (New York: Oxford, 1995), pp. 28–29, and Frank Costigliola, "Lyndon B. Johnson, Germany, and the 'End of the Cold War,'" in *Lyndon Johnson Confronts the World,* ed. Warren Cohen and Nancy Tucker (New York: Cambridge University Press, 1994), p. 210.

20. Lloyd Gardner, *Pay Any Price: Lyndon Johnson and the Wars for Vietnam* (Chicago: Ivan R. Dee, 1995), p. 95.

21. Thomas W. Zeiler, *Dean Rusk: Defending the American Mission Abroad* (Wilmington, Del.: Scholarly Resources, 2000), p. 56.

22. Robert Dallek, "Lyndon Johnson as a World Leader," in H. W. Brands, *Beyond Vietnam: The Foreign Policies of Lyndon Johnson* (College Station: Texas A & M University Press, 1999), p. 8.

23. Correcting this impression of LBJ is not an easy task, in part because LBJ afforded his critics plenty of ammunition. For example, the noted historian Douglas Brinkley, in his account of Dean Acheson's retirement years, discusses Acheson's first meeting with the president in December 1963 and paints LBJ as obsessed with the Soviets' refusal to allow the American musical *Hello Dolly* to be performed in Moscow. Brinkley quotes the imperious Acheson as telling Johnson that "such a trivial issue was not worthy of the attention of the President of the United States." Brinkley concludes that this episode reflected "the aura of insecurity and amateurism emanating from the Oval Office." Douglas Brinkley, *Dean Acheson: The Cold War Years, 1953–1971* (New Haven: Yale University Press, 1992), p. 208. The incident Acheson described took place, but in July 1965, not December 1963. (*Hello Dolly* did not even open in the United States until January 1964.) As Chapter 2 will make clear, by July 1965 Johnson was trying to move the NATO alliance away from the Multilateral Force (MLF) and German nuclear sharing toward a nuclear nonproliferation arrangement. In meeting with Dean Acheson, to whom NATO was akin to a religion and West Germany the most significant country in the world, Johnson may well have wanted to

deflect the former secretary of state from his pro-MLF mission with this tirade against the Soviets. But the story standing by itself hardly speaks well for Johnson's diplomatic acumen.

24. The song was "Luci Baines," and can be found on the Chad Mitchell Trio's album, *That's the Way It's Gonna Be,* produced by Jacob Ander et al. for Mercury Records, 1965. I owe this note to my brother Bob, whose knowledge of the folk music of the 1960s was inexhaustible.

25. Eric Goldman, *The Tragedy of Lyndon Johnson* (New York: Dell, 1969), pp. 447–448.

26. David Fromkin, "Lyndon Johnson and Foreign Policy," *Foreign Affairs* 74, no. 1 (1995): 168–170.

27. Philip Geyelin, *Lyndon B. Johnson and the World* (New York: Praeger, 1966), pp. 13 and 147.

28. Theodore White, *The Making of the President, 1968* (New York: Atheneum, 1969), p. 101.

29. Michael Beschloss, *Taking Charge: The Johnson White House Tapes* (New York: Simon and Schuster, 1997), p. 553. Others attribute this characterization to Hugh Sidey. Johnson's secrecy is also a prominent theme in Robert Caro's work on LBJ. As Caro writes of the young Johnson, "The most striking aspect of Lyndon Johnson's secrecy, however, was not the success with which he imposed it on others but the success with which he imposed it on himself." Robert A. Caro, *The Years of Lyndon Johnson: The Path to Power* (New York: Alfred A. Knopf, 1982), p. 185.

30. George Christian, *The President Steps Down* (New York: Macmillan, 1970), pp. 18–19.

31. Dallek, "Johnson as a World Leader," p. 17.

1. RETREAT FROM THE GRAND DESIGN

1. Douglas Brinkley and Richard T. Griffiths, eds., *John F. Kennedy and Europe* (Baton Rouge: Louisiana State University Press, 1999), p. xvi.

2. *FRUS 1961–1963*, 15, pp. 536–537.

3. *Newsweek*, July 8, 1963, p. 31.

4. Herbert S. Parmet, *JFK: The Presidency of John F. Kennedy* (New York: Viking, 1983), p. 321.

5. *DDF 1963*, 1, 224, pp. 659–662.

6. Frank Costigliola, "The Pursuit of Atlantic Community: Nuclear Arms, Dollars, and Berlin," in *Kennedy's Quest for Victory*, ed. Thomas Paterson (New York: Oxford, 1989), p. 24.

7. Arthur Schlesinger, *A Thousand Days* (Boston: Houghton Mifflin, 1965), p. 888.

8. Henry Brandon, *Special Relationships: A Foreign Correspondent's Memoirs from Roosevelt to Reagan* (New York: Atheneum, 1988), p. 200.

9. Jeffrey Glen Giauque, *Grand Designs and Visions of Unity: The Atlantic Powers and the Reorganization of Western Europe, 1955–1963* (Chapel Hill: University of North Carolina Press, 2002), p. 123.

10. Giauque, *Grand Designs and Visions of Unity*, pp. 112–114. Giauque's impressive study distributes the blame among all the major nations for the fact that "by the end of 1963 the Atlantic Community had largely ground to a halt."

11. For an overview of British-American relations, I have relied on David Reynolds, *Britannia Overruled: British Policy and World Power in the Twentieth Century* (London: Longman, 1991). Other works consulted include Alan Dobson, *Anglo-American Relations in the Twentieth Century* (London: Routledge, 1995), and Sean Greenwood, *Britain and the Cold War, 1945–1991* (New York: St. Martin's, 2000).

12. *DDF 1963*, 1, 77, pp. 221–222. This is a telegram from the ambassador to the United States, Hervé Alphand, to the Foreign Ministry indicating that Robert Kennedy had approached the French with some type of offer of assistance to the French nuclear program. Carl Kaysen, one of the negotiators of the test-ban treaty, claimed that the Kennedy administration was willing to give the French "nuclear warheads for their bombs" if they would sign the Limited Test Ban Treaty. Francis J. Gavin, "The Myth of Flexible Response: United States Strategy in Europe during the 1960s," *International History Review* 23, no. 4 (December 2001): 856–857. In his oral history, Roswell Gilpatric argues the Kennedy administration was attempting to "create something like a special relationship with the French . . . in nuclear weapons matters," but that the project got dropped after Kennedy's assassination. LBJL, Roswell Gilpatric, Oral History, p. 11.

13. This description was offered in the obituary of Douglas-Home, *New York Times*, October 10, 1995.

14. Defense Secretary McNamara frequently made this point. *FRUS 1964–1968*, 12, p. 494.

15. Frédéric Bozo, *Two Strategies for Europe: De Gaulle, the United States, and the Atlantic Alliance*, trans. Susan Emanuel (Lanham: Rowman and Littlefield, 2001), especially chaps. 1 and 2. I have relied heavily on Bozo, although he tends to minimize the general's use of anti-Americanism—both symbolically and on policy questions—as a tool for the restoration of France's *grandeur*. Other recent works on French foreign policy that have influenced this study include Maurice Vaïsse, *Le Grandeur: Politique étrangère du général de Gaulle, 1958–1969* (Paris: Fayard, 1998); Jean Lacouture, *De Gaulle: The Ruler 1945–1970* (New York, 1991); Serge Bernstein, *The Republic of de Gaulle, 1958–1969*, trans. Peter Morris (Paris: Cambridge University Press, 1993); and Frank Costigliola, *France and the United States: The Cold Alliance since World War II* (New York: Twayne, 1992).

16. Charles G. Cogan, *Charles de Gaulle* (New York: Bedford Books, 1996), p. 121.

17. Costigliola, *Cold Alliance*, p. 120.

18. Richard Barnet, *The Alliance* (New York: Simon and Schuster, 1983), p. 249.

19. Alfred Grosser, *The Western Alliance: European-American Relations since 1945* (New York: Vintage, 1982), pp. 227–228.

20. For an overview of Adenauer's chancellorship, I have relied on the extraordinary compilation of research produced by the German Historical Institute in Washington: *Die USA und Deutschland im Zeitalter des Kalten Krieges 1945–1990: Ein Handbuch, Band I, 1945–1968*, ed. Detlef Junker et al. (Stuttgart: Deutsch Verlags-Anstalt, 2001). See also Dennis L. Bark and David R. Gress, *A History of West Germany*, vol. 2: *Democracy and Its Discontents, 1963–1968* (London: Basil Blackwell, 1989); Frank Ninkovich, *Germany and the United States*, 2nd ed. (New York: Twayne, 1995); and Ronald Granier, *The Ambivalent Alliance: Konrad Adenauer, the CDU/CSU, and the West, 1949–1966* (New York: Berghahn, 2002). Granier's study details the internal tensions among Germany's conservatives, between Erhard's Atlanticists and the pro-French Gaullists.

21. Roger Morgan, "Kennedy and Adenauer," in *John F. Kennedy and Europe*, ed. Douglas Brinkley and Richard T. Griffiths (Baton Rouge:

Louisiana State University Press, 1999), pp. 16–17. Adenauer's biographer, Hans-Peter Schwarz, makes it clear how profoundly mistrustful Adenauer was of American policy at this time. Hans-Peter Schwarz, *Adenauer, der Staatsmann: 1952–1967* (Stuttgart: Deutsche Verlags-Anstalt, 1991), pp. 840–853.

22. Terence Prittie, *The Velvet Chancellors: A History of Postwar Germany* (London: Frederick Muller Ltd., 1979), p. 127.

23. Heinrich Krone, quoted in William Glenn Gray, "The Hallstein Doctrine: West Germany's Global Campaign to Isolate East Germany, 1949–1969," Ph.D. diss., Yale University, 1999, p. 246.

24. *FRUS 1961–1963*, 13, p. 624. Marc Trachtenberg argues that the quid pro quo for this commitment of ground forces was that Germany remain nonnuclear. But even he admits that "it took a while before the structure that had taken shape by 1963 was accepted as definitive." Marc Trachtenberg, *A Constructed Peace: The Making of the European Settlement, 1945–1963* (Princeton: Princeton University Press, 1999), pp. 397–398. Indeed the question of the size of the U.S. contingent in Germany, as well as Germany's nuclear status, remained far more open than Trachtenberg admits, especially because of the change in leadership of both superpowers as well as in Great Britain and Germany.

25. Francis J. Gavin, "The Gold Battles within the Cold War: American Monetary Policy and the Defense of Europe, 1960–1963," *Diplomatic History* 26, no. 1 (Winter 2002): 91–92.

26. Leonard Baker, *The Johnson Eclipse: A President's Vice Presidency* (New York: Macmillan, 1966), p. 11.

27. See *The Kennedy Tapes: Inside the White House during the Cuban Missile Crisis*, ed. Ernest R. May and Philip D. Zelikow (Cambridge, Mass.: Harvard University Press, 1997), pp. 42–43.

28. Robert Dallek, *Flawed Giant: Lyndon Johnson and His Times, 1961–1973* (New York: Oxford University Press, 1995), pp. 12–20. Ambassador Kenneth Young, who accompanied LBJ on his trip to Vietnam and three other Asian countries in 1961, reported that the "Vice President dramatically carried the pedestal of power to the open places of the people far better than could long lectures or diplomatic notes." *FRUS 1961–1963*, 1, p. 144. Even his last trip as vice president, to Scandinavia, during which he threw "a Texas barbecue" for

some three thousand guests in Finland, also outlined a more nuanced foreign policy toward the different countries of the region. Jussi Hanhimäki, *Scandinavia and the United States* (New York: Twayne, 1997), p. 117.

29. Robert Caro, *The Years of Lyndon Johnson,* vol. 3: *Master of the Senate* (New York: Alfred A. Knopf, 2002), pp. 519–541. Caro praises Johnson for holding "back a rising isolationist tide" that might have "swept unchecked toward the Marshall Plan, NATO, the United Nations. In his first battle as Democratic leader, Lyndon Johnson had scored a major triumph not only for himself and his party, but for his country as well." Such praise from Caro is both rare and surprising.

30. George Reedy, *Lyndon B. Johnson: A Memoir* (New York: Andrews and McMeel, Inc., 1982), p. 47.

31. Lyndon B. Johnson, *The Vantage Point: Perspectives of the Presidency, 1963–1969* (New York: Holt, Rinehart, and Winston, 1971), p. 24.

32. As with everything about LBJ, there is some dispute about this. Dean Rusk, for example, argues that Johnson "never took a strong personal interest" in arms control, while Clark Clifford notes, "I could see that arms control held the same importance to Lyndon Johnson in international affairs as civil rights did in the domestic arena." Dean Rusk, *As I Saw It* (New York: Norton, 1990), p. 340; Clark Clifford, with Richard Holbrooke, *Counsel to the President: A Memoir* (New York: Random House, 1991), p. 560.

33. Johnson, *Vantage Point,* p. 23. That the fear of a nuclear war remained an overriding theme in the elite and popular discourse of the era is largely forgotten. For example, as late as 1965 one of the most popular songs in the United States was "Eve of Destruction," which forecast just such an apocalypse. Despite being banned from twenty of the nation's fifty largest radio markets, the song spent eleven weeks on the *Billboard* top 100 pop chart and one week at number one. Gregory Dutton, "Music of the Vietnam War," unpublished paper, Vanderbilt University, April 2002, p. 8.

34. Michael R. Beschloss, *Taking Charge: The Johnson White House Tapes, 1963–1964* (New York: Simon and Schuster, 1997), p. 67.

35. Beschloss, *Taking Charge,* pp. 62–63.

36. *FRUS 1961–1963,* 8, p. 544.

37. Jon Margolis, *The Last Innocent Year: America in 1964* (New York: Morrow, 1999), p. 53.
38. Beschloss, *Taking Charge*, p. 145.
39. *FRUS 1964–1968*, 11, p. 22. See also Glenn T. Seaborg, *Stemming the Tide: Arms Control in the Johnson Years* (Lexington, Mass.: Lexington Books, 1987), pp. 39–49.
40. *FRUS 1964–1968*, 11, p. 45.
41. *FRUS 1964–1968*, 17, p. 12.
42. In an influential article written early in the Johnson presidency, McGeorge Bundy emphasized that "the short space of three months is enough to show plainly that the pursuit of peace remains [President Johnson's] central concern." McGeorge Bundy, "The Presidency and Peace," *Foreign Affairs* 42, no. 3 (April 1964): 364.
43. Louis Heren, *No Hail, No Farewell* (New York: Harper and Row, 1970), p. 61.
44. LBJ speech, September 7, 1964, *Public Papers of the President: Lyndon B. Johnson 1963–1964* (Washington, D.C.: G.P.O., 1965), pp. 1049–1052.
45. Johnson, *Vantage Point*, p. 463.
46. W. W. Rostow, *The Diffusion of Power* (New York: Macmillan, 1972), p. 390.
47. In a conversation with George Reedy in July 1964, Johnson noted that one purpose of his bridge building was to lure countries with an independent streak, like Romania, closer to the West. LBJL, LBJ and Reedy, July 15, 1964, Tape WH6407.15. In a September speech, LBJ spoke of how "the solid unity of communism has begun to crack. We have worked to help the nations of Eastern Europe move toward independence." LBJ speech, September 7, 1964, *Public Papers*, p. 1050.
48. Rick Perlstein, *Before the Storm: Barry Goldwater and the Unmaking of the American Consensus* (New York: Hill and Wang, 2001), p. 270.
49. *FRUS 1964–1968*, 14, pp. 8–10.
50. Telegram, Douglas-Home to Foreign Office, February 23, 1964, PREM 11/4794, PRO, London.
51. L. P. Neville-Jones, "Analysis of Fulbright and U.S. Foreign Policy," April 10, 1964, PREM 11/5195, PRO, London.

52. Greenwood, *Britain and the Cold War,* p. 137, and Berstein, *Republic of de Gaulle,* p. 161.

53. Gray, "Hallstein Doctrine," p. 2. Gray's work is the most complete and balanced discussion of the Hallstein Doctrine that we are ever likely to have.

54. On this point I disagree with the conclusions presented in Alexandra Friedrich, "Awakenings: The Impact of the Vietnam War on West German–American Relations in the 1960s," Ph.D. diss. Temple University, 2000, p. 331. The Vietnam War was not directly connected to the Johnson administration's push for the Federal Republic to pursue a more flexible Eastern policy. Johnson's approach predated the escalation of the war and derived from his desire to reduce tensions in Central Europe, the most dangerous location in the Cold War.

55. *Time,* January 10, 1964, p. 23. Kaiser argues that Johnson "failed" to move Erhard toward a more flexible policy toward the Soviets and East Germany. David Kaiser, *American Tragedy: Kennedy, Johnson, and the Origins of the Vietnam War* (Cambridge, Mass.: Belknap Press of Harvard University Press, 2000), p. 286.

56. *FRUS 1961–1963,* 15, p. 670.

57. Document 490 in *AAPD 1963,* vol. 3 (Munich: Oldenbourg, 1994), p. 1703. The literal-minded German foreign secretary underlined Johnson's reference to sixteen or seventeen years and noted, "At most 14, in reality 10!" The account of the Erhard-Johnson talks in the German documents also makes it clear that Erhard was sensitive about any perception of difference in the American-German approach to detente. See also the account in George McGhee, *At the Creation of a New Germany* (New Haven: Yale University Press, 1989), p. 148.

58. *FRUS 1964–1968,* 15, p. 29.

59. Beschloss, *Taking Charge,* p. 200.

60. *FRUS 1964–1968,* 14, pp. 55–58. Johnson did, however, firmly insist that the Soviets should not shoot down such errant planes, and that other methods of deterrence could be used.

61. Letter, Günter Henle to Schröder, July 10, 1964, Nachlass Gerhard Schröder, I-483 100/2, CDU Archive. Henle was a prominent German industrialist who became head of Germany's equivalent of the

Council on Foreign Relations, the Deutscher Gesellschaft für Aus-
wärtige Politik. He was reporting on a trip to the United States in
which the Johnson interview was brought up frequently.

62. *FRUS 1964–1968,* 15, pp. 146–147.
63. Gray, "Hallstein Doctrine," pp. 243–244.
64. Douglas Selvage, "The Warsaw Pact and Nuclear Nonproliferation,
    1963–1965," Working Paper No. 32, Cold War International His-
    tory Project, Woodrow Wilson International Center for Scholars,
    Washington, D.C. (April 2001), p. 10.
65. The Presidium Report, dated October 1964 is quoted in Vladislav
    M. Zubok, "The Multilevel Dynamics of Moscow's German Policy
    from 1953 to 1964," in Patrick M. Morgan and Keith L. Nelson,
    eds., *Reviewing the Cold War: Domestic Factors and Foreign Policy in
    the East-West Confrontation* (Westport: Praeger, 2000), p. 91. Zubok
    makes it clear that Soviet alliance politics and domestic politics came
    together in the ouster of Khrushchev.
66. W. R. Smyser, *From Yalta to Berlin: The Cold War Struggle over Ger-
    many* (New York: St. Martin's Press, 1999), pp. 206–208.
67. Richard Reeves, *President Kennedy: Profile of Power* (New York: Si-
    mon and Schuster, 1993), p. 277.
68. In the aftermath of Kennedy's death, many observers forgot the de-
    gree to which Kennedy's domestic programs had been stalled in
    Congress. James MacGregor Burns, JFK's own biographer, had just
    penned a book, *The Deadlock of Democracy,* that argued that Ameri-
    can governmental machinery needed to be drastically reformed. LBJ's
    success would change the focus of that concern from an all-powerful
    Congress to an all-powerful presidency. Michael Davie, *LBJ: A For-
    eign Observer's Viewpoint* (New York: Duell, Sloan, and Pearce,
    1966), p. 6.
69. Joseph A. Califano, Jr., *The Triumph and Tragedy of Lyndon Johnson*
    (New York: Simon and Schuster, 1991), p. 10.
70. Mary L. Dudziak, *Cold War Civil Rights: Race and the Image of Amer-
    ican Democracy* (Princeton: Princeton University Press, 2000),
    p. 207. Dudziak's impressive study also affirms that in this period,
    "The boundaries of domestic and foreign affairs became blurred,"
    p. 253.
71. Philip Geyelin, *Lyndon B. Johnson and the World* (New York: Praeger,

1966), p. 147. In considering this connection between Johnson's foreign and domestic policies, Lloyd Gardner has argued that there was an "ideological weld between the cold war vision of the world and American beliefs about the capacities of their society," and that "Johnson faced losing the Great Society without going forward in Vietnam." Gardner, *Pay Any Price,* p. 95.

72. Randall Woods, *Fulbright: A Biography* (New York: Cambridge University Press, 1995), p. 323.

73. Geyelin, *Lyndon B. Johnson and the World,* p. 13.

74. Eric Goldman, *The Tragedy of Lyndon Johnson* (New York: Dell, 1969), p. 383.

75. Francis M. Bator, "Lyndon Johnson and Foreign Policy: The Case of Western Europe and the Soviet Union," in *Presidential Judgment: Foreign Policy Decision Making in the White House,* ed. Aaron Lobel (Hollis, N.H.: Hollis Publishing Co., 2001), p. 41.

76. Emmette S. Redford and Richard T. McCulley, *White House Operations: The Johnson Presidency* (Austin: University of Texas Press, 1986), p. 106, note that even though Johnson emphasized his domestic program in his first year, there were significant demands on his time from the foreign crises he encountered.

77. *New York Herald Tribune,* January 29, 1964, quoted in Beschloss, *Taking Charge,* p. 201.

78. LBJ conversation with Ralph Dungan, January 31, 1964, in Beschloss, *Taking Charge,* p. 201.

79. Heren, in his otherwise sympathetic account of Johnson's first days, remarks that his "early approach to foreign affairs was very tentative." Heren, *No Hail, No Farewell,* p. 27.

80. I owe this insight to Professor Robert Johnson, the editor of the Johnson tapes for early 1964.

81. Ormsby Gore to Foreign Secretary Butler, February 4, 1964, PREM 11/4794, PRO, London.

82. Alain Peyrefitte, *C'était de Gaulle,* vol. 2 (Paris: Fayard, 1997), p. 48, and Pierre Galante, *Le Général* (Paris: Presses de la Cité, 1968), p. 162.

83. *New York Times,* March 4, 1968, p. 11.

84. Birrenbach, Report on Trip to the United States, April 4, 1964, Kurt Birrenbach Nachlass (NL) 088/2, CDU Archive, Bonn.

85. Raj Roy, "The Battle over the Pound, 1964–1968," Ph.D. diss., London School of Economics, 2000, p. 40.
86. Memo, Wright to Douglas-Home, February 11, 1964, PREM 11/4794, PRO, London.
87. Memo, Foreign Secretary Butler to Douglas-Home, April 29, 1964, PREM 11/4789, PRO, London.
88. George Herring, *America's Longest War,* 3rd ed.(New York: McGraw-Hill, 1996), p. 121.
89. LBJ, conversation with Robert Kennedy, July 21, 1964, in Beschloss, *Taking Charge,* p. 465.
90. Philip Kaiser, *Journeying Far and Wide: A Political and Diplomatic Memoir.* (New York: Macmillan, 1992), p. 286.
91. Peyrefitte, *C'était de Gaulle,* vol. 2, p. 50.
92. LBJL, LBJ conversation with Richard Russell, January 8, 1964, Tape WH6401.09.
93. *FRUS 1964–1968,* 12, p. 46.
94. LBJ conversation with Richard Russell, January 15, 1964, quoted in Beschloss, *Taking Charge,* p. 162.
95. Logevall, *Choosing War,* pp. 177–178.
96. *Time,* June 12, 1964, p. 42.
97. *Newsweek,* May 25, 1964, p. 48.
98. Bohlen also recommended this course of action to Johnson, telling Johnson that "we should avoid small pinpricks and small actions which look as though they are based upon irritation or ill temper. These could only help de Gaulle without producing any change whatsoever in his attitude or policies." *FRUS 1964–1968,* 12, p. 46. But for reasons that will become clear, this was not simply a case of LBJ's following his smart advisers.
99. LBJ conversation with Walter Heller, February 15, 1964, in Beschloss, *Taking Charge,* p. 243.
100. LBJ conversation with Walter Heller, February 15, 1964, LBJL, WH6402.16. Beschloss leaves out this part of the conversation.
101. Kaiser, *Journeying Far and Wide,* p. 210.
102. Joseph Kraft, *The Grand Design: From Common Market to Atlantic Partnership* (New York: Harper, 1962).
103. Giauque, *Grand Designs and Visions of Unity,* p. 107.

104. Ibid., p. 113.
105. As Table 1 in the Appendix indicates, one of the primary reasons for the overall deficit in the balance of payments was the large deficit in the capital accounts balance, as Americans were investing heavily abroad. By contrast, the current account was continuing to produce a healthy surplus, and the TEA was designed to increase that even further.
106. Ynze Alkema, "European-American Trade Policies, 1961–1963, in Brinkley and Griffiths, eds., *John F. Kennedy and Europe,* p. 226.
107. *New York Times,* January 12, 1962, quoted in Steve Dryden, *Trade Warriors* (New York: Oxford, 1995), p. 49.
108. Dryden, *Trade Warriors,* p. 49.
109. Alkema, "European-American Trade Policies," p. 212.
110. Dryden, *Trade Warriors,* p. 62. The Dillon Round, named for Douglas Dillon, the Eisenhower administration's undersecretary of state for economic affairs and later the Kennedy administration's secretary of the treasury, was the first major trade negotiation between the United States and the European Economic Community. The trade talks began in late 1960 and ended in early 1962 with a modest agreement concerning industrial goods.
111. Ibid., p. 62.
112. LBJL, Memo, Charles Murphy to LBJ, November 25, 1963, WHCF-International Trade, Box 2; Dryden, *Trade Warriors,* p. 77.
113. LBJL, Edward Fried, Oral History, p. 24.
114. Thomas Zeiler, *American Trade and Power in the 1960s* (New York: Columbia University Press, 1992), p. 177.
115. Dryden, *Trade Warriors,* p. 83.
116. LBJL, Bator to LBJ, July 20, 1964, Chronological File, Bator Papers, Box 1. Bator was born in Hungary and came to the United States shortly before World War II. Educated at Groton and MIT, Bator came to national prominence with the publication of his book, *The Question of Government Spending: Public Needs, Private Wants* (New York: Collier, 1960). He came to the White House in April 1964 to handle international economic matters for Bundy, and in the summer of 1965 received the portfolio for European policy.
117. Dryden, *Trade Warriors,* p. 86.

118. *FRUS 1964–1968*, 8, pp. 642–643.
119. *New York Times*, October 19, 1964, quoted in Dryden, *Trade Warriors*, p. 86.
120. *FRUS 1964–1968*, 8, pp. 668–672.
121. Ibid. See also Dryden, *Trade Warriors*, pp. 87–88. Dryden argues that Bundy was being disingenuous by arguing that the president would need to make the final decision, since Ball told the Office of the Special Trade Representative team that LBJ had agreed to "whatever" he and Bundy concluded. But this is a fundamental misunderstanding of the LBJ White House and the role of his advisors. Trade questions were primarily political ones for LBJ, and as it will become clear, the president always reserved the right to a final decision in the deals his negotiators made.
122. *FRUS 1964–1968*, 12, p. 65.
123. Ibid., 8, pp. 690–692.
124. The best recent account of the MLF issue, based on the extensive research done during the Nuclear History Project, is Christoph Hoppe, *Zwischen Teilhabe und Mitsprache: Die Nuklearfrage in der Allianzpolitik Deutschlands 1959–1966* (Baden-Baden: Nomos, 1993). Trachtenberg, *A Constructed Peace,* deals extensively with the MLF, and while I disagree with Trachtenberg on the "finality" of the European settlement reached after 1963, his account is extraordinarily well researched and argued. Another important account is Paul Hammond, *LBJ and the Presidential Management of Foreign Relations* (Austin: University of Texas Press, 1992). An earlier account is John D. Steinbrunner, *The Cybernetic Theory of Decision* (Princeton: Princeton University Press, 1974).
125. Kennedy meeting with Macmillan, December 19, 1962, quoted in Gavin, "Myth of Flexible Response," p. 857. As Gavin makes clear, Kennedy was far more open to nuclear sharing with the French than his State Department advisors, but the issue of how Germany would respond kept him from acting on this point.
126. Johnson speech, November 8, 1963, in *Department of State Bulletin,* Dec. 2, 1963, p. 852.
127. Gerard C. Smith, speech, April 22, 1964, in *American Foreign Policy: Current Documents 1964* (Washington, D.C.: G.P.O., 1967), p. 459.

128. LBJL, NSF Subject File, Box 23, Memo, Discussion of MLF, April 11, 1964.

129. *FRUS 1964–1968*, 13, p. 36, and LBJL, Henry Owen, Oral History, p. 11.

130. LBJL, Gerard Smith, Oral History, p. 7.

131. LBJL, NSF Subject File, Box 23, Rostow to LBJ, December 5, 1963.

132. Barnet, *The Alliance*, p. 240.

133. *FRUS 1964–1968*, 12, p. 50.

134. LBJL, "Wilson Visit and the MLF," memo of conversation, December 6, 1964, Richard Neustadt Papers, Box 2.

135. *FRUS 1964–1968*, 13, p. 36. See also LBJL, memo of conversation, December 8, 1964, Richard Neustadt Papers, Box 2; and Geyelin, *Lyndon B. Johnson and the World*, p. 159.

136. *FRUS 1964–1968*, 11, p. 264.

137. LBJL, NSF Subject File, Box 23, USIA Circular, "MLF Information Activities," June 1, 1964.

138. *FRUS 1964–1968*, 13, pp. 78–83. Haftendorn notes that this may have been one of the events that caused McGeorge Bundy to take an even more critical look at the MLF. Helga Haftendorn, *NATO and the Nuclear Revolution* (Oxford: Clarendon Press, 1996), p. 132.

139. Bundy believed that the French opposition may have been "decisive" in stopping the MLF. McGeorge Bundy, *Danger and Survival* (New York: Random House, 1988), p. 495.

140. Lacouture, *De Gaulle: The Ruler*, p. 359; *FRUS 1964–1968*, 13, p. 107.

141. Wilfried L. Kohl, *French Nuclear Diplomacy* (Princeton: Princeton University Press, 1971), p. 240.

142. Peyrefitte, *C'était de Gaulle*, vol. 2, p. 65. See also Georges-Henri Soutou, *L'Alliance incertaine: Les rapports politico-stratégiques franco-allemands 1954–1966* (Paris: Fayard, 1966), p. 279.

143. Rostow, *The Diffusion of Power*, p. 392.

144. LBJL, Gerard Smith, Oral History, p. 10.

145. *FRUS 1964–1968*, 13, p. 65.

146. Ibid., 14, p. 198.

147. Selvage, "The Warsaw Pact and Nuclear Nonproliferation, 1963–1965," p. 14. Selvage makes it clear that after the Chinese nuclear

test and the ouster of Khrushchev, the Warsaw Pact was able to unite behind a policy that linked the end of the MLF with any progress on nuclear nonproliferation.

148. *FRUS 1964–1968*, 13, p. 105.
149. *Time*, September 25, 1964, p. 17.
150. LBJL, NSF Subject File, Martin Hillenbrand to Klein, November 25, 1964, Box 23.
151. LBJL, NSF, Files of McGeorge Bundy, Kissinger to Bundy, November 27, 1964, Box 15.
152. *FRUS 1964–1968*, 13, p. 113.
153. LBJL, NSF Subject File, Letter, Joseph Clark and eight other senators to Rusk, September 7, 1964, Box 23.
154. *FRUS 1964–1968*, 13, p. 136.
155. Ibid., p. 133. FDR's court-packing plan comes up in a number of Johnson phone conversations. Michael Beschloss, *Reaching for Glory: Lyndon Johnson's Secret White House Tapes, 1964–1965* (New York: Simon and Schuster, 2001), p. 121.
156. *FRUS 1964–1968*, 13, pp. 134–137.
157. LBJL, "Wilson Visit and the MLF," Memo of Conversation, December 6, 1964, Richard Neustadt Papers, Box 2. One wonders why Johnson did not employ this eminently sensible bit of folksy wisdom to his Vietnam decisions.
158. *FRUS 1964–1968*, 13, p. 139.
159. Note for the record, December 7, 1964, PREM 13/103, PRO, London.
160. *FRUS 1964–1968*, 14, p. 199.
161. To make sure that MLF supporters got the message, Johnson deliberately leaked his decision to James Reston of the *New York Times*. Geyelin, *Lyndon B. Johnson and the World*, pp. 171–177.
162. Schlesinger, *A Thousand Days*, p. 797.

2. POLICY IN THE SHADOWS

1. *Newsweek*, January 11, 1965, p. 15.
2. Chen Jian, *Mao's China and the Cold War* (Chapel Hill: University of North Carolina Press, 2001), pp. 211–212. Chen Jian makes it clear

that China's revolutionary posture during these years, and its outspoken support for North Vietnam, was related to "the ambitious Maoist revolutionary program of transforming China and the world."
3. *Newsweek,* January 11, 1965, p. 16.
4. *FRUS 1964–1968,* 14, p. 211, for LBJ's message of January 14, 1965, and p. 229, for the Soviet reply expressing interest in an exchange of visits.
5. *Time,* December 3, 1965, p. 28.
6. Even sympathetic observers perceived this. A cartoon by Bob Taylor in the *Dallas Times Herald* portrayed LBJ soaring toward heaven with his beloved little angel "Domestic Policy," while the abandoned angel "Foreign Policy" struggled to get off the ground. Gary Yarrington, ed., *LBJ Political Cartoons: The Public Years* (Austin: LBJL, 1988), p. 42.
7. *FRUS 1964–1968,* 14, p. 235.
8. Ibid., 13, p. 159.
9. *Time,* December 25, 1964, p. 18.
10. *FRUS 1964–1968,* 13, pp. 169–171.
11. Ibid., 15, pp. 204–206.
12. Ibid., p. 210.
13. Karl Carstens to Schröder, February 28, 1965, Gerhard Schröder Nachlass, I 483, 285/1, CDU Archive, Bonn.
14. *Time,* January 15, 1965, p. 31. Tensions between the United States and West Germany had also developed when, in February 1965, Germany's secret deliveries of tanks—U.S.-built M-48s—to Israel were revealed and created a severe crisis for Bonn in the Arab world. The United States had pressured Germany to provide the tanks in an effort to protect Washington's standing among the Arab states, but the result was damage to Germany's own prominent role in the Middle East and embarrassment for the Erhard government, especially when Egypt decided to retaliate against Bonn and invited the East German leader Walter Ulbricht to visit Cairo. William Glenn Gray, "West Germany's 'Stalingrad on the Nile': Johnson, Erhard, and the Tanks-to-Israel Imbroglio," unpublished paper, June 2002. My thanks to Professor Gray for providing me a copy of his paper.
15. HSTL, Rostow to Tyler, "Germany, March 1965," Papers of Dean Acheson, Box 88.

16. Birrenbach to McCloy, January 25, 1965, McCloy to Birrenbach, January 29, 1965, in Birrenbach NL, I-433, 210/1, CDU Archive, Bonn.

17. The coverage of this issue in the *New York Times* was extensive and included the resignation of one West German cabinet minister after the extension of the statute of limitations was passed. *New York Times,* March 22, 1965.

18. Douglas Brinkley, *Dean Acheson: The Cold War Years, 1953–1971* (New Haven: Yale University Press, 1992), p. 225.

19. Birrenbach, Report on trip to the United States, March 15, 1965, Birrenbach NL, I-433, CDU Archive, Bonn.

20. *FRUS 1964–1968,* 13, pp. 188–189.

21. Ibid., p. 188.

22. Jane E. Stromseth, *The Origins of Flexible Response* (London: Mac-Millan, 1988), p. 80.

23. Helga Haftendorn, *NATO and the Nuclear Revolution* (Oxford: Clarendon Press, 1996), p. 161.

24. *FRUS 1964–1968,* 13, p. 213.

25. Glenn T. Seaborg and Benjamin S. Loeb, *Stemming the Tide: Arms Control in the Johnson Years* (Lexington, Mass.: Lexington Books, 1987), pp. 136–137.

26. *FRUS 1964–1968,* 11, pp. 173–182.

27. Seaborg and Loeb, *Stemming the Tide,* p. 145. Louis Heren comments on Rusk's "extraordinary" relationship with Anatoly Dobrynin, and in this matter Rusk recognized how central the German issue was to Soviet interest in the NPT. Louis Heren, *No Hail, No Farewell* (New York: Harper and Row, 1970), p. 155.

28. Shane Maddock, "The Nth Country Conundrum: The American and Soviet Quest for Nuclear Nonproliferation, 1945–1970," Ph.D. diss., University of Connecticut, 1997, p. 467, and Seaborg and Loeb, *Stemming the Tide,* p. 148.

29. Seaborg and Loeb, *Stemming the Tide,* p. 148.

30. Joseph A. Califano, Jr., *The Triumph and Tragedy of Lyndon Johnson* (New York: Simon and Schuster, 1991), p. 124.

31. In opposition to this view, Maddock argues that "if Johnson had proven more decisive in his early days in office and made a clear decision between the MLF and NPT, an agreement might have been

negotiated as early as 1964 or 1965." Maddock, "Nth Country Conundrum," p. 523. Johnson's reluctance to break decisively with commitments made by two previous presidents on the MLF had obvious parallels with his Vietnam decisions, although his ultimate willingness to do so led to progress on nonproliferation.

32. Seaborg and Loeb, *Stemming the Tide,* p. 158.
33. The speech is in *RFK: Collected Speeches,* ed. Edwin O. Guthman and C. Richard Allen (New York: Viking, 1993), pp. 218–222. See also Jeff Shesol, *Mutual Contempt* (New York: Norton, 1997), pp. 269–273.
34. Edwin O. Guthman and Jeffrey Shulman, *Robert Kennedy: In His Own Words* (New York: Bantam, 1988), p. 327.
35. *RFK: Collected Speeches,* p. 218.
36. Michael R. Beschloss, ed., *Reaching for Glory: Lyndon Johnson's Secret White House Tapes, 1964–1965* (New York: Simon and Schuster, 2001), pp. 368 and 369. These statements were made in two telephone calls with McGeorge Bundy, WH6506.06 PNO15 and WH6506.07 PNO2, which show a more measured reaction by Johnson to Kennedy's speech, a reaction that demonstrates LBJ's understanding of how the speech could be helpful *as well as* his irritation with Kennedy. In parts of the conversations left out of the Beschloss book, Johnson notes that the United States still needs to "sit down with the allies" to discuss an approach to nonproliferation, and regretfully agrees with Bundy's comment that "people will play it as if this was something [Kennedy] prodded us into."
37. Richard N. Goodwin, *Remembering America: A Voice from the Sixties* (Boston: Little, Brown, 1988), p. 397.
38. Beschloss, *Reaching for Glory,* p. 371. Beschloss repeats the argument, also in Shesol's book, that Johnson eliminated from his UN speech "dramatic proposals to reduce nuclear proliferation" solely because of his political rivalry with Kennedy.
39. *FRUS 1964–1968,* 11, p. 216.
40. *New York Times,* July 1, 1965. Johnson knew Kennedy had the Gilpatric report and expected him to leak it. Beschloss, *Reaching for Glory,* p. 368.
41. William C. Foster, "New Directions in Arms Control and Disarmament," *Foreign Affairs* 43, no. 4 (July 1965): 600–601.

42. Bundy, quoted in Seaborg and Loeb, *Stemming the Tide,* p. 149.
43. *AAPD 1965,* II, document 275, July 9, 1965, p. 1157.
44. Ibid., document 311, July 30, 1965, p. 1299.
45. Catherine Kelleher, *Germany and the Politics of Nuclear Weapons* (New York: Columbia University Press, 1975), p. 258. Strauss also attacked the NPT as nuclear colonialism, and demanded an absolutely clear American guarantee for Germany's security. Wolfram Bickerich, *Franz Josef Strauss: Die Biographie* (Düsseldorf: ECON, 1996), p. 204.
46. *AAPD 1965,* II, document 306, July 27, 1965, pp. 1285–1286.
47. LBJL, telegram, Washington to Bonn, July 9, 1965, NSF, Country File Europe and USSR, Boxes 179–186.
48. *FRUS 1964–1968,* 13, p. 245.
49. Ibid.
50. LBJL, NSF, Subject File, "A Reexamination of Premises on the German Problem," December 9, 1965, Box 186.
51. *FRUS 1964–1968,* 13, p. 262.
52. Ibid., 11, pp. 264–267.
53. A. J. Langguth, *Our Vietnam: The War 1954–1975* (New York: Simon and Schuster, 2000), pp. 407–408.
54. Memo, McNamara to Johnson, November 30, 1965, quoted in *Encyclopedia of the Vietnam War,* ed. Spencer C. Tucker (New York: Oxford, 2000), p. 516.
55. George C. Herring, *LBJ and Vietnam: A Different Kind of War* (Austin: University of Texas Press, 1994), pp. 42–43.
56. Stewart to Wilson, December 10, 1965, PREM 13/686, PRO/London.
57. Memorandum, Wilson-LBJ meeting, December 16, 1965, PREM 13/686, PRO/London, and *FRUS 1964–1968,* 13, pp. 284–285.
58. Birrenbach to Erhard, November 16, 1965, Birrenbach NL, I-433, 117/1, CDU Archive, Bonn.
59. Memo, Birrenbach to Foreign Minister Schröder, November 9, 1965, Birrenbach NL, I-433, 117/1, CDU Archive, Bonn.
60. *AAPD 1965,* 3, Document 445, Conversation between Erhard and McCloy, December 6, 1965, p. 1846.
61. Acheson, quoted in Horst Osterheld, *Aussenpolitik unter Bundeskanzler Erhard, 1963–1966* (Düsseldorf: Droste, 1992), p. 268. Acheson stressed the same point to Birrenbach, and was so emphatic

in his support for the MLF that Birrenbach was "sehr ermutigt" (very encouraged). Kurt Birrenbach, *Meine Sondermissionen: Rückblick auf zwei Jahrzehnte bundesdeutscher Aussenpolitik* (Düsseldorf: Econ, 1984), p. 186.

62. Osterheld, *Aussenpolitik unter Bundeskanzler Erhard*, p. 269.
63. For the other issues Johnson addressed in his meeting with Erhard, see the last part of this chapter.
64. *FRUS 1964–1968*, 13, pp. 295–296.
65. For example, see Diane Kunz, *Butter and Guns* (New York: Free Press, 1997), p. 110.
66. Robert M. Collins, *More: The Politics of Economic Growth in Postwar America* (New York: Oxford University Press, 2000), p. 61.
67. Goodwin, *Remembering America*, p. 270.
68. Califano, *Triumph and Tragedy*, p. 75.
69. James E. Anderson and Jared E. Hazelton, *Managing Macroeconomic Policy: The Johnson Presidency* (Austin: University of Texas Press, 1986), p. 227.
70. Arthur Schlesinger, *A Thousand Days: John F. Kennedy in the White House* (Boston: Houghton Mifflin, 1965), p. 601.
71. Francis J. Gavin, "The Myth of Flexible Response: United States Strategy in Europe during the 1960s," *International History Review* 23, no. 4 (December 2001): 847–875. Gavin makes it clear that "flexible response" was far more a political strategy than a military one, and that Kennedy's concern about the balance of payments led him to want cuts that would have reduced U.S. forces in Europe to no more than a "tripwire" against a Soviet invasion and the inevitable nuclear response.
72. Burton Kaufman, "Foreign Aid and the Balance of Payments Problem: Vietnam and Johnson's Foreign Economic Policy," in *The Johnson Years*, vol. 2, ed. Robert A. Divine (Lawrence: University Press of Kansas, 1987), p. 80.
73. Thomas Zoumaras, "Plugging the Dike: The Kennedy Administration Confronts the Balance of Payments Crisis with Europe," in *John F. Kennedy and Europe*, ed. Douglas Brinkley and Richard T. Griffiths (Baton Rouge: Louisiana State University Press, 1999), p. 169.
74. Theodore Sorenson, *Kennedy* (New York: Harper and Row, 1965), p. 458.

75. For an excellent discussion of the political implications of the struggle over gold, see Frank Gavin, "The Gold Battles within the Cold War: American Monetary Policy and the Defense of Europe 1960–1963," *Diplomatic History* 26, no. 1 (Winter 2002): 61–94.

76. Kaufman, "Foreign Aid and the Balance of Payments Problem," p. 83.

77. *AAPD 1963*, III, document 486, Conversation between LBJ and Erhard, December 28, 1963, p. 1673.

78. *FRUS 1964–1968*, 8, p. 26.

79. Kaufman, "Foreign Aid and the Balance of Payments Problem," p. 86.

80. *FRUS 1964–1968*, 8, p. 97.

81. Charles Coombs, *The Arena of International Finance* (New York: John Wiley and Sons, 1976), p. 86.

82. Raj Roy, "The Battle over the Pound, 1964–1968," Ph.D. diss., London School of Economics, 2000, p. 11.

83. James A. Bill, *George Ball: Behind the Scenes in U.S. Foreign Policy* (New Haven: Yale University Press, 1997), pp. 112–119.

84. LBJ to Douglas-Home, December 1, 1963, PREM 11/4794, PRO, London.

85. Bundy memo for the record, December 7, 1964, quoted in Jeremy Fielding, "Coping with Decline: U.S. Policy toward the British Defense Reviews of 1966," *Diplomatic History* 23, no. 4 (Fall 1999): 639.

86. Roy, "Battle over the Pound," p. 15.

87. Kenneth O. Morgan, *Callaghan: A Life* (New York: Oxford University Press, 1997), p. 203.

88. LBJL, Telephone conversation between Ball and James Reston, Papers of George Ball, October 16, 1964, Box 1.

89. Notes from meeting between David Bruce and Patrick Gordon-Walker, October 18, 1964, Diaries of David Bruce, VHS, Richmond.

90. This is the argument put forth cogently and convincingly in Roy, "Battle over the Pound," pp. 47–50.

91. *FRUS 1964–1968*, 8, p. 29. Some in Wilson's government worried that an increase in the bank rate during the same week that Johnson had been embarrassed by the arrest of his close aide, Walter Jenkins,

in a Washington men's restroom might hurt LBJ seriously in the contest with Goldwater. With a reference to one of Britain's 18th-century conflicts—the war of Jenkins' Ear—one wag remarked that "the war of Jenkins' Rear" should not be allowed to contribute to a Republican victory. Alec Cairncross, *The Wilson Years: A Treasury Diary 1964–1969* (London: Historians Press, 1997), p. 19.

92. Califano, *Triumph and Tragedy,* p. 106, and Eric Roll, *Crowded Hours* (London: Faber and Faber, 1985), p. 157. When Roll, the British economic minister in the Washington embassy, tried to defend the increase, LBJ told him, "this is all a lot of chickenshit." Roy, "Battle over the Pound," p. 32.

93. Cairncross, *The Wilson Years,* p. 18.

94. Note for the Record, Conversation between Wilson and Bruce, November 27, 1964, PREM 13/103, PRO, London.

95. *FRUS 1964–1968,* 13, p. 138.

96. Record of meeting, December 7, 1964, PREM 13/252, PRO, London.

97. Georges-Henri Soutou, *L'Alliance incertaine: Les rapports politico-stratégiques franco-allemands 1954–1966* (Paris: Fayard, 1966), p. 287.

98. A Herblock cartoon of March 2, 1965, used the popular James Bond movie *Goldfinger* to parody "Gaullefinger" and his efforts to drain America's gold from Fort Knox. Herbert Bloch, *The Herblock Gallery* (New York: Simon and Schuster, 1968), p. 29.

99. Meeting in Washington, December 7, 1964, PREM 13/104, PRO, London.

100. Note of meeting in Washington, June 29, 1965, PREM 13/216, PRO, London.

101. William Roger Louis, in a presidential address to the American Historical Association, makes the argument that "the United States might have lent support to Britain in a catastrophic war against Indonesia if Sukarno had not followed a path of self-destruction." William Roger Louis, "The Dissolution of the British Empire in the Era of Vietnam," *American Historical Review* 107, no. 1 (February 2002): 16. Although the evidence Louis cites for this conclusion is thin, there is no question that American officials, including LBJ, greatly valued the British protection for Malaysia and the British stance against Sukarno's expansionist threats.

102. Robert Solomon, *The International Monetary System, 1945–1981* (New York: Harper and Row, 1982), pp. 72–73.
103. LBJL, Memorandum to the president, August 10, 1964, Bator Papers, CF, Box 1.
104. *FRUS 1964–1968,* 8, p. 64.
105. *FRUS 1964–1968,* 8, pp. 98–100.
106. Kaufman, "Foreign Aid and the Balance of Payments Problem," p. 87.
107. Ibid., p. 88.
108. Memo from the president to the secretary of the Treasury, June 6, 1965, reprinted in Lyndon B. Johnson, *The Vantage Point: Perspectives of the Presidency, 1963–1969* (New York: Holt, Rinehart, and Winston, 1971), Appendix II, pp. 597–598.
109. *FRUS 1964–1968,* 8, p. 170.
110. John S. Odell, *U.S. International Monetary Policy* (Princeton: Princeton University Press, 1982), p. 130.
111. Ibid., pp. 93–94.
112. *Newsweek,* July 5, 1965, p. 72.
113. Roy, "Battle over the Pound," p. 13.
114. Meeting of Ball, Callaghan, and McNamara, June 30, 1965, PREM 13/253, PRO, London. This was Callaghan's impression from his talks with the French finance minister.
115. *Newsweek,* July 5, 1965, p. 71.
116. Johnson, *Vantage Point,* pp. 597–598.
117. Philip Kaiser, *Journeying Far and Wide: A Political and Diplomatic Memoir* (New York: Macmillan, 1992), p. 226.
118. Telephone conversation between Bundy and Mitchell, March 30, 1965, PREM 13/672, PRO, London.
119. Memo by Wilson of talk with LBJ, April 15, 1965, PREM 13/532, PRO, London.
120. Bruce diary, March 22, 1965, VHS, Richmond.
121. Meeting between Wilson and Fowler, April 15, 1965, PREM 13/532, PRO, London.
122. The United States sent military forces into the island nation of the Dominican Republic in May 1965 to prevent a leftist takeover. The British doubted the seriousness of the threat, and thought the United States had overreacted. Healey objected to the unilateralism of this action as well as to the dispatch of the first Marines to Vietnam in

March 1965. Talks between McNamara and Healey, May 30, 1965, PREM 13/214, PRO, London.

123. Bruce diary, June 24, 1965, VHS, Richmond.

124. Meeting with the president, June 28, 1965, PREM 13/253, PRO, London.

125. Bruce diary, June 29, 1965, VHS, Richmond.

126. Roy, "Battle over the Pound," p. 133.

127. Meeting at the Federal Reserve Bank, June 30, 1965, PREM 13/253, PRO, London.

128. Note of meeting in Washington, June 29, 1965, PREM 13/216, PRO, London.

129. PREM 13/672, Note for the record, July 5, 1965, PRO, London.

130. Bruce diary, July 2, 1965, VHS, Richmond.

131. Memo, Brown to Wilson, July 23, 1965, PREM 13/255, PRO, London.

132. Bruce diary, July 26, 1965, VHS, Richmond.

133. *FRUS 1964–1968,* 8, p. 176.

134. Record of telephone conversation, Mitchell and Bundy, July 27, 1965, PREM 13/255, PRO, London.

135. Meeting with Fowler, July 31, 1965, PREM 13/672, PRO, London.

136. LBJL, Bundy to LBJ, July 28, 1965, Bundy Files, NSF, Box 10.

137. LBJL, Telephone conversation between Ball and Bundy, George Ball Papers, Box 1.

138. LBJL, Notes from meeting with LBJ, July 29, 1965, Bator Papers, Box 23.

139. LBJL, Memo for the president, August 2, 1965, CF, McGeorge Bundy Files, Box 10.

140. *FRUS 1964–1968,* 8, p. 179.

141. Roy, "Battle over the Pound," p. 176.

142. LBJL, Telephone conversation between LBJ and Black, August 5, 1965, WH6508.01.

143. LBJL, Telephone conversation between LBJ and Martin, August 5, 1965, WH6508.02.

144. LBJL, Notes of a meeting with the president, August 6, 1965, Bator Papers, Box 23.

145. LBJL, Bator to Bundy, July 29, 1965, Bator Papers, CF, Box 2.

146. Clive Ponting, *Breach of Promise* (London: Hamish Hamilton, 1989), pp. 48–53.

147. LBJL, Cable from Rusk to Ball, September 7, 1965, Bator Papers, Box 22.

148. Notes of meeting, September 9, 1965, PREM 13/674, PRO, London.

149. Ibid.

150. Roy, "Battle over the Pound," p. 190.

151. LBJL, Bator to LBJ, September 1, 1965, Bator Papers, Box 23.

152. Ilya V. Gaiduk, *The Soviet Union and the Vietnam War* (Chicago: Ivan R. Dee, 1996), p. 36.

153. Michael Mastanduno, *Economic Containment: CoCom and the Politics of East-West Trade* (Ithaca: Cornell University Press, 1992), p. 136.

154. Ibid., pp. 135–139.

155. Walter Lippmann, "The Rest of the World," *Newsweek*, June 21, 1965, p. 21.

156. *Newsweek*, May 17, 1965, p. 30.

157. The *New York Times*, on October 17, 1965, reported on demonstrations with 1,500 people in London, 2,000 in Rome, 900 in Brussels, and 300 in Stockholm.

158. Meeting, French foreign minister Couve de Murville and Romanian president Ceausescu, April 28, 1966, *Cabinet du Ministre/Cabinet Couve de Murville*, MAE, Box 382.

159. Sylvia A. Ellis, "Lyndon Johnson, Harold Wilson and the Vietnam War: A *Not* So Special Relationship?" in Jonathan Hollowell, ed., *Twentieth-Century Anglo-American Relations* (New York: Palgrave, 2001), p. 195.

160. LBJL, Memo of telephone conversation between Wilson and LBJ, February 10, 1965, NSF Memos to the president, Bundy Files, Box 2.

161. Meeting of Bruce and Wilson, March 12, 1965, PREM 13/3021, PRO, London. Louis emphasizes the degree to which LBJ's decision to escalate the war in 1965 "summoned memories in Britain of the Suez crisis of 1956." Louis, "The Dissolution of the British Empire in the Era of Vietnam," p. 24.

162. David Easter, "British Defense Policy in South East Asia and the Confrontation, 1960–1966," Ph.D. diss., London School of Economics, March 1998, p. 412.

163. British political cartoonists frequently lampooned Wilson for his subservience to LBJ. One cartoon pictured the British leader as a di-

minutive Boy Scout asking the giant Texan, "Carry your bags, sir?" with the bags labeled "Vietnam" and "Dominican Republic." Ellis, "Lyndon Johnson, Harold Wilson and the Vietnam War," p. 194.

164. Survey of British elite opinion, December 1965, PREM 13/689, PRO, London. Peter Busch, in his dissertation on British policy toward Vietnam during the Kennedy era, also refutes the myth that the British were always opposed to the U.S. presence there. He notes that the Tory government of Macmillan had been quite sympathetic to the U.S. position in Southeast Asia and that British skepticism became pronounced only with the election of Harold Wilson and the Labour government. Peter Busch, "Britain and Kennedy's War in Vietnam, 1961–1963," Ph.D. diss., London School of Economics, 1999, pp. 304–305.

165. Joachim Arenth, *Johnson, Vietnam und der Westen: Transatlantische Belastungen 1963–1969* (Munich: Olzog, 1994), p. 165, and Alexandra Friedrich, "Awakenings: The Impact of the Vietnam War on West German–American Relations in the 1960s," Ph.D. diss., Temple University, 2000, p. xi.

166. Wilfried Mausbach, "Defending Berlin in Saigon: The Dilemmas of West German Support for America's War," unpublished paper, Vietnam War Symposium, University of California, Santa Barbara, January 1999, p. 2.

167. LBJL, Memo of conversation between Erhard and Rusk, June 4, 1965, NSF, Germany, Box 185.

168. Meeting between Secretary-General of the French Foreign Ministry Hervé Alphand and State Secretary Karl Carstens, February 7, 1966, *Cabinet du Ministre/Cabinet Couve de Murville*, MAE, Box 382.

169. *FRUS 1964–1968*, 3, p. 112.

170. Elisabeth Noelle and Erich Peter Neumann, eds., *Jahrbuch der öffentlichen Meinung 1965–1967* (Allensbach and Bonn: Verlag für Demoskopie, 1967), pp. 475–480.

171. LBJL, Kissinger conversation with Adenauer, June 22, 1965, NSF, Bundy Files, box 15.

172. LBJL, George McGhee, Oral History, p. 19.

173. *FRUS 1964–1968*, 15, p. 112. "More Flags" was the Johnson administration's attempt to get as many countries in the West as possible to send troops or give other support to South Vietnam.

174. Mausbach, "Defending Berlin in Saigon," p. 8.
175. Ibid., p. 9.
176. *FRUS 1964–1968*, 8, p. 199.
177. Ibid., p. 205.
178. Lady Bird Johnson, *A White House Diary* (New York: Holt, Rinehart, and Winston, 1970), p. 342. A recently released telephone conversation also indicates that Secretary of Defense McNamara told the president on the morning of his meeting with Erhard that LBJ would need to tell the chancellor that "we have to have it," referring to the offset, and that his German counterpart, Defense Minister von Hassell, had told McNamara that the chancellor would have to intervene personally to ensure that the United States received its offset payments and that Germany provided aid to Vietnam. LBJL, Telephone conversation between McNamara and LBJ, December 20, 1965, WH6512.03.
179. Goodwin, *Remembering America*, p. 283.
180. NARS, RG 59, McGhee to Leddy, January 13, 1966, State Department Conference Files, Box 393. McGhee's letter begins by noting, "Because of its sensitive nature, I hesitated to write a minute of the meeting between Chancellor Erhard and the President held on December 19 upstairs at the White House following the dinner." McGhee may have worried about the political fallout for Erhard—or for LBJ—should the nature of the meeting become known.
181. George McGhee, *At the Creation of a New Germany* (New Haven: Yale University Press, 1989), p. 184.
182. *AAPD 1965*, III, 469, p. 1941.
183. McGhee, *At the Creation*, p. 185.
184. Lt. Gen. Stanley Robert Larsen and Brig. Gen. James Lawton Collins, Jr., *Allied Participation in Vietnam* (Washington, D.C.: G.P.O., 1975), pp. 164–165. Erhard faced severe criticism within his party for even these small steps on Vietnam. Franz Josef Strauss, *Die Erinnerungen* (Berlin: Siedler, 1989), p. 429.

3. THE FRENCH CHALLENGE

1. Letter, Dean to Sir Paul Gore-Booth, February 26, 1966, FO 371/185010, PRO, London. A few months later Dean noted that the

president "is not a man who likes to make up his mind before he has to." Telegram, Dean to Foreign Office, July 16, 1966, PREM 13/ 1262, PRO, London.

2. Joseph A. Califano, Jr., *The Triumph and Tragedy of Lyndon Johnson* (New York: Simon and Schuster, 1991), p. 173.

3. Douglas Brinkley, *Dean Acheson: The Cold War Years, 1953–1971* (New Haven: Yale University Press, 1992), p. 226.

4. Helga Haftendorn, *NATO and the Nuclear Revolution* (Oxford: Clarendon Press, 1996), p. 1.

5. Ibid., p. 2.

6. Frank Costigliola, *France and the United States: The Cold Alliance since World War II* (New York: Twayne, 1992), p. 142.

7. NARS Record Group 306, USIA, Office of Research, Survey of French opinion, May 1966, Box 2.

8. LBJL, National Security Action Memorandum 336, "Potentially Embarrassing Activities in France or in Areas outside France Which Are Controlled by the French Government," August 6, 1965, Box 171. Much of this NSAM is still classified.

9. Wilfried L. Kohl, *French Nuclear Diplomacy* (Princeton: Princeton University Press, 1971), p. 249.

10. *Newsweek,* November 1, 1965. p. 44.

11. Ibid., December 13, 1965, p. 42.

12. Alain Peyrifitte, *C'était de Gaulle,* vol. 2 (Paris: Fayard, 1997), pp. 48–49.

13. Meeting, de Gaulle and Adenauer, March 10, 1966, *Cabinet du Ministre/Cabinet Couve de Murville,* MAE, Box 382.

14. Thomas W. Zeiler, *Dean Rusk: Defending the American Mission Abroad* (Wilmington, Del.: Scholarly Resources, 2000), p. 221.

15. *FRUS 1964–1968,* 13, p. 226.

16. Ibid.

17. As Charles Cogan has noted, this Gaullist legacy would help to "impede the integration of the EEC for nearly twenty years" after the compromise was reached. Charles G. Cogan, *Charles de Gaulle* (New York: Bedford Books, 1996), p. 161, and *FRUS 1964–1968,* 13, p. 308.

18. *FRUS 1964–1968,* 13, pp. 230–231.

19. LBJL, NSAM 36, August 14, 1965, NSF, France, Box 171.

20. Francis Bator later recalled that both he and Bundy simultaneously

looked up at each other and smiled as others in the meeting made the Article V argument—because they recognized that simple geography—it was impossible for the United States to defend West Germany without defending France—made the threat a pointless one. Interview with Francis Bator, December 16, 1995, Cambridge, Massachusetts.

21. *FRUS 1964–1968,* 13, p. 258.
22. Ibid., p. 309.
23. Francis J. Gavin, "The Myth of Flexible Response: United States Strategy in Europe during the 1960s," *International History Review* 23, no. 4 (December 2001): 865–868.
24. *FRUS 1964–1968,* 13, p. 304.
25. Ibid., pp. 254–257.
26. Kohl, *French Nuclear Diplomacy,* p. 253.
27. Paper, "De Gaulle's Election Victory," January 14, 1966, FO 371/ 189105, PRO, London.
28. *Newsweek,* March 21, 1966, p. 46.
29. Georges-Henri Soutou, *L'Alliance incertaine: Les rapports politico-stratégiques franco-allemands 1954–1966* (Paris: Fayard, 1966), pp. 301–305. Soutou's comment about France and Russia's "natural affinity" refers to a toast offered by de Gaulle in March 1965 on the occasion of the departure from Paris of a Soviet ambassador. Soutou makes the important point that this approach was also a return to the policy de Gaulle tried to follow when he became the leader of France in 1944, demonstrated by the friendship treaty he signed with the Soviet Union at that time.
30. De Gaulle said different things to different people about his ultimate objectives. De Gaulle told *New York Times* correspondent Cyrus Sulzberger that he wanted to move toward bilateral alliances, and then later in 1966 that "we will remain in the Alliance." But he always added that "things can change in the future." Cyrus Sulzberger, *An Age of Mediocrity: Memoirs and Diaries 1963–1972* (New York: Macmillan, 1973), p. 306.
31. Hervé Alphand, *L'Étonnement d'être: Journal 1939–1973* (Paris: Fayard, 1977), p. 453. Bozo argues that de Gaulle did not seek to replace the alliance, only to "relegitimate" it by taking France outside the integrated defense. Frédéric Bozo, *Two Strategies for Europe: De*

Gaulle, the United States, and the Atlantic Alliance, trans. Susan Emanuel (Lanham, Md.: Rowman and Littlefield, 2001), p. 188. My argument with his impressive book is that it mistakes the surprisingly benign results of the French withdrawal for de Gaulle's original intentions, and underestimates the subsequent efforts of the United States to thwart de Gaulle's policies. History could have turned in a very different direction.

32. Cogan, *Charles de Gaulle,* p. 129.
33. *FRUS 1964–1968,* 13, pp. 323–324.
34. LBJL, Bohlen to LBJ, March 11, 1964, NSF, France, Box 169.
35. *FRUS 1964–1968,* 12, p. 56.
36. Ibid.
37. Ibid., p. 45.
38. Bohlen to Rusk, March 7, 1966, NARS, Central Files, DEF 4 NATO, Box 2186. Bohlen's reaction highlights LBJ's restraint. When Johnson was later praised for his "wise judgment" in dealing with de Gaulle, it was still said that LBJ "echoed the opinion of his brilliant, levelheaded Ambassador in Paris, Chip Bohlen." Cyrus Sulzberger, in *New York Times,* June 23, 1968.
39. *FRUS 1964–1968,* 13, p. 325.
40. Memo of conversation with M. de la Rochefordiére, March 18, 1966, FO 371/189105, PRO, London.
41. Rusk to LBJ, June 8, 1966, NARS, DEF 4 NATO, CF, Box 11.
42. *FRUS 1964–1968,* 13, p. 324.
43. LBJL, Bator to LBJ, March 8, 1966, Bator Papers, CF, Box 3.
44. *FRUS 1964–1968,* 13, p. 326.
45. Ibid., p. 327.
46. Ibid., p. 337.
47. Thomas J. Schoenbaum, *Waging Peace and War: Dean Rusk in the Truman, Kennedy, and Johnson Years* (New York: Simon and Schuster, 1988), p. 421.
48. Bill Mauldin, *I've Decided I Want My Seat Back* (New York: Harper and Row, 1965), p. 109.
49. *FRUS 1964–1968,* 13, p. 452.
50. Robert David Johnson, "The Government Operations Committee and Foreign Policy during the Cold War," *Political Science Quarterly* 113, no. 4 (1998–99): 662.

51. *FRUS 1964–1968,* 13, p. 337.

52. Ibid., p. 336.

53. Interview with Francis Bator, December 19, 1995.

54. As respected a historian as Warren Cohen wrote, "Perhaps as a result of advice from men like Bundy and Bohlen, his ambassador to France, Johnson was uncharacteristically tactful in all of his dealings with the French president." Warren Cohen, *Dean Rusk* (Totowa, N.J.: Cooper Square, 1980), p. 262. However, Bundy had left the government by this point, and Bohlen's response to de Gaulle's step broke from his earlier advocacy of restraint. H. W. Brands is a noteworthy exception to this tendency of historians to credit Johnson's advisers for anything he did right in foreign policy. H. W. Brands, *The Wages of Globalism* (New York: Oxford University Press, 1995) p. 102.

55. A Gallup poll found that well over half of all Americans did not believe France was "a dependable ally of the United States," and this figure was almost two-thirds for college-educated Americans. George Gallup, *The Gallup Poll 1935–1971* (Wilmington, Del.: Scholarly Resources, 1972), p. 2017.

56. *New York Times,* March 21, 1966.

57. LBJL, George Ball, Oral History, p. 24.

58. *FRUS 1964–1968,* 13, p. 349. Bator had to fight to keep this sentence in, appealing directly to Johnson over the head of the State Department drafters of the message. He told LBJ that the line was "*not designed to conciliate de Gaulle*" (his emphasis) but was primarily intended to drive home the distinction between de Gaulle and France. It was also, Bator admitted, because he was "thinking what historians will say about this letter in 5–10 years—especially if things go wrong, and America is unfairly blamed by some Europeans for splitting Europe." LBJL, Bator to LBJ, March 18, 1966, Bator Papers, CF, Box 3. Frank Costigliola dissects Bator's language and argues that this sentence contains a "gender-coded" formulation that indicates the continuing American desire to dominate both France and the alliance. Costigliola, *Cold Alliance,* pp. 145–146.

59. *FRUS 1964–1968,* 13, p. 376.

60. George Ball, *The Past Has Another Pattern* (New York: Norton, 1982), p. 336.

61. Lyndon B. Johnson, *The Vantage Point: Perspectives of the Presidency, 1963–1969* (New York: Holt, Rinehart, and Winston, 1971), p. 305.
62. *FRUS 1964–1968*, 13, p. 357.
63. Ibid., p. 376.
64. Telegram 913, Washington to Foreign Office, March 17, 1966, PREM 13/1043, PRO, London.
65. *FRUS 1964–1968*, 13, p. 354.
66. LBJL, NSF, Agency File, NATO, vol. 3, George Ball, Memorandum for the president, "Guidance for John J. McCloy," April 10, 1966.
67. LBJL, Telegram, Bator to LBJ, April 11, 1966, Bator Papers, CF, Box 3.
68. *FRUS 1964–1968*, 13, p. 367.
69. Ibid., p. 441.
70. Lawrence S. Kaplan, *NATO and the United States* (Boston: Twayne, 1988), p. 121.
71. Letter, Acheson to Anthony Eden, March 15, 1967, Papers of Dean Acheson, Box 9, Folder 118, Yale University Library.
72. Interview with Francis Bator, Cambridge, Mass., December 16, 1995.
73. *FRUS 1964–1968*, 13, pp. 391–392. For Acheson's own account of this meeting, and his subsequent rapprochement with LBJ, see his letter to Anthony Eden, June 29, 1966, in *Among Friends: Personal Letters of Dean Acheson*, ed. Davis S. McLellan and David C. Acheson (New York: Dodd, Mead and Co., 1980), p. 279.
74. *FRUS 1964–1968*, 13, pp. 374–375.
75. Brinkley, *Dean Acheson*, p. 234.
76. LBJL, Bator to Moyers, April 12, 1966, Bator Papers, CF, Box 3.
77. *FRUS 1964–1968*, 13, pp. 407–408.
78. LBJL, Bator to LBJ, April 4, 1966, Bator Papers, CF, Box 3.
79. *FRUS 1964–1968*, 13, p. 397.
80. Ibid., p. 396.
81. LBJL, Bator to LBJ, "A Nuclear Role for Germany: What Do the Germans Want?" April 4, 1966, Bator Papers, CF, Box 3.
82. *FRUS 1964–1968*, 13, p. 397.
83. Wilson to LBJ, February 26, 1966, PREM 13/1216, PRO, London.
84. Dean to Hood, April 22, 1966, FO 371/190665, PRO, London.

85. Foreign Minister Stewart to MacLehose, May 11, 1966, FO 371/ 185011, PRO, London.

86. Wilson to LBJ, May 27, 1966, PREM 13/ 1044, PRO, London.

87. Thomas Alan Schwartz, *America's Germany* (Cambridge, Mass.: Harvard University Press, 1991), pp. 269–278.

88. Hubert Zimmermann, *Money and Security: Troops, Monetary Policy, and West Germany's Relations with the United States and Britain, 1950–1971* (Cambridge: Cambridge University Press, 2002), p. 193.

89. Ibid., p. 194.

90. *FRUS 1964–1968,* 15, pp. 385–386.

91. Gregory F. Treverton, *The Dollar Drain and American Forces in Germany* (Athens: Ohio University Press, 1978), p. 65.

92. *FRUS 1964–1968,* 15, p. 372.

93. Treverton, *The Dollar Drain,* p. 35.

94. Meeting with Chancellor Erhard, May 24, 1966, PREM 13/934, PRO, London.

95. Minutes, Callaghan to Wilson, July 15, 1966, PREM 13/934, PRO, London.

96. Memo, Stewart to Callaghan, July 18, 1966, PREM 13/934, PRO, London.

97. Raj Roy, "The Battle over the Pound, 1964–1968" Ph.D. diss., London School of Economics, 2000, pp. 198–224.

98. Dean to Palliser, June 22, 1966, PREM 13/1262, PRO, London.

99. Ibid.

100. LBJL, Bator to LBJ, July 14, 1966, Bator Papers, CF, Box 3.

101. Meeting between LBJ and Wilson, July 29, 1966, PREM 13/855, PRO, London.

102. Fielding, "Coping with Decline," p. 636.

103. Roy, "Battle over the Pound," p. 270.

104. LBJL, Bator to LBJ, July 29, 1966, Bator Papers, CF, Box 3.

105. Dean to Foreign Office, July 21, 1966, PREM 13/1262, PRO, London.

106. Bruce diary, August 3, 1966, VHS, Richmond.

107. Barbara Castle, *The Castle Diaries, 1964–70* (London: Weidenfeld and Nicolson, 1984), p. 156. Castle was the minister of overseas development and one of the minority of left-wingers in the cabinet.

108. *FRUS 1964–1968,* 13, pp. 508–509.
109. Ibid., 15, pp. 398–399.
110. Ibid., p. 403.
111. Ibid., 13, p. 457.
112. Ibid., p. 455.
113. LBJL, Bator to LBJ, August 25, 1966, Bator Papers, CF, Box 3.
114. *FRUS 1964–1968,* 13, p. 453.
115. Ibid., p. 458, and LBJL, Bator to LBJ, September 8, 1966, Bator Papers, CF, Box 3.
116. *FRUS 1964–1968,* 13, p. 461.
117. Ibid., p. 464.
118. *AAPD 1966,* II, Lilienfeld to Carstens, September 13, 1966, Doc. 283, pp. 1182–1183.
119. Treverton, *The Dollar Drain,* p. 73.
120. *FRUS 1964–1968,* 15, p. 408.
121. Ibid., p. 409.
122. Ibid., p. 409.
123. Ibid., p. 417.
124. LBJL, Bator to LBJ, September 25, 1966, NSF, NSC History, Trilateral Negotiations and NATO (TNN), 1966–1967, Box 50.
125. *FRUS 1964–1968,* 15, p. 416.
126. LBJL, McNamara to LBJ, September 19, 1966, NSF, NSC History, TNN, Box 50.
127. *Time,* September 30, 1966, p. 29.
128. *FRUS 1964–1968,* 13, pp. 472–473.
129. Ibid., pp. 475–476.
130. Ibid., 15, p. 435.
131. "Joint Statement Following Discussions between Chancellor Erhard and President Johnson, September 27, 1966," in *Common Values, Common Cause* (New York: German Information Center, 1983), p. 76.
132. On the plane ride back from Cape Kennedy, the German foreign minister, Schröder, wondered why a country as rich as the United States—evidenced by its space program—was so determined to insist on the fulfillment of the offset burden. Bator replied that Schröder should ask his Finance Ministry why they so often lectured the

Americans about the importance of reducing their balance of payments deficit. Schröder could only reply, "That's not my part of the government." Interview with Francis Bator, December 20, 1995.

133. NARS, McGhee to Rusk, October 6, 1966, Central Files, FN 12, Box 861.

134. Zimmermann, *Money and Security,* p. 205.

135. Bonn to Foreign Office, September 30, 1966, FO 371/189185, PRO, London. Thinking Erhard stronger than he was, the British were convinced that the American embassy was "making the State Department's flesh creep" with exaggerated alarms about the German political situation.

136. Theo Sommer, a journalist with close ties to the Social Democrats and Helmut Schmidt, wrote, "It is generally accepted by now that Dr. Erhard's fate was sealed after he returned empty-handed from his last visit with President Johnson . . . in the last analysis, it was American insensitivity which brought him down." Theo Sommer, "Bonn Changes Course," *Foreign Affairs* 45, no. 3 (April 1967): 483.

137. Zimmermann, *Money and Security,* p. 206, and Dennis L. Bark and David R. Gress, *A History of West Germany,* vol. 2: *Democracy and Its Discontents 1963–1988* (Oxford: Basil Blackwell, 1989), p. 57. Although Bark and Gress repeat the argument that American obstinacy caused Erhard's downfall, the evidence they present suggests otherwise.

138. *FRUS 1964–1968,* 13, pp. 406–409.

139. Ibid., p. 409.

140. Ibid., 17, pp. 54–55.

141. LBJL, Bator to LBJ through Robert Kintner, August 16, 1966, Bator Papers, Box 3.

142. LBJL, Press briefing, October 7, 1966, Bator Papers, CF, Box 4.

143. LBJL, Speech to editorial writers, October 7, 1966, NSF Speech File, Box 5.

144. LBJL, Bator to LBJ, October 13, 1966, NSF Speech File, Box 5.

145. *AAPD 1966,* II, Aufzeichnung, "Die problematik unserer Deutschland-Politik," Carstens to Schröder, October 17, 1966, Doc. 333, pp. 1374–1380.

146. I am not arguing that the United States deserves the credit for Ostpolitik, only that at this time it was ahead of Germany on the issue

and capable of lending considerable political support to those Germans who wanted to move in that direction. For the signs of interest in Germany in such a policy, see Roger Morgan, *The United States and West Germany, 1945–1973* (London: Oxford University Press, 1974), pp. 155–158.

147. Wilson to LBJ, July 19, 1966, PREM 13/1218, PRO, London.

148. Max Frankel, *The Times of My Life* (New York: Random House, 1999), p. 296. Frankel reports that Johnson considered opening up a dialogue with China similar to that which Richard Nixon would initiate three years later.

149. *Newsweek,* October 17, 1966, p. 42.

150. Gromyko foreign policy memorandum, January 13, 1967, approved by the Politburo, quoted in Anatoly Dobrynin, *In Confidence: Moscow's Ambassador to America's Six Cold War Presidents* (New York: Random House, 1995), pp. 640–641.

151. Meeting between de Gaulle and Kosygin, December 1, 1966, *Cabinet du Ministre/Cabinet Couve de Murville,* MAE, Box 385.

152. LBJL, Memo, Bator to LBJ, January 12, 1966, Europe Folder, Bator Papers, Box 25. The "pen pal" correspondence had begun with President Kennedy and Premier Khrushchev, and it had helped to ease tensions after the Cuban missile crisis.

153. *FRUS 1964–1968,* 11, p. 387.

154. Robert Dallek's Johnson biography, *Flawed Giant,* more than 600 pages long, contains no reference to the European speech.

155. *Newsweek,* October 17, 1966, p. 42.

156. LBJL, Reactions to European speech, Bator Papers, Box 21. Wilson's message is dated October 10, 1966.

157. LBJL, Rostow to LBJ, October 6, 1966, NSF Speech File, Box 5.

158. *Newsweek,* October 17, 1966, p. 44.

4. THE YEAR OF ACHIEVEMENTS

1. *FRUS 1964–1968,* 13, p. 512.

2. NARS, RG 306, USIA Reports, "Some Recent West German Public Opinion on Issues Relating to German-American Relations," September 11, 1968, Reports of the Office of Research, Box 5.

3. Speech of September 1, 1966, in Charles de Gaulle, *Discours et messages*, vol. 5: *Vers le terme Janvier 1966 Avril 1969* (Paris: Plon, 1970), p. 76.

4. Telegram, Reilly to Foreign Office, September 2, 1966, FO 371/189107, PRO, London.

5. LBJL, Memo, "France," Winthrop Knowlton to Fowler, July 11, 1966, Henry Fowler Papers, Box 68. Knowlton's memo suggests some possible U.S. actions, but notes that *overt* action would come at "exceedingly heavy cost to other U.S. objectives," including the cohesion of the alliance. Knowlton did suggest that *covert* action, including a *"high level approach to individual executives of the largest corporations doing business with France,"* might have some effect, although, he added, "we would be pouring fuel on the fire of anti-French feeling and also building pressures upon ourselves for *overt* action covering all aspects of French-American relations." (Emphasis in the original.)

6. The correspondent Hedley Donovan, who visited with Johnson in December 1966, engaged in an argument with the president about whether the midterm losses were a defeat for LBJ or a normal off-year result. Despite LBJ's best attempt to argue that the losses were normal, he could see the decline in his standing with the public. Hedley Donovan, *Roosevelt to Reagan: A Reporter's Encounters with Nine Presidents* (New York: Harper & Row, 1985), pp. 100–101.

7. George Gallup, *The Gallup Poll, 1935–1971* (Wilmington, Del.: Scholarly Resources, 1972), p. 2038.

8. *New York Times,* November 10, 1966.

9. *Time,* November 18, 1966, p. 24.

10. *New York Times,* November 9, 1966.

11. For a treatment of McCloy as high commissioner, see Thomas Alan Schwartz, *America's Germany* (Cambridge, Mass.: Harvard University Press, 1991).

12. Kai Bird, *The Chairman: John J. McCloy and the Making of the American Establishment* (New York: Simon and Schuster, 1992), p. 589.

13. *FRUS 1964–1968,* 13, pp. 495–498.

14. Ibid., p. 485.

15. Ibid., p. 486.

16. Bowie understood that the other members of NATO felt excluded by

the trilateral negotiations, but he hoped they would understand that the crisis situation had left the United States no choice but to proceed with only the "Big Three." Earlier in his career, he had played a crucial role in negotiating the treaty under which Germany regained her sovereignty, and his role in defining the issues for both McCloy and the Germans should not be underestimated. See Schwartz, *America's Germany,* pp. 43, 269–278.

17. UK delegation to NATO to Foreign Office, October 22, 1966, FO 371/190641, PRO, London.

18. Barnes to Lord Hood, October 5, 1966, FO 371/190640, PRO, London.

19. Dean to George Thomson, February 4, 1967, PREM 13/1525, PRO, London.

20. Record of conversation, Wilson, Rostow, Callaghan, Kaiser, and Enders, November 21, 1966, PREM 13/1525, PRO, London.

21. *FRUS 1964–1968,* 13, p. 492.

22. Ibid.

23. Meeting, December 8, 1966, CAB 128/41, PRO, London.

24. Wolfram Kaiser, "Party Games: The British EEC Applications of 1961 and 1967," in *Moored to the Continent? Britain and European Integration,* ed. Roger Broad and Virginia Preston (London: Institute of Historical Research, 2001), p. 71. Kaiser comments that "Wilson never had any strong feelings about Europe."

25. Raj Roy, "The Battle over the Pound, 1964–1968" Ph.D. diss., London School of Economics, 2000, p. 283.

26. *FRUS 1964–1968,* 13, p. 491.

27. Ibid., 15, pp. 477–478.

28. Birrenbach to Kiesinger, December 2, 1966, Birrenbach NL, I-433, 019/1, CDU Archive, Bonn.

29. Steven J. Brady, "Der amerikanische Kongress und Deutschland," in *Die USA und Deutschland im Zeitalter des Kalten Krieges 1945–1990,* ed. Detlef Junker et al. (Stuttgart: Deutsch Verlags-Anstalt, 2001), p. 223.

30. Memo of conversation, Wilson and Kosygin, February 7, 1967, PREM 13/1530, PRO, London.

31. *Washington Post,* November 5, 1966.

32. Dirk Kroegel, *Einen Anfang Finden! Kurt Georg Kiesinger in der*

Aussen-und Deutschlandpolitik der Grossen Koalition (Munich: Oldenbourg, 1997), p. 28.

33. Harald Rosenbach, "Der Preis der Freiheit: Die deutsch-amerikanischen Verhandlungen über den Devisenausgleich (1961–1967)," *Vierteljahresheft für Zeitgeschichte* 46 (1998): 746.

34. Willy Brandt, *My Life in Politics* (New York: Viking, 1992), p. 176.

35. *FRUS 1964–1968*, 13, p. 517.

36. Theo Sommer, "Bonn Changes Course," *Foreign Affairs* 45, no. 3 (April 1967): p. 488.

37. *FRUS 1964–1968*, 13, p. 517.

38. Gottfried Niedhart, "The Federal Republic's Ostpolitik and the United States: Initiatives and Constraints," in *The United States and the European Alliance since 1945*, ed., Kathleen Burk and Melvyn Stokes (New York: Oxford, 1999), p. 292.

39. *FRUS 1964–1968*, 13, p. 521.

40. W. R. Smyser, *From Yalta to Berlin: The Cold War Struggle over Germany* (New York: St. Martin's Press, 1999), p. 216.

41. *FRUS 1964–1968*, 15, p. 485.

42. *AAPD 1967*, I, Document 52, pp. 262–264.

43. Ibid., Document 78, p. 359.

44. *FRUS 1964–1968*, 15, p. 488.

45. LBJL, Memo of conversation, LBJ and McCloy, March 2, 1967, NSF Histories, Trilateral Negotiations and NATO 1966–1967, Box 50.

46. LBJL, Memo for secretary of defense from Earle Wheeler, Chairman, JCS, NSF Histories, TNN 1966–1967, Box 50.

47. *FRUS 1964–1968*, 13, pp. 536–537.

48. LBJL, Memo of conversation, LBJ and McCloy, March 2, 1967, NSF Histories, TNN 1966–1967, Box 50.

49. LBJL, Memo of conversation, LBJ and McCloy, March 2, 1967, NSF Histories, TNN 1966–1967, Box 50.

50. Palliser to Wilson, March 2, 1967, PREM 13/1525, PRO, London.

51. Memo of conversation, Wilson and Rostow, PREM 13/1525, February 25, 1967, PRO, London.

52. *FRUS 1964–1968*, 13, pp. 538–545, and *AAPD 1967*, I, Document 87, pp. 396–411. The German version makes it even more clear how

anxious Kiesinger was to correct any misunderstandings about his comments.

53. LBJL, Bator to LBJ, March 10, 1967, Bator Papers, CF, Box 4.

54. *FRUS 1964–1968,* 13, pp. 546–549.

55. LBJL, Bator to LBJ, "Trilaterals—Status Report," March 17, 1967, Bator Papers, CF, Box 4.

56. Minute, March 21, 1967, PREM 13/1526, PRO, London.

57. LBJL, Bator to LBJ, "Trilaterals—Status Report," March 17, 1967, Bator Papers, CF, Box 4.

58. LBJL, Bator to LBJ, March 8, 1967, Bator Papers, CF, Box 4.

59. *AAPD 1967,* II, Document 117, pp. 530–533.

60. LBJL, Bator to LBJ, April 27, 1967, Bator Papers, CF, Box 5.

61. LBJL, Bator to LBJ, April 4, 1967, Bator Papers, CF, Box 5.

62. Zuckerman to Wilson, March 14, 1967, PREM 13/1888, PRO, London. Zuckerman noted that the Germans were now referring to Article III of the NPT as the "General Electric article." In the late 1960s, the civilian nuclear power industry was perceived as being at the cutting edge of technology, and the ecological and environmental movements had not yet countered this image. For a sense of the importance of this technology to the Germans, see *Newsweek,* January 15, 1968, p. 59.

63. *FRUS 1964–1968,* 13, p. 540.

64. Ibid., 15, p. 513.

65. George McGhee, *At the Creation of a New Germany* (New Haven: Yale University Press, 1989), p. 220.

66. Robert L. Hardesty, *The Johnson Years: The Difference He Made* (Austin: Lyndon B. Johnson Library, 1993), p. 190.

67. McGhee, *At the Creation of a New Germany,* p. 221.

68. Martin J. Hillenbrand, *Fragments of Our Time: Memoirs of a Diplomat* (Athens: University of Georgia Press, 1998), pp. 241–242.

69. *FRUS 1964–1968,* 15, pp. 514–522.

70. Roberts to Hood, April 28, 1967, PREM 13/1528, PRO, London.

71. Dean to Lord Hood, April 28, 1967, PREM 13/1528, PRO, London. Dean's thoughts were based on a conversation with Walt Rostow after their return to Washington.

72. LBJL, Bator to LBJ, April 27, 1967, Bator Papers, CF, Box 5.

73. LBJL, John J. McCloy, Oral History, p. 14.
74. Lyndon B. Johnson, *The Vantage Point: Perspectives of the Presidency, 1963–1969* (New York: Holt, Rinehart, and Winston, 1970), p. 311.
75. Kennedy told Kiesinger on February 2, 1967, that the Kennedy Round had considerable significance for the United States, and that failure would not lead the United States to try again. *AAPD 1967,* I, Document 48, p. 253.
76. Patrick Dean to Foreign Office, May 10, 1967, PREM 13/1869, PRO, London.
77. Andrew Moravcsik, *The Choice for Europe* (Ithaca: Cornell University Press, 1998), p. 208.
78. *FRUS 1964–1968,* 8, p. 839.
79. Ibid., p. 840.
80. Steve Dryden, *Trade Warriors* (New York: Oxford University Press, 1995), p. 94. Dirksen considered his attacks on trade policy fair game in his otherwise stout defense of the ideal of a bipartisan foreign policy and his good personal relationship with LBJ. Byron C. Hulsey, *Everett Dirksen and His Presidents: How a Senate Giant Shaped American Politics* (Lawrence: University Press of Kansas, 2000), pp. 207ff.
81. Dryden, *Trade Warriors,* p. 102.
82. *FRUS 1964–1968,* 8, p. 889.
83. LBJL, Harry McPherson Oral History, Tape V, p. 15. McPherson makes it clear that although Johnson delegated the negotiating details, he was in full command on the respective decisions.
84. Benzenoid chemicals were those hydrocarbon chemicals used in organic synthesis, solvents, and motor fuels.
85. LBJL, NSF, NSC Histories, Kennedy Round Crisis, 1967, p. 3, Box 52.
86. *FRUS 1964–1968,* 8, p. 879.
87. LBJL, NSF, NSC Histories, Kennedy Round Crisis, 1967, pp. 9–10, Box 52. See also Dryden, *Trade Warriors,* pp. 104–105.
88. *FRUS 1964–1968,* 8, p. 916.
89. Powell to London, May 8, 1967, PREM 13/1869, PRO, London.
90. *FRUS 1964–1968,* 8, p. 923.
91. Gould notes that because of farmer dissatisfaction with administra-

tion policies, in May 1967 the White House believed it would lose every nonsouthern state with a farm-voter population of 9 percent or more. Lewis L. Gould, *1968: The Election That Changed America* (Chicago: Ivan R. Dee, 1993), p. 16.

92. *FRUS 1964–1968*, 8, p. 923.

93. Ibid., p. 927.

94. Palliser, Note for the record, May 16, 1967, PREM 13/1869, PRO, London.

95. Powell, "Kennedy Round," May 16, 1967, PREM 13/1869, PRO, London.

96. *FRUS 1964–1968*, 8, p. 933.

97. Dryden, *Trade Warriors*, p. 112.

98. Powell, Kennedy Round, May 16, 1967, PREM 13/1869, PRO, London.

99. *AAPD 1967*, II, Document 170, p. 746.

100. Moravcsik, *Choice for Europe*, pp. 159–237, especially pp. 162–163. Moravcsik's work demonstrates how essential the CAP was to the French. Ironically enough, the American reluctance to push to break the CAP undoubtedly delayed another American objective, getting Britain into Europe.

101. *FRUS 1964–1968*, 8, p. 974.

102. Ernest Preeg, *Traders and Diplomats* (Washington: Brookings, 1970), pp. 256–260.

103. Alfred E. Eckes, Jr., *Opening America's Market: U.S. Foreign Trade Policy since 1776* (Chapel Hill: University of North Carolina Press, 1995), p. 200. Eckes also provides other indexes to show that certain sectors of the American economy were adversely affected by the Kennedy Round.

104. Thomas Zeiler, *American Trade and Power in the 1960s* (New York: Columbia University Press, 1992), pp. 244–245.

105. Thomas Ilgen, *Autonomy and Interdependence: U.S.–Western European Monetary and Trade Relations, 1958–1984* (Totowa, N.J.: Rowman and Allenheld, 1985), p. 68.

106. Eckes, *Opening America's Market*, p. 203.

107. Ilgen, *Autonomy and Interdependence*, p. 68.

108. Geir Lundestad, *"Empire" by Integration: The United States and Euro-*

pean Integration, 1945–1997 (New York: Oxford, 1998), p. 164. Lundestad's book makes a convincing case for the value of any trade-offs the United States made to strengthen European unity.

109. Eckes, *Opening America's Market,* p. 197.
110. Memo of conversation, Bator and Palliser, May 31, 1967, WO 16/1468, PRO, London.
111. Burton Kaufman, "Foreign Aid and the Balance of Payments Problem: Vietnam and Johnson's Foreign Economic Policy," in *The Johnson Years,* vol. 2, ed. Robert A. Divine (Lawrence: University Press of Kansas, 1987), p. 90.
112. Francis M. Bator, "Lyndon Johnson and Foreign Policy: The Case of Western Europe and the Soviet Union," in *Presidential Judgment: Foreign Policy Decision Making in the White House,* ed. Aaron Lobel, (Hollis, N.H.: Hollis Publishing Co., 2001), p. 63.
113. *FRUS 1964–1968,* 8, p. 283.
114. Ibid., p. 351.
115. LBJL, Memo, Deming to McCloy, May 17, 1967, Liquidity Exercise—McCloy Trip folder, June 1967, Bator Papers, Box 8.
116. *New York Times,* April 19, 1967.
117. *FRUS 1964–1968,* 15, pp. 541–542.
118. Ibid., 8, p. 360.
119. Ibid., p. 361.
120. Ibid., p. 375. The Group of Ten comprised the finance ministers of the noncommunist world's major industrial countries.
121. Ibid., pp. 376 and 384.
122. Ibid., p. 381.
123. Ibid., p. 383.
124. Conversation between de Gaulle and Kiesinger, July 12, 1967, and conversation between de Gaulle, Kiesinger, and Brandt, July 12, 1967, *Cabinet du Ministre/Maurice Couve de Murville* (1958–1968), MAE, Box 382.
125. *FRUS 1964–1968,* 8, p. 412.
126. Ilgen, *Autonomy and Interdependence,* p. 35.
127. *New York Times,* August 29, 1967. As a sign of the president's own increasing difficulties with the press, the *Times* editorialized that the president was "overselling monetary reform."
128. Harold James, *International Monetary Cooperation since Bretton*

Woods (Washington, D.C.: International Monetary Fund; New York: Oxford University Press, 1996), p. 174.

129. Barry Eichengreen, *Globalizing Capital* (Princeton: Princeton University Press, 1996), p. 135.
130. Johnson, *Vantage Point,* pp. 480–481.
131. Ibid., p. 483.
132. Glenn T. Seaborg and Benjamin S. Loeb, *Stemming the Tide: Arms Control in the Johnson Years* (Lexington, Mass.: Lexington Books, 1987), p. 291.
133. *FRUS 1964–1968,* 11, pp. 494–495.
134. The magazine's conclusions are cited in Louis Heren, *No Hail No Farewell* (New York: Harper and Row, 1970), p. 159.
135. Record, Kiesinger conversation with Schröder, July 21, 1967, Gerhard Schröder NL, I-483, 287/4, CDU Archive.
136. *FRUS 1964–1968,* 15, pp. 558–560.
137. Ibid., 13, pp. 602–605.
138. LBJL, Hubert Humphrey, Oral History, Interview III, p. 5.
139. *FRUS 1964–1968,* 15, p. 581.

5. THE LONG 1968

1. *Time,* January 5, 1968, p. 13.
2. *New York Times,* October 3, 1967.
3. Ibid., October 27, 1967.
4. Lewis L. Gould, *1968: The Election That Changed America* (Chicago: Ivan R. Dee, 1993), pp. 12–21.
5. *New York Times,* December 8, 1967, and Wilson Miscamble, "Francis Cardinal Spellman and 'Spellman's War,'" in *The Human Tradition in the Vietnam Era,* ed. David L. Anderson (Wilmington, Del.: Scholarly Resources, 2000), p. 18.
6. *Time,* January 5, 1968, p. 13.
7. Joseph A. Califano, Jr., *The Triumph and Tragedy of Lyndon Johnson* (New York: Simon and Schuster, 1991), p. 251, and Diane Kunz, "The American Economic Consequences of 1968," in *1968: The World Transformed,* ed. Carole Fink, Philipp Gassert, and Detlef Junker (New York: Cambridge University Press, 1998), p. 83.

8. Lyndon B. Johnson, *The Vantage Point: Perspectives of the Presidency, 1963–1969* (New York: Holt, Rinehart, and Winston, 1970), p. 492.

9. Irving Bernstein, *Guns or Butter: The Presidency of Lyndon Johnson* (New York: Oxford University Press, 1996), pp. 368–369.

10. Ibid., p. 358. However, there is a considerable debate about this question that Bernstein's categorical statement ignores. See John F. Walker and Harold G. Vatter, "The Princess and the Pea; or The Alleged Vietnam War Origins of the Current Inflation," *Journal of Economic Issues* 16, no. 2 (June 1982): 597–608. This article precipitated a critical commentary on and further restatement of the original thesis in *Journal of Economic Issues* 17, no. 1 (March 1983): 175–196.

11. David Halberstam's article is the best known account that makes this charge. David Halberstam, "How the Economy Went Haywire," *Atlantic Monthly* 230, no. 3 (September 1972): 56–60. However, as Donald Kettl makes clear, the evidence is much more complex than the simple "devil theory" of Halberstam and others. Donald F. Kettl, "The Economic Education of Lyndon Johnson: Guns, Butter, and Taxes," in *The Johnson Years,* vol. 2, ed. Robert Divine (Lawrence: University Press of Kansas, 1987), p. 54.

12. Lester Thurow, *The Zero Sum Society* (New York: Basic Books, 1980), p. 43.

13. Jeffrey W. Helsing, *Johnson's War / Johnson's Great Society: The Guns and Butter Trap* (Westport, Conn.: Praeger, 2000), p. 256.

14. David Hackett Fischer, *The Great Wave: Price Revolutions and the Rhythm of History* (New York: Oxford University Press, 1996), pp. 203–205. Table 3 in the Appendix of this volume makes it clear that inflation was higher in Western Europe than in the United States from 1961 to 1966.

15. LBJL, Frederik L. Deming, Oral History, tape 3, p. 4.

16. LBJL, Arthur Okun, Oral History, p. 19.

17. Johnson, *Vantage Point,* p. 325.

18. Robert M. Collins, "The Economic Crisis and the Waning of the 'American Century,'" *American Historical Review* 101, no. 2 (April 1996): 402.

19. LBJL, Wilbur Mills, Oral History, p. 14. Mills thought Johnson knew little of economics and "always was a spender," p. 21.

20. Bernstein, *Guns or Butter,* p. 370.

21. Raj Roy, "The Battle over the Pound, 1964–1968," Ph.D. diss., London School of Economics, 2000, p. 294.
22. *FRUS 1964–1968*, 8, p. 434. See also Harold Wilson, *The Labour Government, 1964–1970: A Personal Record* (London: Weidenfeld and Nicolson, 1971), p. 400.
23. *FRUS 1964–1968*, 8, pp. 434–435 (emphasis in the original).
24. Alec Cairncross, *The Wilson Years: A Treasury Diary 1964–1969* (London: Historians' Press, 1997), p. 229. Wilson's misunderstanding of the significance of devaluation for American politics must have been encouraged by LBJ's worries in 1964, before that election. Any British diplomat in the United States in 1967 could have told Wilson that the circumstances had changed dramatically since then, and that the value of the British pound was not as important as it once was.
25. Wilson minute, November 5, 1967, PREM 13/1447, PRO, London. Wilson acknowledged to David Bruce that LBJ would be reluctant to see him on Vietnam. But he wanted to assure the president that they could dispose of the subject "in a few minutes on a basis which would help me to hold the House of Commons and on public opinion here despite its recent and alarming hardening at all levels." The real reason for the meeting would be the pound sterling.
26. Bruce diary, November 8, 1967, VHS.
27. Dean to FO, November 11, 1967, PREM 13/1854, PRO, London.
28. FO to Washington, November 9, 1967, PREM 13/1854, PRO, London.
29. Cairncross, *Wilson Years,* p. 244.
30. *FRUS 1964–1968*, 8, pp. 435–437.
31. Telegram, Paris to FO, November 14, 1967, PREM 13/1854, PRO, London.
32. *FRUS 1964–1968*, 8, p. 438.
33. Paris to FO, November 21, 1967, PREM 13/1856, PRO, London.
34. Roy, "Battle over the Pound," p. 306. See also Raj Roy, "The Battle for Bretton Woods: America, Britain and the International Financial Crisis of October 1967–March 1968," *Cold War History* 2, 2 (January 2002): 46.
35. Wilson to LBJ, November 17, 1967, PREM 13/1447, PRO, London.
36. Johnson, *Vantage Point,* p. 315.

37. Gordon L. Weil and Ian Davidson, *The Gold War* (New York: Holt, Rinehart, and Winston, 1970), p. 127.
38. *FRUS 1964–1968*, 8, p. 441.
39. Ibid., p. 442. LBJ had used the same expression in his press conference the previous day, and it had already become a rallying cry for the Republican opposition.
40. Collins, "The Economic Crisis," p. 405.
41. The members of the gold pool were the United States, Great Britain, France, Germany, Italy, Switzerland, Canada, the Netherlands, and Belgium.
42. Weil and Davidson, *The Gold War*, p. 126.
43. LBJL, Ackley to LBJ, November 27, 1967, in "The Gold Crisis," NSF History, Box 53. See also Kunz, "American Economic Consequences," p. 96.
44. LBJL, "The 1968 Balance of Payments Program," NSF History, Box 54.
45. *Newsweek*, July 24, 1967, pp. 32–33.
46. Serge Berstein, *The Republic of de Gaulle, 1958–1969*, trans. Peter Morris (Paris: Cambridge University Press, 1993), pp. 181–182.
47. Donald Cook, *Charles de Gaulle: A Biography* (New York: Putnam, 1983), pp. 392–393.
48. Paris to FO, December 8, 1967, PREM 13/1515, PRO, London.
49. For a recent treatment of de Gaulle's more extreme positions in 1967, in a much less reverential tone than that of previous biographers, see Éric Roussel, *Charles de Gaulle* (Paris: Gallimard, 2002), pp. 817–849.
50. Johnson, *Vantage Point*, p. 317.
51. *FRUS 1964–1968*, 8, p. 453.
52. Ibid., p. 431 and p. 456.
53. LBJL, "The Gold Crisis," NSF History, Box 53.
54. LBJL, "The 1968 Balance of Payments Program," NSF History, Box 54.
55. LBJL, Telegram from the president to Califano, December 23, 1967, "The 1968 Balance of Payments Program," NSF History, Box 54.
56. Kunz, "American Economic Consequences," p. 98.
57. "Sacrificial Rite in Darkest Washington," January 4, 1968, reprinted in Herbert Block, *The Herblock Gallery* (New York: Simon and Schuster, 1968), p. 29.

58. LBJL, "The 1968 Balance of Payments Program," NSF History, Box 54.

59. *Newsweek,* January 29, 1968.

60. Ackley to Johnson, January 6, 1968, quoted in Collins, "The Economic Crisis," p. 406.

61. Conversation between Katzenbach and Wilson, January 6, 1968, PREM 13/2452, PRO, London.

62. *FRUS 1964–1968,* 8, p. 504.

63. Ibid., p. 500.

64. See also Mitchell Lerner, "A Failure of Perception: Lyndon Johnson, North Korean Ideology, and the *Pueblo* Incident," *Diplomatic History* 25, no. 4 (Fall 2001): 647–675. Lerner is critical of the Johnson administration for interpreting the North Korean action "within a global Cold War framework" rather than recognizing its roots within the North Korean domestic context. However, given the bizarre and secretive nature of the regime in Pyongyang, the administration's caution was understandable.

65. Dean to Gore-Booth, January 31, 1968, PREM 13/2454, PRO, London.

66. NARS, Memo of conversation, Rusk and George Brown, January 11, 1968, Central Foreign Policy Files, 1967–1969, Economic FN 15—UK, Box 833.

67. Record of talks, LBJ and Wilson, February 8 and 9, 1968, PREM 13/2455, PRO, London. Wilson, not one to offer praise for Johnson to non-American listeners, told NATO secretary general Broslio that he was impressed with Johnson's "relaxed and restrained mood" despite the crises he faced, and with his "considerable courage in the face of the pressure of public opinion." Wilson conversation with Broslio, February 1968, PREM 13/2836, PRO, London.

68. Telegram, Palliser to Dean, February 12, 1968, PREM 13/2454, PRO, London.

69. Wilson to LBJ, March 15, 1968, PREM 13/2051, PRO, London.

70. Collins, "The Economic Crisis," p. 396.

71. Warren Cohen, *America in the Age of Soviet Power, 1945–1991* (New York: Cambridge University Press, 1993), p. 172.

72. *Time,* March 24, 1968, p. 24.

73. Califano, *Triumph and Tragedy,* pp. 260–262, indicates that Johnson's cool reaction to the commission's report was influenced by the

sense that it was leaked in order to "box him in" and force him to make large spending commitments.

74. Robert Dallek, *Flawed Giant: Lyndon Johnson and His Times, 1961–1973* (New York: Oxford University Press, 1998), p. 516.

75. Wilson to LBJ, March 18, 1968, PREM 13/2051, PRO, London. Wilson's adviser Thomas Balogh told him later that "the present acute crisis was unquestionably caused by France stimulating a drain on gold from America, and, at the same time, advertising the weakness of the American balance of payments." Balogh to Wilson, March 26, 1968, PREM 13/2052, PRO, London.

76. *FRUS 1964–1968,* 8, p. 535.

77. Ibid., p. 538.

78. Dallek, *Flawed Giant,* p. 512. As Dallek correctly writes, Johnson's shift came not from losing the establishment but "from a recognition of the reality that the war was stalemated and unwinnable without an escalation that would risk a domestic and international crisis unwarranted by the country's national security."

79. LBJ to Wilson, March 15, 1968, PREM 13/2051, PRO, London.

80. Roy, "The Battle for Bretton Woods," p. 56.

81. LBJL, Frederick L. Deming, Oral History, p. 29.

82. LBJL, "The Gold Crisis," NSF History, Box 53.

83. On March 16, 1968, Robert Kennedy began his campaign for the presidency in the wake of the strong showing by Eugene McCarthy in the New Hampshire primary only four days earlier.

84. *FRUS 1964–1968,* 8, p. 544.

85. Michel Debré, *Gouverner autrement: Mémoires 1962–1970* (Paris: Albin Michel, 1993), p. 176.

86. *AAPD 1968,* Document 100, Kiesinger conversation with McGhee and Schaetzel, March 21, 1968, p. 370.

87. Alain Peyrefitte, *C'était de Gaulle,* vol. 3 (Paris: Fayard, 2000), p. 287. That Debré would refer to the American edict with a word from czarist Russia is revealing of the French attitude toward the United States.

88. *FRUS 1964–1968,* 8, p. 543.

89. Chancellor of the Exchequer to prime minister, March 30, 1968, PREM 13/2050, PRO, London.

90. Weil and Davidson, *The Gold War,* p. 202.

91. Ibid., p. 100.
92. Cook, *Charles de Gaulle*, p. 397.
93. Robert Soloman, *The International Monetary System 1945–1981* (New York: Harper and Row), p. 155.
94. Kunz, "American Economic Consequences," p. 106.
95. Johnson, *Vantage Point*, p. 321.
96. *FRUS 1964–1968*, 8, p. 544.
97. Harvey C. Mansfield, Sr., *Illustrations of Presidential Management* (Austin: University of Texas, 1988), p. 59.
98. Califano, *Triumph and Tragedy*, p. 288. Table 2 in the Appendix demonstrates how LBJ's tax increase was able to shift the budget deficit into a surplus, the last federal surplus until the late 1990s.
99. Diane Kunz, *Butter and Guns: America's Cold War Economic Diplomacy* (New York: Free Press, 1997), p. 114.
100. John Connally with Mickey Herskowitz, *In History's Shadow* (New York: Hyperion, 1953), p. 214.
101. *FRUS 1964–1968*, 11, pp. 431–432.
102. Anatoly Dobrynin, *In Confidence: Moscow's Ambassador to Six Cold War Presidents* (New York: Times Books, Random House, 1995), p. 165.
103. *FRUS 1964–1968*, 14, p. 529.
104. Ibid., p. 566.
105. Dobrynin, *In Confidence*, p. 166. Dobrynin believes this was one example of the Kremlin's missing "a historic opportunity" to reach an agreement with the Johnson administration to stop ABM development.
106. McNamara's speech of September 18, 1967, can be found in LBJL, Papers of Spurgeon Keeny, ABM II folder, Deployment Decision, Box 1.
107. Paul Nitze, *From Hiroshima to Glasnost: At the Center of Decision* (New York: Grove Weidenfeld, 1989), p. 290. Nitze's account suggests that Johnson's push forward with appropriations for the ABM brought forth a Soviet response.
108. *FRUS 1964–1968*, 14, pp. 627–628.
109. Ibid., p. 641.
110. Ibid., 15, p. 633.
111. Ibid., p. 646.

112. Ibid., 11, p. 601.
113. Speech at Glassboro State College, June 4, 1968, *Public Papers of the President: Lyndon B. Johnson 1968–1969* (Washington, D.C.: G.P.O., 1969), pp. 679–684.
114. Robert Divine, "Lyndon Johnson and Strategic Arms Limitation," in *The Johnson Years*, vol. 3: *LBJ at Home and Abroad*, ed. Robert Divine (Lawrence: University Press of Kansas, 1994), p. 267. Divine makes it clear that the American proposal would have preserved U.S. superiority in nuclear warheads, and emphasizes that it did not include a ban on MIRVs.
115. Donald to Palliser, July 2, 1968, PREM 13/2442, PRO, London.
116. LBJL, Bator to LBJ, November 30, 1966, Bator Papers, CF, Box 3.
117. International Institute for Applied Systems Analysis, *Annual Report*, 1991, quoted in Frank Costigliola, "LBJ, Germany, and the 'End of the Cold War,'" in *Lyndon Johnson Confronts the World*, ed. Warren Cohen and Nancy Tucker (New York: Cambridge University Press, 1994), p. 207.
118. I have drawn my account largely from Alan McDonald, "The International Institute for Applied Systems Analysis," unpublished case study, Harvard University, March 13, 1997. My thanks to Professor Francis Bator for providing me with a copy.
119. Writing in 1988, a year before the Berlin Wall fell, one of the British founders of IIASA, Solly Zuckerman, commented, "Only time will tell whether IIASA will succeed in fulfilling the main hope that brought it about—that of helping bring about East-West understanding. So far there is little to boast about." Solly Zuckerman, *Monkeys, Men, and Missiles: An Autobiography, 1946–1988* (London: Collins, 1988), p. 435.
120. Johnson made his comments at a meeting of the National Security Council on May 3, 1967. *FRUS 1964–1968,* 8, p. 573.
121. *FRUS 1964–1968,* 8, p. 618.
122. Ibid., pp. 641–643.
123. Frédéric Bozo, "Detente versus Alliance: France, the United States and the Politics of the Harmel Report (1964–1968)," *Contemporary European History* 7, no. 3 (1998): 358.
124. Ibid., p. 357. Bozo regards the Harmel report as a "definite victory" by the U.S.-led alliance over de Gaulle and the French vision of Europe's future.

125. LBJL, Notes of Clifford's staff conferences, May 13, 1968, George Elsey Papers, Box 1.
126. *FRUS 1964–1968*, 17, p. 195. RIAS was Radio in the American Sector, an important radio station in Germany.
127. Ibid., p. 196.
128. Ibid., p. 214.
129. *DBPO*, series I, vol. 1: Britain and the Soviet Union, 1968–1972, no. 12, p. 65.
130. Ibid., no. 13, p. 67.
131. Ibid.
132. Jaromir Navratil et al., *The Prague Spring 1968* (Budapest: C.E.U. Press, 1998), xviii.
133. LBJL, Eugene Rostow, Oral History, p. 23.
134. Brady, "Der amerikanische Kongress und Deutschland," in Detlef Junker, et al., eds., *Die USA und Deutschland im Zeitalter des Kallen Krieges 1945–1990: Ein Handbuch* (Stuttgart: Deutsche Verlag, 2001), p. 223.
135. George C. Herring, "Tet and the Crisis of Hegemony," in *1968: The World Transformed*, ed. Fink, Gassert, and Junker, p. 50.
136. Dobrynin, *In Confidence*, p. 181.
137. Herring, "Tet and the Crisis of Hegemony," p. 50.
138. LBJL, Tom Johnson's Notes on Meetings, July 24, 1968.
139. Dean Rusk, *As I Saw It* (New York: Penguin, 1990), p. 351.
140. *FRUS 1964–1968*, 17, p. 248.
141. Ibid., p. 248.
142. Herring, "Tet and the Crisis of Hegemony," p. 50.
143. Rusk, *As I Saw It*, p. 365.
144. Some critics have gone so far as to liken the U.S. response to the British and French appeasement of Hitler in Munich in 1938. Kenneth N. Skoug, Jr., *Czechoslovakia's Lost Fight for Freedom, 1967–1969: An American Embassy Perspective* (Westport, Conn.: Praeger, 1999), p. 245.
145. *DBPO*, no. 15, p. 79.
146. Frédéric Bozo, *Two Strategies for Europe: De Gaulle, the United States, and the Atlantic Alliance*, trans. Susan Emanuel (Lanham, Md.: Rowman and Littlefield, 2001), pp. 223–225.
147. LBJL, Notes of Clifford's staff conferences, September 21, 1968, George Elsey Papers, Box 1.

148. Herring, "Tet and the Crisis of Hegemony," p. 51.

149. George Christian, *The President Steps Down* (New York: Macmillan, 1970), p. 145.

150. Ibid., p. 144. Given that Dobrynin offered Hubert Humphrey financial assistance for his campaign—an offer Humphrey quickly declined—it is not far-fetched to presume that the Russians were concerned about what a Nixon presidency would bring. Dobrynin, *In Confidence,* p. 192.

151. LBJL, Notes of Clifford's staff conferences, September 11, 1968, George Elsey Papers, Box 1.

152. Herring, "Tet and the Crisis of Hegemony," p. 51.

153. Christian, *President Steps Down,* p. 145.

154. John Prados, "Prague Spring and SALT," in H. W. Brands, *The Foreign Policies of Lyndon Johnson: Beyond Vietnam* (College Station: Texas A & M University Press, 1999), pp. 32–35. The Bush-Putin agreement of May 2002 will finally bring the nuclear arsenals of both countries below where they stood in 1967.

155. Glenn T. Seaborg, *A Chemist in the White House* (Washington, D.C.: American Chemical Society, 1998), p. 153.

EPILOGUE

1. George Christian, *The President Steps Down* (New York: Macmillan, 1970), p. 2.

2. Ibid., p. 269.

3. *Public Papers of the President: Lyndon Johnson,* vol. 2: 1968–1969 (Washington, D.C.: G.P.O., 1969), p. 1270.

4. Christian, *President Steps Down,* p. 272.

5. Robert Caro, *The Years of Lyndon Johnson: The Path to Power* (New York: Alfred A. Knopf, 1982), pp. xix–xx. Caro was equally harsh on Johnson in the second volume of his biography, *The Years of Lyndon Johnson: Means of Ascent* (New York: Alfred A. Knopf, 1990). In the third volume, *Master of the Senate,* he does give Johnson credit for the Civil Rights Act of 1957, but he continues to portray Johnson as a completely unprincipled politician interested only in his own advancement.

6. George Reedy, *Lyndon B. Johnson: A Memoir* (New York: Andrews and McMeel, 1982), p. 157.

7. Robert Dallek, *Lone Star Rising: Lyndon Johnson and His Times, 1908–1960* (New York: Oxford University Press, 1991), p. 3.

8. Ibid., p. 4.

9. Books such as Paul Conkin, *Big Daddy from the Pedernales: Lyndon Johnson* (1987), Dallek's *Lone Star Rising*, and Irwin and Debi Unger, *LBJ: A Life* (1999) offer a much more balanced portrait than Caro's. See Lewis L. Gould, "The Revised LBJ," *Wilson Quarterly* 24, no. 2, (Spring 2000): 81. It may be, as Gould argues, that Johnson's stock has risen somewhat in recent years, with the release of his tape recordings and increasing distance from the Vietnam years. The recent John Frankenheimer movie *Path to War*, created for Home Box Office and televised in May 2002, presented a largely sympathetic portrait of Johnson's agonizing dilemmas on Vietnam, although because it relied heavily on the Clifford and Goodwin memoirs, it portrayed a Johnson almost psychologically unhinged by the war.

   On the other hand, Oliver Stone still plans a movie that will blame LBJ for the Martin Luther King assassination, an event that could deal a fatal blow to the one area of Johnson's legacy, civil rights, for which he is usually praised. And consider this letter to the editor of the *Wilson Quarterly* after the article by Lewis Gould appeared urging a reconsideration of LBJ: "We don't need a nuanced view of Lyndon Johnson from historians. Whatever positive accomplishments the man may have had apart from his prosecution of the war are offset a hundred times, no, a thousand times, by the swath of death, disillusionment, sadness, cynicism, and self-loathing this war left in its wake. In his life he was called upon to make one supremely important decision, and he failed." *Wilson Quarterly* 24, no. 3 (Summer 2000): 7. In the wake of September 11, a magazine article titled "15 Presidents Who Changed the World" contrasted Johnson unfavorably with other chief executives who have taken the nation to war, describing the "narcissism" and "paranoia" he exhibited in his decision to commit American forces to Vietnam. *U.S. News and World Report*, February 25 and March 4, 2002, p. 67.

10. Arthur Schlesinger, Jr., "The Ultimate Approval Rating," *New York Times Magazine*, December 15, 1996, p. 48. A survey conducted

by C-SPAN in 1999 found that its viewers ranked LBJ nineteenth among the forty-one presidents, including Bill Clinton, while professional historians ranked him tenth. Interestingly enough, both groups saw LBJ's foreign policy as a failure, ranking him thirty-sixth of the forty-one presidents in the conduct of international relations. These results are available on the Web at *www.americanpresidents.org/survey.*

11. Quoted in Gould, "The Revised LBJ," p. 80.

12. *New York Times,* November 27, 1999, p. 14. George Reedy wrote, "No matter how much can be chalked up to his credit, [LBJ] is irrevocably attached to the war." Reedy, *Lyndon Johnson,* p. 152.

13. Anatoly Dobrynin, *In Confidence: Moscow's Ambassador to America's Six Cold War Presidents* (New York: Times Books, Random House, 1995), p. 189.

14. It is simply misleading and simplistic to assert that "Johnson believed, however—and probably more deeply than Joe McCarthy—in a worldwide, monolithic Communist conspiracy." Larry L. King, "Machismo in the White House: Lyndon B. Johnson and Vietnam," *American Heritage* 27, no. 5 (August 1976): 12. Recent historical treatments stress the degree to which the Johnson administration furthered the process of detente. Thomas W. Zeiler, *Dean Rusk: Defending the American Mission Abroad* (Wilmington, Del.: Scholarly Resources, 2000), pp. 60–61.

15. For example, Johnson rejected advice to use nuclear weapons in Vietnam, even when it came from close friends like John Connally. John Connally with Mickey Herskowitz, *In History's Shadow* (New York: Hyperion, 1993), pp. 205–206.

16. Thomas C. Schelling, "A Half-Century without Nuclear War," *Key Reporter* 65, no. 3 (Spring 2000): 4.

17. Leon Carter, *Arms Control and Nonproliferation: Issues and Analysis* (Huntington, N.Y.: Nova Science Publications, 2000), p. 33. When a recent policy review suggested a greater willingness to use nuclear weapons in the war on terrorism, there was a strong reaction. As one editorial put it, "Nuclear weapons are not just another part of the military arsenal. They are different, and lowering the threshold for their use is reckless folly." Editorial, *New York Times,* March 12, 2002, p. 28.

18. Bator, "Lyndon Johnson and Foreign Policy," p. 51.

19. Caro, *Master of the Senate,* p. iv.

20. John Ikenberry, *After Victory: Institutions, Strategic Restraint, and the Rebuilding of Order after Major Wars* (Princeton: Princeton University Press, 2001), p. 203.

21. Ibid., p. 204.

22. Andrew Moravcsik, "Introduction," in *Doubled-Edged Diplomacy: International Bargaining and Domestic Politics,* ed. Peter B. Evans, Harold K. Jacobson, and Robert D. Putnam (Berkeley: University of California Press, 1993), p. 15. If, as Odd Arne Westad has recently argued, historians have given insufficient attention to the manner in which the United States undertook a "conscious and comprehensive attempt at changing Europe (and Japan) in the direction of U.S. ideas and models," and that "over a period of fifty years [the U.S.] transformed its main capitalist competitors according to its own image," one approach might be to examine the manner in which these states had to learn how to play within the American international system, to understand its rules and norms, and to adjust their politics—and systems of political economy—accordingly. Odd Arne Westad, "The New International History of the Cold War: Three (Possible) Paradigms," *Diplomatic History* 24, no. 4 (Fall 2000): 554–556.

23. Doris Kearns, *Lyndon Johnson and the American Dream* (New York: Harper and Row, 1976), p. 195.

24. Lawrence S. Kaplan, "The U.S. and NATO in the Johnson Years," in *The Johnson Years,* vol. 3: *LBJ at Home and Abroad,* ed. Robert Divine (Lawrence: University Press of Kansas, 1994), p. 143.

25. Richard L. Kugler, *Commitment to Purpose: How Alliance Partnership Won the Cold War* (Santa Monica, Calif.: Rand Corporation, 1993), pp. 205–207.

26. Wilfried L. Kohl, *French Nuclear Diplomacy* (Princeton: Princeton University Press, 1971), pp. 263–264.

27. Indeed, President George Bush would use this formulation—"let Europe be whole and free"—in his May 1989 address on the eve of the great changes in Europe. Philip Zelikow and Condoleezza Rice, *Germany Unified and Europe Transformed* (Cambridge, Mass.: Harvard University Press, 1995), p. 31.

28. Timothy Garton Ash, *In Europe's Name: Germany and the Divided Continent* (New York: Random House, 1993), pp. 23–24.
29. Kugler, *Commitment to Purpose,* p. 196.
30. Ibid., p. 168.
31. For examples of Johnson's irritation with Wilson's mediation, see Michael Beschloss, ed., *Reaching for Glory: Lyndon Johnson's Secret White House Tapes, 1964–1965* (New York: Simon and Schuster, 2001), p. 214 and p. 366.
32. Philip Ziegler, *Wilson: The Authorised Life of Lord Wilson of Rievaulx* (London: Weidenfeld and Nicolson, 1993), pp. 228–229.
33. Wilson conversation with Kiesinger, April 25, 1967, PREM 13/1528, PRO, London.
34. Sylvia Ellis, "Lyndon Johnson, Harold Wilson, and the Vietnam War," in *Twentieth Century Anglo-American Relations,* ed. Jonathan Hollowell (New York: Palgrave, 2001), p. 182. Sir Michael Palliser, one of the senior British diplomats of this period, believed that there was something of a "Walter Mitty quality" in Wilson, that he thought his relationship with Johnson was better than it was. Raj Roy, "The Battle over the Pound, 1964–1968," Ph.D. diss., London School of Economics, 2000, p. 166.
35. If the British had announced their withdrawal east of Suez before the October 1965 coup in Indonesia, the U.S. position in Southeast Asia might have become untenable. R. B. Smith, *An International History of the Vietnam War,* vol. 3: *The Making of a Limited War, 1965–66* (New York: St. Martin's Press, 1991), pp. 185ff.
36. John Kenneth Galbraith, *A Life in Our Times* (Boston: Houghton Mifflin, 1981), p. 450.
37. Burton Kaufman, "Foreign Aid and the Balance of Payments Problem," in *The Johnson Years,* vol. 2, ed. Robert Divine (Lawrence: University Press of Kansas, 1987), p. 105.
38. Richard Cooper, "Comment," in *A Retrospective on the Bretton Woods System: Lessons for International Monetary Reform,* ed. Michael D. Bordo and Barry Eichengreen (Chicago: University of Chicago Press, 1993), p. 106. See also Thomas Ilgen, *Autonomy or Independence: U.S.–Western European Monetary and Trade Relations, 1958–1984* (Totowa, N.J.: Rowman and Allanheld, 1985), p. 49.
39. As Diane Kunz rightly points out, Richard Nixon, though almost al-

ways given high marks for his understanding of diplomacy and foreign policy, chose to reform the system with unilateral American measures that rattled all of America's allies. See Diane Kunz, *Butter and Guns: America's Cold War Economic Diplomacy* (New York: Free Press, 1997), pp. 192–222.

40. This study does not dispute that the Vietnam War damaged the image and popularity of the United States in Western Europe. However, images and popularity rates are volatile and subject to change. For example, in France, the country most adamantly opposed to American policy in Vietnam, the image of the brutality of the American intervention was superceded in the late 1970s and 1980s by images of the boat people of Vietnam and the killing fields of Cambodia.

41. Brian Van DeMark, *Into the Quagmire: Lyndon Johnson and the Escalation of the Vietnam War* (New York: Oxford University Press, 1991), p. 213.

42. George Herring, the dean of American historians of the Vietnam War, uses this formulation of Johnson's "gambling" on a limited war to avoid a larger war with the Soviet Union and China, because he feared that such a larger war would push the two communist giants back together. However, Herring does not suggest that Johnson's gamble might also have been motivated by his desire to continue a process of detente with the Soviets. George C. Herring, *LBJ and Vietnam: A Different Kind of War* (Austin: University of Texas, 1994), p. 131.

43. Heren, in his contemporary account, remarked perceptively that "the first principle of American national security policy . . . [was] . . . that the balance of power, both military and ideological, must not be violently disturbed." Heren, *No Hail, No Farewell,* p. 151.

44. Jack F. Matlock, Jr., the former U.S. ambassador to the Soviet Union, makes this argument in his review of Logevall's book *Choosing War.* Logevall argues that an American settlement of the war in 1965 would have allowed for an earlier and more robust detente with the Soviet Union. Matlock responds that it was far more likely that a communist takeover of Saigon in 1965 would have led to calls for a renewed anticommunist crusade by Nixon and the Republicans. "To think that rapprochement with China or arms control agreements would have been possible under such conditions, as Logevall does, is

an exercise in fantasy." Matlock, "Why Were We in Vietnam?" *New York Times Book Review,* August 8, 1999, pp. 11–12.

45. Chen Jian, *Mao's China and the Cold War* (Chapel Hill: University of North Carolina, 2001), p. 217, and Qiang Zhai, *China and the Vietnam Wars, 1950–1975* (Chapel Hill: University of North Carolina Press, 2000), p. 156. The latter concludes that "it appears that Johnson had drawn the correct lesson from the Korean War and had been prudent in his approach to the Vietnam conflict." The American decision not to invade North Vietnam, however, provided the communists with a crucial advantage on the ground and can be considered part of Beijing's contribution to Hanoi's war effort.

46. Harry Middleton, *LBJ: The White House Years* (New York: Harry N. Abrams, 1989), p. 144. The phrase "in cold blood" is quoted in Herring, *LBJ and Vietnam,* p. 131. Lady Bird Johnson put it even more succinctly: "It is unbearably hard to fight a limited war."

47. Michael Lind, *Vietnam, The Necessary War: A Reinterpretation of America's Most Disastrous Military Conflict* (New York: Free Press, 1999). Although Lind's book is much more of a polemic than a historical study, I believe that he raises some extremely important questions about the Vietnam War that many historians have neglected. In terms of this study, I disagree with Lind's assessment of how Johnson saw the international situation in 1965. Johnson did not think, as Lind puts it, that the United States had been "humiliated" by the Soviet bloc in Berlin and Cuba (p. 17). Rather, Johnson believed that the stability created in Europe by the Berlin Wall and the aftermath of the Cuban missile crisis allowed for a reasonable coexistence with the Soviet Union based on the preservation of the status quo in Europe. The problems were the absence of such a clear line in Southeast Asia and the danger of rewarding what seemed to be China's version of violent revolutionary communism.

48. Pierre Galante, *Le Général* (Paris: Presses de la Cité, 1968), p. 162. De Gaulle added that "if he [LBJ] did not exist, we'd have to invent him," a statement that makes it clear how a simplistic caricature of Johnson was instrumental to de Gaulle's own policies.

Bibliography

In the interest of space, I have left out the secondary sources used in this book. A complete list can be found on my Website, accessible at www.vanderbilt.edu/AnS/history.

ARCHIVAL COLLECTIONS

United States

Lyndon Baines Johnson Library, Austin, Texas

National Security File
    Country Files
    Files of McGeorge Bundy
    Files of Spurgeon Keeny
    Files of Walt Rostow
    Head of State Correspondence
    Memos to the President
    National Security Council Histories
    National Security Council Meetings File
Personal Papers
    George Ball Papers
    Francis M. Bator Papers
    George Elsey Papers
    Henry Fowler Papers
    Tom Johnson's Notes on Meetings
    Spurgeon Keeny Papers

Oral Histories:
  George Ball
  Joseph Barr
  Charles Bohlen
  Zbigniew Brzezinski
  David Bruce
  William Camp
  Frederick L. Deming
  Douglas Dillon
  Thomas Finletter
  Adrian Fisher
  Henry Fowler
  Edward Fried
  Roswell Gilpatric
  Hubert Humphrey
  Nicholas Katzenbach
  John Leddy
  Lyman Lemnitzer
  John McCloy
  George McGhee
  Robert McNamara
  Harry McPherson
  Lawrence McQuade
  Wilbur Mills
  Richard Neustadt
  Karl Mundt
  Arthur Okun
  Henry Owen
  Robert Roosa
  Eugene Rostow
  Walt Rostow
  Dean Rusk
  Anthony Soloman
  Gerard Smith
  Alexander Trowbridge
  William White

National Archives and Records Administration, Washington, D.C.

Record Group 59
Office of the Executive Secretariat, Conference Files, 1964–1966
Central Files, 1964–1966
Central Foreign Policy Files, 1967–1969
Record Group 306
United States Information Agency, Reports of the Office of Research

Virginia Historical Society, Richmond, Virginia

Papers of David Bruce

Harry S. Truman Library, Independence, Missouri

Papers of Dean Acheson

Yale University, New Haven, Connecticut

Papers of Dean Acheson

Georgetown University, Washington, D.C.

Papers of George McGhee
Foreign Service Officers, Oral History Collection

United Kingdom

Public Record Office, Kew Gardens, Surrey

FO 371: Foreign Office, Political Correspondence
PREM 11 and 13: Prime Minister's Office Files

France

Ministère des Affaires Étrangères, Paris

Federal Republic of Germany

Politisches Archiv des Auswärtigen Amtes, Bonn (now Berlin)

Archiv für christlich-demokratische Politik, St. Augustin

Nachlässe
    I-433 Kurt Birrenbach
    I-483 Gerhard Schröder

OFFICIAL DOCUMENT PUBLICATIONS

Foreign Relations of the United States (Washington, D.C.: Government Printing Office, for the Department of State)

1961–1963
    1: Vietnam 1961
    7: Arms Control and Disarmament
    8: National Security Policy
    9: Foreign Economic Policy
    13: Western Europe and Canada
    15: Berlin Crisis, 1962–1963

1964–1968
    8: International Monetary and Trade Policy
    9: International Development and Economic Defense Policy; Commodities
    11: Arms Control and Disarmament
    12: Western Europe
    13: Western Europe Region
    14: Soviet Union
    15: Berlin; Germany
    17: Eastern Europe; Austria; Finland

Public Papers of the President: Lyndon B. Johnson, 5 volumes (Washington, D.C.: Government Printing Office, 1965–1969)

Akten zur Auswärtigen Politik der Bundesrepublik Deutschland (Munich: Oldenbourg Verlag, for the Institut für Zeitgeschichte, 1994–1999)

1963: Ed. Rainer Blasius, Mechthild Lindemann, Ilse Dorothee
Pautsch.
1964: Ed. Rainer Blasius, Wolfgang Hölscher, Daniel Kosthorst.
1965: Ed. Mechthild Lindemann and Ilse Dorothee Pautsch.
1966: Ed. Matthias Peter and Harald Rosenbach.
1967: Ed. Ilse Dorothee Pautsch, Jürgen Klöckler, Matthias Peter, and
Harald Rosenbach.
1968: Ed. Mechthild Lindemann and Matthias Peter.

Documents diplomatique français 1963 (Paris: Imprimerie nationale)

Documents on British Policy Overseas (London: Stationary Office, for the
Foreign and Commonwealth Office)
Series 3, volume 1: *Britain and the Soviet Union, 1968–1972*

NEWSPAPERS AND PERIODICALS

Newsweek
New York Times
Time
U.S. News and World Report

MEMOIRS, CORRESPONDENCE, CONVERSATIONS, AND DIARIES

Alphand, Hervé. *L'étonnement d'être: Journal (1939–1973).* Paris: Fayard,
1977.
Ball, George. *The Past Has Another Pattern.* New York: Norton, 1982.
Bator, Francis M. "Lyndon Johnson and Foreign Policy: The Case of West-
ern Europe and the Soviet Union," in Aaron Lobel, ed., *Presidential
Judgment: Foreign Policy Decision Making in the White House.* Hollis,
N.H.: Hollis Publishing Co., 2001.
Beschloss, Michael R., ed. *Reaching for Glory: Lyndon Johnson's Secret White
House Tapes, 1964–1965.* New York: Simon and Schuster, 2001.
Beschloss, Michael R., ed. *Taking Charge: The Johnson White House Tapes,
1963–1964.* New York: Simon and Schuster, 1997.

Birrenbach, Kurt. *Meine Sondermissionen: Rückblick auf zwei Jahrzehnte bundesdeutscher Aussenpolitik.* Düsseldorf: Econ Verlag, 1984.

Blessing, Karl. *Im Kampf um gutes Geld.* Frankfurt: Fritz Knapp Verlag, 1966.

Bohlen, Charles. *Witness to History, 1929–1969.* New York: Norton, 1973.

Brandon, Henry. *Special Relationships: A Foreign Correspondent's Memoirs from Roosevelt to Reagan.* New York: Atheneum, 1988.

Brandt, Willy. *My Life in Politics.* New York: Viking, 1992.

Cairncross, Alec. *The Wilson Years: A Treasury Diary 1964–1969.* London: Historians' Press, 1997.

Califano, Joseph A., Jr., *The Triumph and Tragedy of Lyndon Johnson.* New York: Simon and Schuster, 1991.

Callaghan, James. *Time and Chance.* London: Collins, 1987.

Castle, Barbara. *The Castle Diaries, 1964–1970.* London: Weidenfeld and Nicolson, 1984.

Christian, George. *The President Steps Down.* New York: Macmillan, 1970.

Clifford, Clark, and Richard Holbrooke. *Counsel to the President: A Memoir.* New York: Random House, 1991.

Connally, John, with Mickey Herskowitz. *In History's Shadow.* New York: Hyperion, 1993.

Couve de Murville, Maurice. *Une politique étrangère, 1958–1969.* Paris: Plon, 1971.

Debré, Michel. *Gouverner autrement: Mémoires, 1962–1970.* Paris: Albin Michel, 1993.

De Gaulle, Charles. *Discours et messages,* vol. 5: *Vers le terme Janvier 1966–Avril 1969.* Paris: Plon, 1970.

Dobrynin, Anatoly. *In Confidence: Moscow's Ambassador to America's Six Cold War Presidents.* New York: Times Books, Random House, 1995.

Donovan, Hedley. *Roosevelt to Reagan: A Reporter's Encounters with Nine Presidents.* New York: Harper and Row, 1985.

Frankel, Max. *The Times of My Life and My Life with the* Times. New York: Random House, 1999.

Galbraith, John Kenneth. *A Life in Our Times.* Boston: Houghton Mifflin, 1981.

Goodwin, Richard N. *Remembering America: A Voice from the Sixties.* Boston: Little, Brown, 1988.

Guthman, Edwin O., and C. Richard Allen. eds. *RFK: Collected Speeches.* New York: Viking, 1993.

Guthman, Edwin O., and Jeffrey Shulman, eds. *Robert Kennedy in His*

Own Words: The Unpublished Recollections of the Kennedy Years. New York: Bantam, 1988.

Heren, Louis. *No Hail, No Farewell*. New York: Harper and Row, 1970.

Hillenbrand, Martin J. *Fragments of Our Time: Memoirs of a Diplomat*. Athens: University of Georgia Press, 1998.

Humphrey, Hubert H. *The Education of a Public Man*. Garden City, N.Y.: Doubleday, 1976.

Johnson, Lady Bird. *A White House Diary*. New York: Holt, Rinehart, and Winston, 1970.

Johnson, Lyndon B. *The Vantage Point: Perspectives of the Presidency, 1963–1969*. New York: Holt, Rinehart, and Winston, 1971.

Kaiser, Philip. *Journeying Far and Wide: A Political and Diplomatic Memoir*. New York: Macmillan, 1992.

Kissinger, Henry. *White House Years*. Boston: Little, Brown, 1979.

McGhee, George. *At the Creation of a New Germany*. New Haven: Yale University Press, 1989.

McLellan, David S., and David C. Acheson. *Among Friends: Personal Letters of Dean Acheson*. New York: Dodd, Mead and Co., 1980.

Middleton, Harry. *LBJ: The White House Years*. New York: Harry N. Abrams, 1990.

Nitze, Paul. *From Hiroshima to Glasnost: At the Center of Decision*. New York: Grove Weidenfeld, 1989.

Osterheld, Horst. *Aussenpolitik unter Bundeskanzler Ludwig Erhard 1963–1966: Ein dokumentarischer Bericht aus dem Kanzleramt*. Düsseldorf: Droste, 1992.

Peyrefitte, Alain. *C'était de Gaulle*, vol. 2. Paris: Fayard, 1997.

Peyrefitte, Alain. *C'était de Gaulle*, vol. 3. Paris: Fayard, 2000.

Reedy, George. *Lyndon B. Johnson: A Memoir*. New York: Andrews and McMeel, 1982.

Roll, Eric. *Crowded Hours*. London: Faber and Faber, 1985.

Rostow, W. W. *The Diffusion of Power*. New York: Macmillan, 1972.

Rusk, Dean. *As I Saw It*. New York: Norton, 1990.

Schlesinger, Arthur. *A Thousand Days: John F. Kennedy in the White House*. Boston: Houghton Mifflin, 1965.

Seaborg, Glenn T. *A Chemist in the White House*. Washington, D.C.: American Chemical Society, 1988.

Seaborg, Glenn T., and Benjamin S. Loeb. *Stemming the Tide: Arms Control in the Johnson Years*. Lexington, Mass.: Lexington Books, 1987.

Solomon, Robert J. *The International Monetary System, 1945–1981.* New York: Harper and Row, 1982.

Strauss, Franz Josef. *Die Erinnerungen.* Berlin: Siedler, 1989.

Sulzberger, Cyrus L. *An Age of Mediocrity: Memoirs and Diaries 1963–1972.* New York: Macmillan, 1973.

Volcker, Paul A., and Toyoo Gyohten. *Changing Fortunes: The World's Money and the Threat to American Leadership.* New York: Times Books, 1992.

Wilson, Harold. *The Labour Government, 1964–1970: A Personal Record.* London: Weidenfeld and Nicolson, 1971.

Zuckerman, Solly. *Monkeys, Men, and Missiles.* London: Collins, 1988.

UNPUBLISHED DOCTORAL DISSERTATIONS AND PAPERS

Busch, Peter. "Britain and Kennedy's War in Vietnam, 1961–1963," Ph.D. diss., London School of Economics, 1999.

Easter, David. "British Defense Policy in South East Asia and the Confrontation, 1960–1966," Ph.D. diss., London School of Economics, 1998.

Friedrich, Alexandra. "Awakenings: The Impact of the Vietnam War on West German–American Relations in the 1960s," Ph.D. diss., Temple University, 2000.

Gray, William Glenn. "The Hallstein Doctrine: West Germany's Global Campaign to Isolate East Germany, 1949–1969," Ph.D. diss., Yale University, 1999.

Maddock, Shane. "The Nth Country Conundrum: The American and Soviet Quest for Nuclear Nonproliferation, 1945–1970," Ph.D. diss., University of Connecticut, 1997.

Mausbach, Wilfried. "Defending Berlin in Saigon: The Dilemmas of West German Support for America's War," unpublished paper, Vietnam War Symposium, University of California, Santa Barbara, January 1999.

McDonald, Alan, "The International Institute for Applied Systems Analysis," unpublished case study, March 13, 1997.

Roy, Raj. "The Battle over the Pound, 1964–1968," Ph.D. diss., London School of Economics, 2000.

Acknowledgments

All books have a story behind them. This one began with a request by my friend Professor Diane Kunz that I contribute an essay to a volume she was editing on United States foreign policy in the 1960s. I accepted the challenge and somehow, despite starting a family and a new job, the essay got written, although the conclusions were based on a very limited documentary record. My essay did lead, however, to a phone call from Professor Francis M. Bator, who challenged me on a number of critical points I had made about President Lyndon Johnson's policies toward Europe. Bator's arguments provoked my curiosity, and I soon found myself back at the Johnson Library investigating the documents. Some years later, after considerable travel, archival work, and lots of thinking, the end result is this book, an attempt at some historical—and even personal—revisionism.

Many institutions and individuals have made this book possible. The Norwegian Nobel Institute, led by the noted Cold War scholar Geir Lundestad, gave me a fellowship to pursue research on this subject and then present my early findings in the beautiful city of Oslo. The Woodrow Wilson International Center for Scholars awarded me a fellowship that enabled me to research these issues during a year in Washington. The presence at the Wilson Center of the Cold War International History Project, under the exceptional leadership of Christian Ostermann, also proved highly valuable. The Center for the Study of European Integration in Bonn, directed by Professor Ludgar Kühnhardt, offered me a senior fellowship that enabled me to research and present my findings in Germany. I have also been the very fortunate recipient of a NATO Fellowship, which allowed for travel to London and Paris. The Vanderbilt University Research Council has generously assisted this research as well. Finally, I was able to complete the writing of this book in the very supportive and scholarly atmosphere of the Robert Penn Warren Center for the Humanities at Vanderbilt.

Among my many debts to archivists, I must single out the extremely helpful staff of the Lyndon Baines Johnson Library, especially Regina Greenwell, Linda Seelke, Phil Scott, and Jennifer Cuddeback.

Responsibility for the content of this work rests with me alone, but many people have helped me in its production. Francis Bator was always generous with his time and encouragement, explaining and debating with me the various issues of the Johnson presidency. My Harvard mentors Ernest May and Charles Maier supported this project in many ways. The Vanderbilt History Department is a wonderful place to work, and one could not have better colleagues and friends than the ones I have found there. (How many academics can honestly say that?) In particular, Paul Conkin, himself a biographer of LBJ, encouraged me when the project was still in a very fragile and early state. The late Hugh Graham, who knew more about Johnson's domestic policies than anyone, helped me find the financial assistance necessary to complete this project. Sam McSeveney was a constant source of encouragement and put up with my tendency to find a Johnson quote for every occasion. Elsewhere, historians of the Cold War years, among them Marc Trachtenberg, Frank Gavin, Max Guderzo, Günter Bischof, Detlef Junker, Odd Arne Westad, Jussi Hahnimaki, Diane Kunz, Ilya Gaiduk, Priscilla Roberts, Alexandra Friedrich, Willi Mausbach, Fred Logevall, and Robert Bothwell, have helped keep me honest, forcing me to think and rethink my conclusions about the Johnson era. My friends Bill Miscamble, Robert "KC" Johnson, and Michael Creswell read and commented on drafts of this manuscript. The graduate students I have worked with at Vanderbilt, most notably Appu Soman, Darlene Rivas, Michael Davis, Rob Spinney, Caroline Pruden, Yijia Wang, Sean Smith, Justin Wilson, Doug Kasischke, Craig Kaplowitz, Rob Lawson, Amy Sturgis, and Chris Caplinger, have assisted me in a wide variety of ways, including reading and commenting on many drafts of the book. In London, Raj Roy offered both friendship and a willingness to teach me everything he knew about Harold Wilson and British foreign policy during this era, and I am immensely grateful for his insights. Deborah Kisatsky and her husband, Shane Maddock, helped make my stay in Germany more rewarding. Frédéric Bozo and Philippe Vial helped me get started with my research in Paris. A number of my Vanderbilt undergraduates, especially Lauren O'Neill, Andreea Prodhan, Claire Holloway, Sebastian Arango, Bradley Cordes, Justin Memmott, Curtis Austin, and Keith Nunn, have been constant in their encouragement. Two Vanderbilt students, Matthew Buesching and Tim Shuman, were excellent research assistants. Odette Bonnet provided me with generous hospitality during my time in Washington. And the fifth- and sixth-graders in Michael Stewart's social studies class at Saint Bernard Academy in Nashville patiently allowed me to teach them about the Johnson era, and asked the questions children do about recent history that made me think twice about many of my assumptions.

At Harvard University Press I have had the constant encouragement and enthusiasm of my editor, Kathleen McDermott, as well as that of her predecessor, Aida Donald. My copy editor, Julie Hagen, has saved me from many embarrassing errors and made the book more readable. Lyndon Johnson may have believed that he would never get any credit in foreign policy because he didn't go to Harvard, but Harvard University Press has treated this manuscript with great professionalism and care.

My family sustained me throughout this work. My children, Helene, Evie, and Marigny, put up with their father's absences and his occasional distracted looks as he thought about Lyndon Johnson during their basketball practices. My mother-in-law, Jane Bruce, came to help during my many absences, as did our family friend, Sean O'Rourke. My father-in-law, Harry Kirschke, and his wife, Jan, have been supportive throughout. My sister-in-law, Melissa Stockdale, and her husband, Tom, and son, Nic, have made Norman, Oklahoma, a second home to us. My own parents, John and Mary Schwartz, passed away during the time I was researching this book, but their interest in the events of their time and their devotion to education helped to produce a historian. My older brother, Bob, who delighted in Lyndon Johnson stories and loved discussing the 1960s, died of cancer before he could see this book, but his courage and humor in the face of his illness continues to inspire me. My other siblings—John, Mary, Joe, Geri, and Rose—and in-laws—Carol, Pat, Ed, Donna, and John—and my nieces and nephews have been through all of this joy and sadness with me, and I am grateful for their love and support.

This book is dedicated to my wife, Amy Helene Kirschke, a scholar in her own right and my best friend. She has kept our day-to-day life together during my many absences, and has been my greatest and most loyal supporter. I can never hope to repay the sacrifices she has made to see that this book would eventually appear.

Index

Czechoslovakia, 220; and Wilson, 232. *See also* Germany
Kissinger, Henry, 2, 43
Knappstein, Heinrich, 57, 58
Kosygin, Alexei: and Germany, 26, 147; and North Vietnam, 48–49; and Vietnam War, 136, 207; and France, 137; and Multilateral Force, 137; and LBJ, 137, 143, 181–182, 183, 206, 207, 208, 209, 226; and United States, 147; and Nazism, 148–149; and Wilson, 148–149; and nuclear nonproliferation, 181, 182–183; and nuclear arms control, 181–182, 206–207, 208, 220, 221; and Glassboro meeting, 226
Kraft, Joseph, 34
Krone, Heinrich, 16
Krushchev, Nikita, 20, 25–26, 42, 47
Kuklick, Bruce, 2
Kunz, Diane, 196

Labour Party (Great Britain), 44, 45, 48, 67, 68, 81, 86, 119, 233
Leddy, John, 58
Lederer, William J., 3; *The Ugly American*, 1
Lilienfeld, Georg von, 126
Limited Test Ban Treaty, 14, 15, 16, 30, 56
Lind, Michael, 236
Lippmann, Walter, 84
Logevall, Fredrik, 3
Long, Russell, 122
Luxembourg Compromise, 95–96

Macmillan, Harold, 11, 12
Malaysia, 12, 71, 85, 86
Manchester, William, 7

Mansfield, Mike, 31, 121–122, 147–148, 154, 156, 184, 195, 233
Mansfield Resolution, 121–122, 144, 146, 148
Marshall Plan, 70
Martin, William McChesney, 80–81, 175
Mauldin, Bill, 103
McCarthy, Eugene, 187
McCloy, John J.: and Nuclear Nonproliferation Treaty, 61; and France-NATO relationship, 103, 107, 108; and Germany, 111; and German offset payments, 124–125; and trilateral negotiations, 143–145, 165; and Great Britain, 144, 145, 155; and NATO, 144–145; and Brandt, 147–148; and National Democratic Party of Germany, 148; and LBJ, 152, 153–155, 156; and Kiesinger, 152, 155–156; and military in Germany, 152–153, 158; and international monetary system, 177, 178
McCormack, John, 21
McGhee, George: and Soviet-German relations, 24; and U.S.-German relations, 50; and German Vietnam policy, 87; and offset payments, 89, 90, 126, 132; and Franco-German relationship, 97, 106; and Erhard, 127; and Brandt, 151; and LBJ, 159; and international monetary system, 176–177; and Germany, 184–185; and Nuclear Nonproliferation Treaty, 208
McGovern, George, 225
McMaster, H. R., 3
McNamara, Robert: and Multilateral Force, 43; and Nuclear Planning